Alexander III of Russia

Alexander III of Russia

Charles Lowe

With an introduction by John Van der Kiste

A & F Reprints

First published by Heinemann 1895
First published by A & F 2016

Introduction copyright © John Van der Kiste 2016
All rights reserved

A & F Publications
South Brent, Devon, England TQ10 9AS

Cover: *Coronation of Tsar Alexander III*, by George Becker

ISBN (13-digit) 978-1522840725
ISBN (10-digit) 1522840729

Typeset 11/10.5pt Garamond
Printed by CreateSpace

CONTENTS

Illustrations   7

Chronology   9

Introduction   11

Chapter I   PREDECESSORS   15

The Romanoffs - Holstein-Gottorps - Paul, the Madman - Alexander I - Tale of a sucking-pig - Nicholas I - Instances of his despotism - Alexander II - Character-sketch - 'Sasha' the 'Military Tailor' - The 'Tsar Emancipator' - Cycle of autocratic reforms

Chapter II   HEIR-APPARENT   22

Death of the Tsarevitch Nicholas - Alexander heir-apparent - His first Rescript - 'My son, my heir' - Youthful Characteristics - Marriage - Marie Feodorovna - A Teutophobe - 'Thank God for Woronzoff!' - In opposition - Franco-German War - Visit to England - Anglo-Russian Press amenities - Marie Alexandrovna - Alexander II in London - The Eastern Question - A Panslavist champion - Russo-Turkish War - Army of the Lom - Character as a commander - Courageous or cowardly? - The foe of falsehood and corruption - Under arrest - The eve of action

Chapter III   CIRCUMSTANCES OF HIS ACCESSION   37

March 13, 1881 - The Anitchkoff Palace - An Equerry's message - Assassination of Alexander II - Alexander III's Manifesto - Accession formalities - Imperial funeral - English sympathy - Nihilist ultimatum - National slip between cup and lip - Loris-Melikoff's Constitution - A tap-room Parliament - Reform or Reaction? - Despotism by Divine Right - The choice of Hercules-Alexander

Chapter IV   THE LORD'S ANOINTED   49

Autocrat of All the Russias - Moscow - Triumphal entry - Oath to Imperial Standard - Proclamation *Urbi et Orbi* - Ambassadors of the Press - Church of the Assumption - Coronation Ceremony - Second burning of Moscow - The Kazan Cathedral

Chapter V   THE TSAR PEACE-KEEPER   56

Foreign Policy Circular - Imperial meeting at Danzig - Its results - Skobeleff the Teutophobe - M. de Giers - His meetings with Bismarck - Mr Gladstone and the Tsar - Russo-German *rapprochement* - The Three Emperors at Skierniwiece - The Tsar and Francis Joseph - Germany's 'Hecuba' - Fresh Russo-German misunderstanding - The Tsar in Berlin - His interview with Bismarck - The Forged Despatches - Friends once more - Bismarck on the Tsar - 'Printer's Ink' - The Kaiser in St Petersburg - The Tsar in Berlin – 'Hurrah for the Russian Army!' - Results of the meeting - Russia's 'One Friend' - The 'Key of your House' - The Kaiser at Narva - The Tsar at Kiel – 'Long live the German Navy!' - *'Vive la Marine Française!'* - Beauty and the Beast - Franco-Russian relations - A Petersbourg! à Petersbourg! - The French at Cronstadt - 'For the sake of our dear France' - 'You *must* marry me' - The Russians at Toulon - Gold *versus Gloire* - *'Souvenirs de Sebastopol'* - Customs-War - *'La France, c'est l'Ennemi!'* - Russia in Central Asia - Skobeleff's prophecy - English 'Mervousness' again - *'Beati possidentes!'* - The Penjdeh Incident - *Si vis pacem, para bellum* - John Bull puts on his Boots - Arms or Arbitration? - The Russo-Afghan Frontier – Central Asian and Siberian Railways - The Black Sea Fleet - Masterful Declaration of the Tsar - Batoum *versus* Bulgaria

Chapter VI   THE TWO ALEXANDERS   103

The two cousins - Prince Alexander of Battenberg - A glimpse of him at Bucharest - Prince of Bulgaria Elect - Explosion at the Winter Palace - The Tsar says, 'Do your best!' - Muscovite art of managing men - A Russian Satrapy - The Prince and his Nessus-shirt - 'Good, as long as it lasts' - *Pour décourager les autres* - Fat on the Russian fire - Kaulbars and Soboleff - Tactics of the Duumvirs – 'Cowardly King Milan' - 'Power into Russian hands' - Prince Alexander at Moscow - Turning of the Russian tide - The two deputations - 'Not at home!' - *'Aut Caesar, aut nullus!'* - M. Jonin bullies the Battenberger - The Prince takes the trick - *'Je suis heureux et tranquillisé'* - 'Swine, rascals, perjured rabble!' - 'The Tsar is not Russia' - Military quarrels - The Prince dances with Madame Jonin - The Prince in England and Austria - His confidences to Herr von Huhn - The Tsar cannot stand liars - A thunderbolt from Russia - The Servians rush to arms - But have to reel back on their pig-styes and their Russian patrons - The two Bulgarias - Climax and anti-climax - *La Russie boude* - Conspiracies to 'remove' the Prince - 'Beware of the Struma regiment!' - The *Prinzenraub* - 'Here may you see a traitor!' - Muscovite 'stoutbrief and hamesucken' - An exchange of telegrams - 'Farewell to Bulgaria!' - The Prince's Seven Years' War - Worried to death - A thunder-loud 'No!'

Chapter VII   THE TSAR PANSLAVIST   128

The 'Father of Lies' - Shuffling of the pack - Domestic policy - Ignatieff's circular - The Tsar bad at figures - His sovereign responsibility - 'One King, one Faith, one Law' - 'Russia for the Russians' - Character of Finland and the Finns - The hall-mark of Muscovy - 'Violation of Finnish rights' - The Baltic Provinces - 'A bear's skin on the Teutonic bird - German 'a foreign language' - Vladimir at Dorpat - Anti-German edicts - Panslavism in Poland - High-handed measures - The Tsar 'the best cosmopolite' - Ignorance the pillar of Autocracy - The Tsar as Press Censor - His second sceptre a blacking-brush - The demoralisation of Russia - Famine, fetters and finance - *'C'est à prendre, ou à laisser!'* - 'The Russian army' - Duelling decree - Another ukase

Chapter VIII   THE TSAR PERSECUTOR   142

A new King over Egypt - M. Pobedonostseff - Are the Jews Revolutionists? - Anti-Semitic riots - Ignatieff's circular - The Tsar Jew-baiter - Race or religion? - The Russian Ghetto - The 'May Laws' - Prince Metchersky on microbes - Mr Gladstone and the conscience of England - Guildhall meeting and Memorial - Returned by the Tsar unopened - The Russian Herod - The Tsar Persecutor - Polish Catholics - Baltic Province Lutherans - Barclay de Tolly - The Stundists - History and progress of the sect - Their principles and character - An archiepiscopal anathema - Anti-Stundist alliance between Church and State - 'Gentle pressure' - A modern Torquemada - Mr Swinburne's counter-anathema

Chapter IX   A REIGN OF TERROR   160

Assassination and executions - A Terrorist ultimatum - What the Nihilists want - A chat with 'Stepniak' - Party of the 'People's Will' - And of the 'People's Rights' - Spiritual and material means – *De propaganda fide* - Congress of Lipètak - Nihilist organisation - Mass trial of Terrorists - Suchanoff executed - General Strelikoff shot - A basketful of eggs - Coronation of the Tsar -

Tactics of the Terrorists at Moscow – 'Nor I either' - Nihilism in the Army - Murder of Colonel Sudeikin - Colonel Aschenbrenner and Baron Stromberg - Vera Filipoff, a tempting Terrorist - Arrests and assassinations - Plots against the Emperor - A life of fear and precaution - Anecdotes - The Grand Morskaia plot, and the Executive Committee - Another mass trial - 'Education to be abolished!' - The Borki catastrophe - 'Oh, papa, they'll come and murder us all!' - A bomb factory at Zurich - 'A paper bullet of the brain' - Madame Tzebrikova's letter - Its consequences to her - Sophie Gunsberg - General Seliverskoff shot at Paris - A French Exhibition at Moscow - Dynamite one of its exhibits - Proof against bribes - The Moujik Tsar - Shaken nerves - A Ministry of personal protection - The greatest Terrorist of all - A revolting manifesto

Chapter X   ILLNESS AND DEATH   181

'Weep, Russia!' - A Sore Saint - Monseigneur of Kharkoff *versus* Professor Zacharin - Origin and Course of Illness - Belovishaya - Spala - Story of a Duck - Professor Leyden - Livadia, the Russian Cannes - Father Ivan, the 'Wonder-Worker' - Corfu - Princess Alix of Hesse - Diary of Disease - An Angel on Earth - Death - Last Hours - Nature of Malady - A Funeral-Drama in Five Acts - Yalta - Sebastopol - Moscow - St Petersburg - Processional Pageant - Scene in the Fortress Church - A Prayer *by* the dead – 'The Tsar is dead! Long live the Tsar!'

Chapter XI   CHARACTERISTICS   198

A 'Psychological Enigma' - A Compound Monarch - Not a Military One - The 'Peace-keeper' of Europe - Examination of his Claim to the Title - A Treaty-breaker if a Peace-keeper - European Peace and Russian War - A Second Ivan the Terrible - A 'Moujik Tsar' - The 'Tsar Prisoner' - Truth-lover and Truth-teller - His real Feelings towards France -The Great Mistake of his Reign - The Dumb Ruler of a Voiceless People - Model Husband and Father - Family Life - Denmark an Asylum - 'Uncle Sasha' - Contemporary, not of Queen Victoria, but of Queen Isabel - The 'Two Alexanders' - Opinions of Lords Rosebery and Salisbury - M. Leroy-Beaulieu - Mr Harold Frederic - Professor Geffcken - The *Times* - A Personal as well as a Political Autocrat - Lady Randolph Churchill - His daily Habits described by Mr 'Lanin' - General Richter, the 'Sandalphon of the Empire' - Great Physical Strength - Fondness for Animals - 'Sullen, Taciturn, Curt' - Intellectual Tastes - Domestic Habits – *De mortuis nil nisi bonum* - Canon Wilberforce - 'Resistance to Tyranny is Obedience to God'

Chapter XII NICHOLAS II 216

'What is Nicholas II?' - His Teachers - A Panslavist Tutor - General Danilovitch and his Method - Not much of a Soldier - Youthful Characteristics - His Tastes and Reading - Nothing but good to say of Him' - 'Good all Round' - A 'Globe-trotter' - Visit to India - In Japan - Narrow Escape at Ossu - His Saviour describes the Incident - 'I admired Nicky's Pluck' - At Vladivostock - The Trans-Siberian Railway - The Great Famine Anecdote by 'An Englishman' - The Princesses of Hesse-Darmstadt – 'Every one to Heaven in his own way!' - Betrothal - The Royal Wedding at Coburg - Second Visit to England - Sketch of in the House of Commons - Accession Manifesto - What will he do? - The Finns - The Jews - Dr Geffcken on the New Tsar - His Foreign Policy - The Kaiser and the Tsar - Nicholas II less anti-German than his Father - Two Thousand Telegrams from France - The Emperor and the President – 'Grovelling before the Tsar' - England and Russia - Marriage - 'Nonsense about me' — See-saw System of Russian Government - A Tsar-Emancipator of his subjects' souls?

ILLUSTRATIONS

Between pp. 84-103

Tsar Alexander II

Tsarina Marie Alexandrovna

Tsarevitch Nicholas and Grand Duke Alexander

Tsarevitch Alexander and Princess Dagmar of Denmark

Tsar Alexander II and Tsarina Marie Alexandrovna

Tsar Alexander II and his family

Tsar Alexander II and Tsarina Marie Alexandrovna with the Tsarevitch and Tsarevna

Tsar Alexander II and the Tsarevitch with the Duke and Duchess of Edinburgh

The Winter Palace, St Petersburg

The Tsarevitch and Tsarevna with their children

The assassination of Tsar Alexander II

Tsar Alexander III rouble

Constantin Pobedonostseff

Prince Alexander of Battenberg

Gatchina Palace and Park

The imperial train after the accident at Borki

Tsar Alexander III, Tsarina Marie Feodorovna and Princess Alexandra

Tsar Alexander III, Tsarina Marie Feodorovna and their children

Tsar Alexander III and Tsarina Marie Feodorovna

Tsar Alexander III and Princess Marie

Livadia Palace

Funeral procession of Tsar Alexander III

Tsar Alexander III and Tsarevitch Nicholas

CHRONOLOGY

1845 Birth of Grand Duke Alexander, 10 Mar (O.S. 26 Feb) at the Winter Palace, St Petersburg, second son of Tsar Alexander II and Tsarina Marie Alexandrovna, the other children being Alexandra (1842-9), Nicholas (1843-65), Vladimir (1847-1909), Alexei (1850-1908), Marie (1853-1920), Sergei (1857-1905), and Paul (1860-1919)

1865 Death of Nicholas, 24 Apr (O.S. 12 Apr), at Nice, makes Alexander Tsarevitch

1866 Marriage of Tsarevitch Alexander and Princess Dagmar of Denmark, second daughter of King Christian IX, 9 Nov (O.S. 28 Oct) in the Imperial Chapel, Winter Palace

1868 Birth of Grand Duke Nicholas, Tsarevitch and later Tsar Nicholas II, 18 May (O.S. 6 May), followed by Alexander (1869-70), George (1871-99), Xenia (1875-1960), Michael (1878-1918), and Olga (1882-1960)

1880 Death of Tsarina Marie Alexandrovna, aged 55, 3 Jun (O.S. 22 May); marriage of Tsar Alexander II and Princess Dolgoruki, 6 Jul (O.S. 24 Jun)

1881 Assassination of Tsar Alexander II, aged 62, at St Petersburg, 13 Mar (O.S. 1 Mar), brings Alexander III to throne

1882 Temporary regulations banning Jews from inhabiting rural areas and restricting occupations in which they could engage, or 'May Laws', enacted

1883 Coronation of Alexander and Marie Feodorovna at the Cathedral Church of the Assumption, Moscow, 26 May (O.S. 14 May)

1886 Alexander, Sovereign Prince of Bulgaria, abdicates after incurring Alexander's enmity, 21 Aug

1887 Reinsurance Treaty signed by Foreign Minister Nikolai de Giers with Germany and Austria, 18 June (O.S. 6 June), expires in 1890

1888 Imperial train crash derailed in accident at Borki, with imperial family aboard, 29 Oct (O.S. 17 Oct)

1894 Death of Alexander, aged 49, at Livadia Palace, 1 Nov (O.S. 20 Oct), buried at Peter and Paul Cathedral, St Petersburg, 19 Nov (O.S. 7 Nov)

1917 Russian revolution, fall of Romanov Empire and abdication of Tsar Nicholas II, 15 Mar (O.S. 2 Mar), murdered with his wife and children at Ekaterinburg the following year

1928 Death of Dowager Empress Marie Feodorovna, aged 80, at Hvidore, Denmark, 13 Oct

INTRODUCTION

(The following is adapted in part from the article 'Mischievous beyond measure: Charles Lowe, correspondent and biographer', *Royalty Digest*, January 1998)

CHARLES Lowe was born at Balconnel, Forfarshire, in 1848, and educated at Edinburgh University. After travelling and working in France and Germany, he returned to Britain, settling in London, and entering Gray's Inn in 1874. He joined *The Times* as foreign sub-editor two years later. In December 1878 he was appointed the newspaper's correspondent in Berlin, with instructions to cover Russia and Scandinavia as well.

When Tsar Alexander III was crowned in 1883, he was the only British correspondent admitted to the cathedral at Moscow. After sending his account of the events and pageantry to the local telegraph office, he fell asleep exhausted in his hotel bedroom. On being woken by the 'stirring clarion notes of the Chevalier Guards' passing from the Kremlin under his window the next morning, he found a telegram from the Editor thanking him for the safe arrival of his report. Less happily, he also discovered that his wallet and gold watch were missing. An angry complaint to the landlord and a thorough search of the servants' quarters led to reports in the Moscow press, and reached the ear of the Tsar himself. When the governor of Moscow threatened some of the most notorious thieves in the city with a one-way ticket to Siberia if the watch was not recovered, it soon reappeared, although the culprit was never apprehended.

Four years later Lowe was in Berlin, with responsibility for filing the newspaper's official reports on the illness of Crown Prince Frederick William, who was suffering from cancer of the larynx. An admirer of Prince Otto von Bismarck, the German Chancellor, he took the general view of many others at Berlin that Dr Morell Mackenzie, the British laryngologist who had been summoned to take charge of the Crown Prince, was misleading everybody with regard to the severity of his condition because he wanted to set himself up as a 'kingmaker', intent on helping his patient to survive long enough to outlive his nonagenarian father, Emperor William, ascend the throne as a dying man, and thus permit him to exercise 'a decisive influence upon the destiny of the German nation'. Ironically the two men had initially met when Mackenzie was asked to treat Mrs Lowe for a throat ailment. But the correspondent's vindictive campaign against Mackenzie distressed the Crown

Princess, who was Empress during her husband's brief reign as Emperor Frederick III and then known as Empress Frederick after his death in June 1888. Her brother the Prince of Wales, later King Edward VII, was infuriated by the behaviour and attitude of Lowe, whom he called 'a horrible fellow and mischievous beyond measure,' and he promised his sister he would let George Earle Buckle, then Editor of *The Times*, of her feelings about him (Giles St Aubyn, *Edward VII, Prince and King*, 1979, 274-5).

A couple of years later Lowe fell out with the management of *The Times* on an unrelated matter, although the Prince of Wales's complaints about him had undoubtedly placed him in some jeopardy. When he was informed that his employment would be terminated at the end of June 1891, he brought an action for wrongful dismissal and lost. He dedicated the rest of his career to freelance writing, and published books on Bismarck and the German Emperor William II, regarded as potboilers and hardly remembered today.

His only book of lasting value was his biography of Tsar Alexander III, published in 1895, the year after its subject's death. The last but one imperial ruler of Russia, he noted, was 'a mass of apparent contradictions', who deserved praise for keeping the peace throughout his reign and sparing Europe the calamity of war. Yet he 'plunged his own Empire into domestic struggles', and his reign was 'one tragedy of racial and religious persecutions, which can scarcely be paralleled out of the cruellest page of history'. Despite his failings as an autocrat, he was a devoted husband and a doting father, an exception and an example to all the other Grand Dukes of the house of Romanov who in some cases had not been noted for their marital fidelity. He deserved sympathy as a man lacking in intellectual and leadership qualities, ill-fitted to be an Emperor, and at heart a devoted family man who however allowed himself to be influenced unduly by his advisers, not always to advantage.

Lowe's last book was a memoir, *The Tale of a 'Times' Correspondent*, published in 1927. According to Dr Mackenzie's biographer, the volume reflects its author's 'self-centred, truculent and jealous character' (R. Scott Stevenson, *Morell Mackenzie*, 1946, 20). Much of it reeks of self-congratulation, especially when writing about his own books and inserting laudatory quotes from reviews of them.

Having outlived his wife, one of their two sons who was killed in the First World War, and one of their daughters, he died in a London nursing home in 1931 at the age of 82. An obituary in the newspaper with which he had made his name before falling out of favour acknowledged that he 'frankly admitted that he was a hero-worshipper, but, unfortunately, he was not always discriminating in his choice of objects of worship'. (*The Times*, 19.1.1931)

Whatever one may think of Lowe as a person and biographer in general, posterity owes him a debt of gratitude for his life of Tsar Alexander III. His judgments were perspicacious, his analysis shrewd, and his research into contemporary sources thorough. Unlike his other titles, the book remains a valuable source of information on his life and times to this day. Moreover, only a few months after Tsar Nicholas II had succeeded his father, his judgment was far-sighted indeed. In the last chapter, he observed that if the young ruler 'continues to tread in the domestic tracks of his father, he will be laying up for himself a still more insufferable crown of thorns than that which galled his father to the grave.' It was in part an acknowledgement that his hero surely carried some share of the blame for the collapse of the Russian empire.

This edition retains the complete text of the original, apart from the addition of a few more names to the simplified genealogical table in Chapter 1. Original spellings have been retained, though in some cases the punctuation has been modernised, such as the replacement of double quotation marks by single quotes, and footnotes have been moved to the end of their respective chapters. Finally, illustrations have been added to a volume which initially included only a frontispiece, and a brief chronology is also included.

John Van der Kiste

CHAPTER I

PREDECESSORS

The Romanoffs - Holstein-Gottorps - Paul, the Madman - Alexander I - Tale of a sucking-pig - Nicholas I - Instances of his despotism - Alexander II - Character-sketch - 'Sasha' the 'Military Tailor' - The 'Tsar Emancipator' - Cycle of autocratic reforms

ALEXANDER Alexandrovitch Romanoff, the third of his name who ruled All the Russias, was born at St Petersburg on March 10 (OS February 26), 1845. He was the second son of Alexander II, who will be known in history as the 'Emancipator of the Serfs' and Princess Maria of Hesse-Darmstadt. For more than a century the Russian Tsars had come to Germany for their wives, so that the dynasty of the Romanoffs had now little or no Russian blood left in it, as the poet Pushkin used to exemplify by the ingenious process of adding tumbler after tumbler of water to a glass of wine till the mixture at last retained no taste of the original juice of the grape. It was a curious circumstance that the founder of the dynasty, which was henceforth to rule by divine right alone in Russia, should have been elevated to the Imperial throne by an elective assembly of the various estates. But I do not intend to ask the company of my readers into the mediaeval mists of Muscovite history.

Peter the Great was the last of the pure Russian Tsars, who thenceforth became merged by marriage into the Holstein-Gottorps to such an extent that German blood at last usurped that of the Romanoffs as much as it also replaced that of the Stuarts with us in England. When Prince Peter Dolgoruki, acting as secretary to the Russian Embassy in Paris, was summoned home by the Emperor Nicholas, in consequence of something he had written, he replied by offering to send his photograph instead, and by begging his Majesty to remember that his (Dolgoruki's) ancestors 'were Grand Dukes of Moscow, when those of his Majesty were not even Dukes of Holstein-Gottorp.'

It will be well to remember the fact of this predominance of the German element in the race of the modem Romanoffs when we come to consider the marked antipathy of some of their number, the subject of the present sketch included, to the country of their origin. For the American naval lieutenant was not entirely right when he said, at the taking of the Taku forts, that blood was always thicker than water. It is a curious circumstance, this tendency of modem nations to fall under the sway of alien races and dynasties, as witness the Guelph-Saxe-Coburgs in England, the Danes in Greece, the Italian Napoleons and Gambettas in France, the French Bemadottes in Norway-Sweden, the Hapsburgs in Mexico, the English in India, the Battenbergs in Bulgaria, and the Holstein-Gottorps in Russia.

The subjoined genealogical table shows the descent of Alexander III as far as from Catherine II, of notorious memory, and further back we need not go. As a man must naturally inherit some of the qualities of his ancestors, it may be well to say just a few words about the immediate predecessors of Alexander III.

CATHERINE II
|
PAUL
|
ALEXANDER I; NICHOLAS I
|
ALEXANDER II; Constantine; Nicholas; Michael
|
Alexandra; Nicholas; ALEXANDER III; Vladimir; Alexis; Marie; Sergius; Paul
|
NICHOLAS II; Alexander; George; Xenia; Michael; Olga

Paul, the son of Catherine II (though it is not quite so certain that her legitimate husband was his father), was a wildly insane despot. He knouted his subjects into the observance of his slightest caprices. Once asked by a foreign visitor who were the most important men in Russia, he replied that there were none save those he happened to be speaking to, and that their importance lasted only just as long as his conversation with them. Unlike his mother, he was incapable of literature; but he once wrote a paragraph for his own official gazette in which he proposed that quarrels between States should in future be settled by personal encounters between their Sovereigns, each combatant to be attended by his Premier in the character of second. He then caused the paragraph to be copied into a Hamburg print, with the remark that this was apparently some notion of that madman, Paul.' Among other mad things, he conceived the idea of helping Napoleon to expel the English from India. His hatred of the modern spirit was so great that he enjoined the players to use the word 'permission' instead of 'liberty' on their bills, and forbade the Academy of Science to use the word 'revolution' when speaking of the courses of the heavenly bodies. Eventually he succumbed to a *révolution du palais*. Some of his courtiers thought him much too mad even for a Russian despot, and forced him to abdicate - strangling him to death in the process.

His son and successor, Alexander I (who had been privy to the conspiracy for dethroning his father, but guiltless of his murder), was of a gentle and affectionate disposition, mildly mannered, and sympathetic - weirdly made up of strength and softness, of 'manly qualities and feminine weakness' as was written of him by Metternich. Madame de Staël once told him that his character in itself was 'a charter and constitution for his subjects.' Like Frederick the Great, he had been educated by a French tutor (La Harpe), by whom his mind had been imbued with very liberal, almost republican, ideas. He was honestly concerned for the welfare of his subjects; but, while intent on the work of domestic reform, he kept a steady eye on the external aggrandisement of his Empire. With this latter object he entered into a compact with Napoleon for the pursuit of a common career of conquest, but ultimately he fell out with the Satanic Corsican - as robbers generally do - over the distribution of their spoil, and then banded himself with Prussia and other foes of the French. 'Napoleon,' says an inscription on the battlefield of Borodino, 'entered Moscow, 1812; Alexander entered Paris, 1814.'

In the latter year he came over to London, and was immensely fêted, as he well deserved to be; and public curiosity was strongly excited by the Cossacks, mounted on their small white horses with their long spears grounded, keeping guard at the door of Lawrence, the painter, while he took the portrait of their Hetman, Platoff. The Senate at St Petersburg voted his political canonisation, and begged him to accept the title 'Blessed.' 'I have always endeavoured,' replied Alexander I, 'to set the nation an example of simplicity and moderation. I could not accept the title you offer me without departing from my principles.' It was then proposed to erect a monument to him. 'It is for posterity,' he said, 'to honour my memory in that way if it deems me worthy of it.' His solicitude for the weal of his subjects was warm and genuine, though his good intentions were frequently thwarted by the apathy, the falsehood, and the corruption of his officials. One story will serve to show what he and all the Tsars of Russia have ever had to contend with in this respect.

On paying a visit to one of the military colonies, Alexander resolved to inspect every house, so as to satisfy himself as to the condition of the establishment. On every table he found a commissariat dinner prepared, one of the staple articles of which was a sucking-pig. At last, one of his Majesty's attendants, Prince Volkhonski, suspecting some trick, slily cut off the pig's tail and slipped it into his pocket. On entering the next house, there again was a roast pig on the table - but this time *without a tail!* 'I think," said the Prince, 'that we have an old friend here.' On being questioned as to his meaning, he produced the missing tail, and fitted it to the place from which it had been sliced. Disheartened and disgusted by innumerable frauds of this kind, Alexander I abandoned the helm in despair to his Minister, Araktcheief, and the Empire returned to its old routine. He died in 1825, and was succeeded by his second younger brother, Nicholas; for the real heir to the crown, Constantine, was such a startling copy, in mind and person, of his mad father, Paul, that he had to be passed over and allowed to indulge his brutal and eccentric passions in the innocuous obscurity of private life.

Now came the reign of Nicholas, who, forming a singular contrast to his predecessor on the throne, was a despot of the most ancient and approved type. Tall, well-built, handsome, imperious, and impressive, he might have sat to a painter as the incarnation of human pride and autocratic will. Having managed to insert the thin end of the wedge in. the reign of Alexander, the friends of freedom in Russia thought they could not have a better opportunity than the present change of sceptre, with all its uncertainties, for widening the rift. But they soon found out that Nicholas was not a man to be trifled with in this respect. For the echoes of the cannon that had saluted his accession had barely died away when the streets of St Petersburg were again reverberating with the roar of guns, which the new Emperor had turned with terrible effect upon the revolutionists of his capital. Great numbers were killed, and their bodies thrust into the Neva through holes cut in the ice; while hundreds of the other conspirators were at once packed off to Siberia. Many of these victims of the insurrection had not the faintest notion what they wanted. Some of them had cried: 'Long live Constantine! The Constitution for ever!' and then inquired: 'But who is this *Constituzia*? Is she the wife of the Emperor?'

'Let there be no mind in Russia - I, Nicholas the Tsar, so will it' - such was the ukase practically ascribed to him by a foreign noble. His whole administration was well illustrated by an incident connected with the construction of the railway between St Petersburg and Moscow. The engineers had wrangled and jangled so long over the precise direction which this line should take, that at last the Emperor grew utterly sick of the discussion. 'Give me a ruler,' said his Majesty ; and with that he sharply drew a straight line between his two capitals, adding, 'Let that be the route.' And to this day it is the route, with the result that considerable towns and centres of commerce, which it ought to be the function of a railway to connect, are left *en l'air*, so to speak, at several miles' distance on either side of the line. Once, as head of the Russian Church, he was requested by the Holy Synod, in a long memorandum, to declare whether or not the existence of purgatory was an Orthodox doctrine. 'No purgatory,' was all he wrote on the margin of the memorial. During his reign which lasted about thirty years, he engaged in four campaigns - that of 1828-29 against Turkey; that of 1831 for the suppression of the Poles, who had writhed under and risen against his iron rule; that of 1848-49, in which he joined hands with his fellow-despot at Vienna in order to quench the flames of Hungarian liberty and independence, which had been kindled by Kossuth; and that of the Crimea, of which the failure broke his proud and sensitive heart. Yet on his death-bed - and this seems to be an authenticated fact - he exhorted his son and successor to liberate the serfs.

This son was Alexander II, who was just as unlike his father Nicholas, as the latter had been unlike his brother Alexander I. On the other hand, the two first Alexanders, uncle and nephew, had a good deal in common, both being humane, cultured, upright, and indulgent, comparatively speaking, towards their subjects. The first half-dozen years of Alexander II's reign formed a period less of reform than of relief; and it was not till 1861 that he managed to act on the advice of his father by issuing what was called 'the law for the amelioration of the peasantry,' or, in other words, for the emancipation of the serfs. 'Of a kind-hearted, humane disposition,' wrote Sir Donald Mackenzie Wallace of him, 'sincerely desirous of maintaining the national honour, but singularly free from military ambition, and imbued with no fanatical belief in the drill-sergeant system of government, Alexander II was by no means insensible to the spirit of the time. He was well aware of the existing abuses, many of which had been partially concealed from his father, and he had seen how fruitless had been the attempts to eradicate them by a mere repressive system of administration. As heir-apparent, he had taken no part in public affairs, and was consequently in no way bound by antecedents. He had, however, none of the sentimental enthusiasm for liberal institutions which had characterised his uncle, Alexander I. On the contrary, he had inherited from his father a strong dislike to sentimentalism and rhetoric of all kinds. This dislike, joined to a goodly portion of sober common sense and a consciousness of enormous responsibility, prevented him from being carried away by the prevailing excitement. With all that was generous and humane in the movement he thoroughly sympathised, and he allowed the popular ideas and aspirations to find free utterance; but he did not at once commit himself to any definite policy, and carefully refrained from all exaggerated expressions of reforming zeal.'

'Though possessing,' said a writer in the *Times*, 'neither the transcendent genius and Herculean energy of Peter the Great, nor the wonderful intelligence and far-sighted political wisdom of Catherine II, he did, perhaps, as much as either of these great Sovereigns towards raising his country to the level of West European civilisation. His early life gave little indication of his subsequent activity, and, up till the moment of his accession, no one ever imagined that he would one day play the part of a great reformer.' 'My son Sasha is an old woman (baba),' said his very father Nicholas of him. 'There will be nothing great done in his time.' At first, too, that began to be the opinion of 'Sasha's' own subjects, who could see nothing in their new Sovereign but the making of a 'military tailor' - the nickname applied to him from his passion for altering the uniforms of his troops. 'I suppose you fancy we have little freedom of speech,' said a liberal-minded Russian to M. Leroy-Beaulieu. 'Well, one day a student of one of the great Crown colleges, in talking over with his comrades the reforms of Alexander II, declared that the

Emperor was nothing but a tailor, meaning to insinuate that he was too fond of altering military uniforms. These words came to the ears of the police, who carried them to the Sovereign. The imprudent youth was summoned by Imperial order to the palace. His parents already saw him on the road to Siberia. And what punishment do you think was inflicted on him? The Emperor ordered him to be presented with a complete uniform!'

But it was not long before the 'military tailor' bloomed out into the 'Emancipator of the Serfs.' One evening he came into his wife's *salon* very much excited, and, showing a paper which he held in his hand, remarked in a tone of vehemence, quite at variance with his usual demeanour, 'Here is a description of the inhuman treatment a proprietress has been inflicting on her domestic serfs. I shall never sleep calmly till I have put a stop to all that!' Involving as it did the reconstruction, so to speak, of the whole of Russian society, the emancipation of the serfs was not a thing that could be done with a mere '*sic volo, sic jubeo*' on the part of the Emperor. The main point at issue was whether the serfs should become agricultural labourers dependent economically and administratively on the landlords, or should be transformed into a class of independent communal proprietors. The Emperor favoured the latter proposal, and the Russian peasantry acquired privileges such as are enjoyed by no others of their class in Europe. Beside this great and sweeping change, which gained for Alexander II the title of 'Tsar Emancipator,' his Majesty also appointed and personally presided over a variety of Commissions for the elaboration of other reforms, which included a judicial organisation on the French model; a new penal code, and a greatly simplified system of civil and criminal procedure; a system of local self-government, in which each district and province had its elective assembly, possessing a restricted right of taxation; a new rural and municipal police under the direction of the Minister of the Interior; and new municipal institutions, more in accordance with modem notions of civic equality.

'The reign of Nicholas,' says M. Leroy-Beaulieu in his deep and elaborate work on 'The Empire of the Tsars,' 'had shown that, with all its omnipotence, autocracy was not strong enough to keep Russia from rolling down the incline on which Peter the Great had started her. The Crimean War made patent to all eyes, together with the feebleness of the stationary system, the necessity for Russia of placing herself, socially, if not as yet politically, on a level with the West, if only to be in a condition to stand her own against it. Under Alexander II the gates were thrown open, and the reform came at last that was to reconcile Russia to herself as well as with Europe. This time it was not a white-washing or a patching-up of the facade-stucco, or mere outer-casing; it was an upheaving and a remodelling of the very foundations of society; it was the whole people, not one class, that was called to liberty and civilisation. Until the emancipation of the serfs, the work of Peter I having left out the bulk of the nation, lacked a basis; the emancipation gave it one.

The reign of Alexander II may be considered as the closing of a long historical cycle - the cycle of autocratic reforms.

The Emperor Paul had been little better than a madman. Alexander I was little better than a dreamer. In Nicholas 'the old Muscovite Tsars appeared to revive, rejuvenated and polished up after the modern fashion.' Alexander II was a benevolent if cautious reformer, and his son, Alexander III - what was he? The following pages will attempt to show.

CHAPTER II

HEIR APPARENT

Death of the Tsarevitch Nicholas - Alexander heir-apparent - His first Rescript - 'My son, my heir' - Youthful Characteristics - Marriage - Marie Feodorovna - A Teutophobe - 'Thank God for Woronzoff!' - In opposition - Franco-German War - Visit to England - Anglo-Russian Press amenities - Marie Alexandrovna - Alexander II in London - The Eastern Question - A Panslavist champion - Russo-Turkish War — Army of the Lom - Character as a commander - Courageous or cowardly? - The foe of falsehood and corruption - Under arrest - The eve of action

AS the second son of his father, the Grand Duke Alexander received the training of a soldier more than of a Sovereign. His elder brother, Nicholas, a fine, tall, amiable Prince, was Tsarevitch, and a very promising heir-apparent he was. But he died at Nice in April 1865 just about the time of President Lincoln's assassination, and. then his brother, Alexander, became heir to the throne. The disease - cerebro-spinal meningitis - which carried off the Grand Duke Nicholas had been lurking in his system for several years. It had been aggravated by a fall from his horse, but it was said to have originated in the overstrain of a wrestling match to which the Tsarevitch had challenged his cousin, Prince Nicholas of Leuchtenberg. 'A post-mortem examination,' wrote the *Lancet*, 'showed that a tubercular tendency exists in the constitution of a Royal family likely to exercise a most important influence on the history of Europe and the world.'[1]

The Tsar himself had hurried to Nice with several members of his family (the Empress was there already), and it is said that the special train which carried the Imperial party from the French frontier to the shore of the Mediterranean was driven by a Polish exile! Among others who had hastened to Nice on the illness of the Tsarevitch taking so serious a turn were the Queen, and Crown Prince, and Princess Dagmar of Denmark, who had been affianced to the Grand Duke Nicholas. With his bride-elect the dying Prince had an interview immediately on her arrival, and confided her to the love and care of his brother Alexander, whom he described as a much better man than himself. His obsequies were celebrated at Nice with great ceremony, after which his remains were taken by sea to St Petersburg in a Russian man-of-war, and deposited with gorgeous funeral pomp in the Fortress Church of

Saints Peter and Paul, which forms the mausoleum of the Romanoffs. The house at Nice where he had died was bought by the Emperor and turned into a Russian chapel.

Three months later the new Tsarevitch attained his majority and took the oath to his father, amid a scene of great ceremony, in the chapel of the Winter Palace. On this occasion he issued his first rescript, addressed to the Governor-General of St Petersburg, and it is worth quotation for the character of the sentiments therein expressed:

'In taking the most important step of my life, and vowing devotion to my father, and in his person to all Russia, my first thought was to mark this day by an act of charity. I herewith transmit to you the sum of 6000 roubles, requesting you to distribute the same among the poorest inhabitants of the country. I shall be happy if it serve to dry but a few tears, or to provide bread for a few needy families; and God will listen to the prayers they will offer up in common with me for the long life of our Emperor-Lord, and for the prosperity of the country.'

It was popularly rumoured that the Emperor meant to pass over Alexander and vest the succession in his third son, Vladimir, a much more gifted Prince; and we have already seen how this was done in the case of Nicholas I, who superseded his elder brother, Constantine, the son and facsimile of the crazy Emperor, Paul. But the rumour was at once disposed of by the manifesto in which the Tsar called upon all his subjects to take the oath of allegiance to the new Tsarevitch, Alexander, as well as by the words which he addressed to a deputation of Polish nobles, who had come to condole with him on the death of his eldest son. 'Here stands my son Alexander, my heir,' said his Majesty, after reading the nobles a very sharp lecture on the political sins of their misguided countrymen, whom he solemnly counselled to have done with their dreams of recovering their lost independence. 'He bears the name of the Emperor who formerly established the kingdom of Poland. I hope he will know how to govern his inheritance worthily, and that he will not endure that which I myself have not tolerated.'

'Brought up hitherto as a dashing officer of the Guards,' as was written of him by a Baltic Province man 'without any political education, with but a scanty knowledge of languages for a man in his position, and with a disposition more given to self-indulgence than to work, the new heir-apparent found that time was above all things necessary to adapt himself to the altered state of things.'[2] He was but a poor linguist compared with his father, who had learnt in his youth to write English, French, and German with perfect fluency and correctness. His quick ear had even caught up peculiarities of dialect, and in after-life he sometimes surprised Scotsmen 'by addressing them in the language and accent of an 'auld nurse,' to whom he had been much attached in his childhood.

'Alexander Alexandrovitch,' wrote a keen, incisive critic,[3] who had ample opportunities of judging his character, 'not having become heir-apparent to the throne before his twenty-first year, was not brought up to the calling of monarch any more than he was trained to the profession of surgery. The role for which Nature, grace, and education had fitted him could be equally well played by any one of a million 'supers' on the world's stage, and his consciousness of his shortcomings, before his coronation, was as keen as that of the inebriated Irishman who declared himself sober enough to know that he was not sober. His elder brother's death, which the nation viewed as the finger of cruel fate, he regarded with awe as that of a paternal providence shaping his destiny; and bowing before the inscrutable decree which thus marked him out as the Pope of a vast Empire and the autocrat of a national church, he wisely left the puzzling question of ways and means to be worked out by Omnipotence, who alone could grapple with the insoluble problem.'

The following story was told of him before he became heir-apparent. Shortly after he had been appointed tutor to the two Grand Dukes (Nicholas and Alexander), M. Pobedonostseff (who was afterwards to become Procurator of the Holy Synod and trusted counsellor of Alexander III) penned a letter to his friend Admiral Shastakoff, in which he described the occupations and progress of his imperial pupils. 'After having descanted in enthusiastic terms on the marvellous talents of the elder brother, the Russian Fenelon struck a minor key in his allusions to Alexander, regretting that 'our darling dove' had been so badly misused by Nature, who sent him into the world with the shabbiest of intellectual outfits. Whether the story be true or false, the personal appreciation that underlies it is acquiesced in by all the preceptors of the Grand Duke, who was considered, as was David Hume by his mother, to be 'a fine, good-natured creature, but uncommon wake-minded.'

'...In the midst of congenial surroundings, and with such mental and moral equipment, Alexander Alexandrovitch was trained to the profession of arms. The story of his youth is that of most Grand Dukes of that day and this, and is contained in a wearisome record of reviews, races, routs, balls, and those freaks of fashionable folly which modern modesty is wont to describe by the euphemism of sowing wild oats. The Grand Duke never posed as a saint, and possessed little claim to the aureole; but the effects of temperament are sometimes similar to the fruits of virtue, and, dull and phlegmatic as he was, with the 'melancholy juices redundant all over,' his propensities never assumed the form of passions, and his sins never acquired the peculiar deep shade connoted by the epithet Oriental....The massive build, the slow *tempo*, awkward bearing, and bovine butting of the head, suggested 'bullock' as a term of endearment which his father first conferred upon him in his childhood, and his people altered to 'bull' after his accession to the throne.'

'Contemporary history the Grand Duke studied in the most Liberal text-book of the day - the once famous *Golos* newspaper. Its proprietor found in him a willing and powerful protector against the Censor-General, Grigorieff, who, desirous to promote the success of its rival (the *Novoe Vremya*), frequently superseded it for weeks and months on the flimsiest of pretexts. To my own knowledge, arbitrary sentences of this kind were several times reversed, or mitigated, owing to the personal intercession of the heir-apparent, who professed to relish the plain speaking of that journal. Indeed, his utterances on some of the burning questions of the day were of the frank and sweeping kind which would, at the present moment, endanger the liberty of an ordinary citizen; and his political leanings were generally assumed to be Liberal enough to clash with the system of government pursued by his father's advisers - General Timasheff and Count Tolstoi. This belief was sufficiently probable, seeing that he drew his facts from the chronicle, and his commentaries from the leaders, of the *Golos*.'

Until the time of his marriage, the Grand Duke Alexander Alexandrovitch paid little, if any, attention to politics. It was not until his wife impressed upon him the necessity of preparing for the lofty duties which one day awaited him, whatever in the way of literature, history, and economical science he acquired, was learned in association with her, if not absolutely under her guidance. An historical work of considerable importance is known to have been written expressly for his instruction and edification. This was, in the first instance, a narrative of the relations between Russia and the different European Powers, from the peace of 1815 until the Crimean War. But it was afterwards extended so as to include the history of Russian diplomacy from the end of the Crimean War until the denunciation, in 1871, of the most **important clause in the Treaty of Paris - the one which forbade Russia to keep war-ships in the Black Sea.** The work, still further developed, was published not many years ago by the Russian Foreign Office, under the title of 'Etude Diplomatique sur la Guerre de Crimée.' Its author is understood to have been Baron Jomini.[4]

On November 9, 1866, the Tsarevitch was married to the Princess Dagmar of Denmark, sister of the Princess of Wales, who had previously been baptised into the Orthodox Church under the name of Marie Feodorovna.[5] She had been betrothed to the Tsarevitch Nicholas, who, on his death-bed, as we have seen, had entrusted her to the love and care of his brother Alexander. The union was one of duty as well as affection, and furnished a precedent for the marriage of our own Duke of York in precisely similar circumstances. The wedding *fêtes* at St Petersburg were of the most gorgeous kind, and were graced, among other illustrious guests, by the presence of the Prince of Wales, who afterwards spent a month in travelling over the Russian Empire, where he was everywhere treated with the greatest distinction and hospitality.

The union into which the Tsarevitch had now entered was destined to prove one of the happiest of its kind, for, whatever may have been his failings in other respects, he ever, at least, set a shining example to the rest of his family in the singleness of his affections and the absolute purity of his domestic life. His consort, on her part, proved as good an Empress as she was a wife, as witness the following sketch of her character from the pen of 'Comte Paul Vasili' in his 'Société de Saint Petersbourg.'

She was no political woman, and had not the slightest desire to appear such. Concerning the affairs of State and Government, there was ever complete silence between her and the Emperor; intriguing, at a Court where intrigue has ever played a formidable part, was as far from her as prying into political affairs, and she enjoyed life with the love of a girl at fifteen for dress and dancing and all things amusing. 'The Empress exercised the same fascination on one and all who approached her. Adore her, as an exceptionally graceful creature, and do not look to her for grave intellectual faculties. Say to yourself that she has realised all that could be expected of her; that, with marvellous intuition, feeling that she had not the necessary resources to play a great part, she had abstained from prying into anything outside her circle. Marie Feodorovna has correctly judged herself and acted accordingly, and it is for this reason that no one can reproach her with the machinations of certain Sovereigns. She never descends to the intrigues of the ante-chamber, and is content to be the angel of her home, the protectress of numerous benevolent establishments in which she is interested in her capacity as a compassionate woman. She visits these establishments, delights her protégés by her presence, and produces wherever she appears the effect of a sunbeam in the dark sky.'

The year of his marriage was otherwise an eventful one for the Tsarevitch, for it marked the first of the long series of attempts to take the life of his father, and he was profoundly moved by this revelation of the active forces of revolution. He himself had lived through an excited and exciting time. He had been a witness of the crises of 1860-61, the first 'students' disturbances,' the emancipation of the serfs, the peasant rising, the hostile demonstration of the nobility, the 'May fires' of 1862, the Polish revolution and its bloody repression; but he had viewed all these things with the comparative insouciance of a young Prince who had no thought of ever succeeding to his father and was content to view life from the easy, careless standpoint of an officer in the Guards. But the prospect that was opened up to him by the death of his brother completely changed the spirit of his dream, and forced him to make a serious effort to understand the political tendency of the time. In making this effort he fell into the hands of the malcontents, who, as always happens, tried to ingratiate themselves with the heir to the throne, and 'to perplex and entangle his straightforward nature in the meshes of their interminable intrigues.' As the Prince of Wales was generally in opposition in the time of our own Georges, so the heir of Alexander II gradually drifted into an attitude of something very like oppugnancy to his Imperial father.

Identifying himself with some of the chief currents of his time as the easiest road to popularity, the Tsarevitch, for one thing, allowed himself to be drawn into the anti-German movement, which was then a 'noble passion' with the party opposed to the reigning Tsar, Alexander II, who was still, as he ever remained, under the influence of the German traditions dating from the time of the brotherhood-in-arms between Russia and Prussia .at the beginning of the century. It was believed, and not without reason that these anti-German feelings of the Tsarevitch found at once their chief source of sympathy and encouragement in the breast of his Danish spouse, of whom, quite naturally enough, it could scarcely have been expected that she should love the nation which had deprived her father of his Schleswig-Holstein sceptre, and slaughtered her gallant countrymen at the redoubts of Düppel. And what the Germans had done with the Elbe Duchies they might equally seek to do with the Baltic Provinces.

A story was told of his Teutophobia, which, even if not true, was at least most expressive of his well-known sentiments on this subject. Soon after assuming command of the famous Preobrajenski regiment, the list of its officers was one day read out in his hearing for some purpose or other, and his countenance was observed to fall, and fall, and further fall as the reader gradually approached the end of the alphabet without reciting a single genuine Russian name; all were German. At last the letter 'W' was reached, and 'Woronzoff' was sung out. 'Thank God for Woronzoff!' exclaimed the Tsarevitch, with a sigh of relief, and a look which seemed to convey his determination of thenceforth supporting a policy of Russia for the Russians.

For these and other reasons, therefore, the Tsarevitch at first became an ardent adherent of the national party, and a great admirer of its mouthpiece, Katkoff, the Moscow editor. With the view also of testifying his concern for the public weal he placed himself at the head of the committee which was formed during the winter of 1867-68 for relieving the famine distress in the north of the Empire; while at the same time he did his best to make the Minister of the Interior the scapegoat of all the evils which had thus overtaken the country. But, like the Crown Prince of Prussia, afterwards Emperor Frederick, who placed himself in opposition to the reactionary policy of his father during the famous 'Conflict Time,' and was virtually banished from Court for some time in consequence, the Tsarevitch also incurred the displeasure of his Imperial sire, and, what was even more unfortunate, of Count Schouvaloff, chief of the 'Third Section,' or secret police. Some correspondence between the Tsarevitch and his political partisans had fallen into the hands of the 'Third Section,' and the heir to the throne made a bitter complaint to his father about this police interference with the private affairs of members of the Imperial family. But the incident was closed by Count Schouvaloff declaring that he could only do his duty as supreme guardian of the monarch's safety, and the authority of his

Government, if his powers of control extended to all His Majesty's subjects without distinction of persons.

For some time now the person of the Tsarevitch receded into the background, and it was only on the outbreak of the Franco-German War that he again stepped forward to play a party *rôle*. At the head of the whole youth of Russia he made no secret of his strong sympathy with the cause of the French, which, indeed, became a shibboleth with the Slavophiles. This national partisanship of his was all the more striking as his father's heart was known to be wholly on the side of the Germans in their tremendous struggle. For did Alexander II, on hearing of Sedan, not give a grand banquet at Moscow to celebrate the event, and subsequently send the Cross of St George to Moltke, the vanquisher of the French? But when the war ended with the Commune, the Tsarevitch was said to have exclaimed, with a sigh: *'C'est là que mènent ces idées?'* - 'It is to this, then, is it, that all these ideas lead?' - and to have taken temporary farewell of some of his youthful French dreams.

The French war had aroused Russia, as most other countries, to the necessity of reorganising her army, and into this question the Tsarevitch threw himself with his wonted ardour. The War Minister, General Milutin, was for doing the work of military reform gradually; but that would not satisfy the heir to the throne, who, in order to evince his patriotic solicitude, ordered, at his own private cost, several thousand rifles and a number of field-guns, so as thus to expedite the work of re-armament. The incident caused a great sensation at the time - the more so, as the friends of the Tsarevitch had sought to engage an English expert at a very high salary to superintend the work of making rifles.

A memorable and important incident in the life of the Tsarevitch was his visit to England in June 1873 with his wife and two boys. For it enabled him to see and better understand the people who were now fast becoming the neighbours of Russia in Central Asia; and even on the very day of his arrival in London an official report announced, under the heading, 'On the way to Khiva,' that 'the enemy, numbering 3600 Turcomans, Khirgiz, and Khan's troops, had been defeated without any loss on the Russian side' (not even of the traditional three Cossacks!) 'by General von Kaufmann.'

This visit of the Tsarevitch was coincident with that of the Shah of Persia, in whose honour such *fêtes* and national demonstrations were organised as had not been seen in England since the days of the allied monarchs before and after Waterloo; and, on the very day of the grand military review at Windsor, the *Times* quoted a long article from the St Petersburg *Mír* as a specimen of the bitterly anti-British tone which was then pervading all the Russian Press, on account of our very natural solicitude about the march of events in Central Asia. This was one of its sentences:

'In a word, proud Albion is doing all she can to astonish the Shah by the pomp and luxury of his reception - and all this only in order to outdo Russia, and to efface from his mind the pleasing reminiscence he took with him from St Petersburg. From the naive language of the English papers it is clear that, in all the festivities in honour of the Shah, England is showing her spite against Russia rather than her friendship for Persia,' &c.

To which the *Times* replied:

'Such acrimonious rant as the comments of the Mir, it has seldom been our lot to read...Yet we fear it only exaggerates and does not misrepresent a national feeling...The article may be taken as evidence that there is a portion of the public in St Petersburg which likes to hear England spoken of as 'Bloody Albion,' which enjoys such delicate figures of speech as 'the hidden growl of the perfidious and cruel tiger,' and is able to tolerate as a true version of history the description of the Sepoy Mutiny as of the general rebellion, excited by English policy and sustained by English gold, to supply an opportunity for the 'plunder of the Indian Princes.'....Our Russian friends must not suppose that we are always thinking about them. Our Queen, her Ministers, and those who are set in authority among us, including the Lord Mayor, the Lessee of the Opera, the Directors of the Albert Hall and the Crystal Palace, have not the slightest desire to make a demonstration against the Russian Government or any other. In fact, their Imperial Highnesses the Tsarevitch and the Tsarevna have borne a chief part in all these ceremonials. Is it to be supposed that they, too, have been aiding the moral conquest of the **British tiger?**'

It was during the exchange of these journalistic amenities that the Heir of All the Russias paid his first visit to England, where he remained for the greater part of a month, he and his consort, as the guests of the Prince and Princess of Wales at Marlborough House. Had the Court of Persia not transferred itself to London, the Tsarevitch and Tsarevna would have been the chief attractions of the London season; but, as it was, they figured at all the splendid pageants given in honour of the Shah, and lent additional lustre to the great social gatherings which marked that eventful summer. At Spithead, the Tsarevitch had an exceptional opportunity of being impressed with the naval power of England, while at Windsor, Aldershot, and Woolwich, he was equally present at reviews and sham-fights, which enabled him to judge of the quality of our little army. When the Guards in magnificent array went past at the Grand Review in Windsor Park, the Tsarevna, turning to her sister, the Princess of Wales, 'straightened her hand in illustration of the level ranks' while the Shah motioned to the Duke of Cambridge and the Queen 'with an animated gesture of admiration,' which was shared by the Tsarevitch, when by there swept the 93rd Highlanders, who had formed the 'thin red line' at Balaclava.

In the intervals left him by the balls, operas, banquets, and other social functions which made the season of 1873 one of the most brilliant on record, the Tsarevitch sought to complete his knowledge of English life and institutions by a display of energy which could not even have been surpassed by an eager American tourist. Everything that was characteristic of our national life, be made a point of seeing. Prisons, picture-galleries, hospitals, banks, race-courses, polo-grounds, the Tower, the docks, the Post-office, and all the other sights of London were in turn the objects of his intelligent curiosity, and he even spent an afternoon in the Court of the Lord Chief Justice, listening to the trial of the Tichborne case.

He saw something of the country, too. For he went to Hull for a couple of days to inspect a new yacht, the 'Tsarevna,' which had been devised for him by Sir E.T. Reed, of whom he was the guest; and he bestowed on some ironclads that were being built in the Humber a degree of attention such as only his ancestor, Peter the Great, was wont to pay to our ships of war at Deptford. Before leaving England, after a pleasant and instructive stay of about four weeks, the Tsarevitch dined with the Duke of Edinburgh and the Elder Brethren of Trinity House, when his health was drunk with the utmost enthusiasm. Speaking in French, his Imperial Highness thanked the Prince of Wales for the cordial manner in which he had been received in England, adding, 'and I trust that our cordial and affectionate relations may continue to the end of our lives. I trust also that the same affectionate cordiality with which I have been received by my brother-in-law may be extended to me by the English nation.' It cannot be doubted that this visit of the Russian heir-apparent to the Court of the Empress of India, of whom he had also been the honoured guest for a couple of days at Windsor Castle, had a beneficent effect that was destined to make itself felt on the future relations of the two countries.

The Tsarevitch had referred to the Prince of Wales as his 'brother-in-law'; and now the title was to become applicable in a double sense. For by this time it was known, though not yet officially announced, that a marriage was being arranged between the only daughter of the Russian Emperor and the second son of Queen Victoria.

> 'The son of him with whom we strove for power -
> Whose will is lord thro' all his world domain -
> Who made the serf a man, and burst his chain -
> Has given our Prince his own imperial flower, Alexandrowna.'

'No private family in this country are more attached to each other than the Imperial family of Russia,' said the Prime Minister when asking the House of Commons for the usual marriage grant. 'It is for her happiness, but the light of my life has gone out,' sadly remarked the Emperor, after the gorgeous marriage ceremony in the Winter Palace, on the 23rd of January of the following year (1874).

A few months later the Tsar Liberator came to England (as Alexander I and Nicholas had done before him) on a visit to his dearly beloved daughter; and at a luncheon which was offered him at the Guildhall, his Majesty, speaking with much emotion, trusted 'that, with the blessing of Divine Providence, the affectionate home she finds in your country will strengthen the friendly relations now established between Russia and Great Britain for the mutual advantage of their **prosperity and peace.**' I think it was Lord Granville who said that, even if such dynastic alliances were powerless to prevent war, they could, at least, help to preserve peace; and, indeed, such had been the impression produced by the union of the Duke of Edinburgh with the only daughter of the Tsar, that several towns in England hastened to return to the Government the Russian guns captured at Sebastopol, which had been sent to them as trophies of the Crimean war, as wishing it to be understood that they no longer felt anything but good-will towards their former foe. But these millennial acts were premature. For at this very time the Eastern horizon of Europe was beginning to be darkened by gathering storm-clouds, which, gradually overspreading the Balkan skies, ended in a war that had the effect of making England send her threatening ironclads up through the Dardanelles, so as to prevent the Russians from seizing on the city of the Sultans, which Napoleon had well described as the 'capital of the world.'

When these black clouds began to gather over the Balkan peninsula, it was only in keeping with the antecedents of the Tsarevitch that he should have hastened to identify himself with the Pan-Slavonic party of action - that is to say, of war. 'Any one,' said a writer in the *Times*, 'who ventured to counsel prudence, pointing to the danger of grave European complications, and to the sacrifices which even a war in Turkey alone would inevitably entail, was held up to public scorn as a pusillanimous, unworthy son of the Fatherland, who did not know the inexhaustible resources of the country and the unbounded patriotic devotion of the people. The popular feeling naturally found its way to the Emperor through the various unofficial channels. Every morning his Majesty read the fierce diatribes of the Press, and afterwards heard them re-echoed in fainter, more respectful tones by those with whom he conversed, especially in the vicinity of the Empress and the Tsarevitch.'

On two occasions already, Alexander II, though not a military monarch like his father Nicholas, had braced himself up to the prospect of war - once in 1863, when he was firmly determined to resist all interference of the Powers in the settlement of the Polish question; and again in 1870-71, when he resolved at all hazards to free Russia from the hampering Black Sea clauses of the Treaty of Paris. But in 1876-77 the Tsar himself was much less bellicose than the party of extreme Panslavists which claimed the Tsarevitch as one of its leading members. On the two former occasions, the Emperor himself had headed the national movement; in the present case, he was hurried along by it, and, in spite of all his autocratic power, he found it impossible to stem the current of the popular tide, which was setting, deep and strong, for a war with the 'unspeakable' Turks. The Tsarevitch thrilled with the triumph of his own convictions when, standing by the side of his father in the St George's Hall of the Kremlin at Moscow, he heard his Majesty at last declare: 'My most ardent wish is to arrive at a general agreement. Should this not be achieved, and should I see that we cannot obtain such guarantees as are necessary for carrying out what we have a right to demand of the Porte, I am firmly resolved to act independently, and am convinced that in this case the whole of Russia will respond to my summons, should I consider it necessary, and should the honour of Russia require it.'

Immediately after the passage of the Danube by the Russian troops, the 12th and 13th Corps were detached under the Tsarevitch to take up position along the line of the Lom, in order to secure the left of the army advancing across the Balkans from molestation by Mehemet Ali (a Magdeburg German by birth), who, with about 50,000 troops, was holding the Quadrilateral of Turkish fortresses - Rustchuk, Shumla, Varna, and Silistria. The army of the Tsarevitch - numbering about 40,000 infantry, 500 cavalry, and 200 guns - was scattered over a length of more than fifty miles behind the White Lom, and its duties were of a strictly defensive kind.

'The achievements of the Tsarevitch's detachment,' wrote Lieutenant Greene, US., the most accurate if most colourless historian of the war, 'have been somewhat obscured by the more bloody engagements around Plevna, and the subsequent brilliant advance over the Balkans. But it must not be forgotten that throughout the campaign it fulfilled to the letter, and without drawing reinforcements from the other parts of the army, the task which was assigned to it, viz, to assure the safety of the left flank of the army, and to weaken the Quadrilateral of Turkish fortresses.'

Whatever may have been thought of the generalship of the Tsarevitch on the line of the Lom, he could at least boast that the Turks were never able to break through this lengthy line. Several times, indeed, he had to fall back before his Turkish foes - notably at Karahassankoi, Popkoi, Opaka, and Kaceljevo - engagements which were always claimed as great victories by the Ottomans; but it was a curious kind of victory which ultimately ended in the transfer of Mehemet Ali from his command, 'because he had refused to break his neck against a stone wall,' as he said to an English correspondent at Varna. 'Of the generalship on the Russian side (Tsarevitch),' wrote the same correspondent, 'it is unnecessary to speak, for it is a matter of universal comment and criticism, and I need only refer to the descriptions of the different movements which I have sent from time to time, and let every one judge for himself.' The truth is that the Tsarevitch, who had indulged in 'unaccountable movements and wild manoeuvres,' did not exhibit anything like inborn genius for the art of war - far from it; though he now showed himself, to the surprise of many of his friends, to be *un homme sérieux* who could command esteem, if not, perhaps, love. It was certainly much less owing to his own brilliant generalship than to the strategical blunders of the Turks that he had kept intact the line of the Lom.

But if the Tsarevitch did not display anything like military genius at the head, of the army of the Lom, did he at least exhibit the ordinary courage of the soldier? In a brilliant article on the character of Alexander III, Mr 'Lanin' said: 'Marvellous personal courage is not a striking characteristic of the dynasty of the Romanoffs as it was of the English Tudors....The Tsar has been frequently accused of cowardice, an indictment to which, it must be admitted, many undeniable facts lend a strong colouring of probability.' He further spoke of the Emperor's aversion to ride on horseback, and of his dread of a horse even when the animal is harnessed to a vehicle.' Commenting on these statements, Mr Archibald Forbes in an article on the 'Military Courage of Royalty,' wrote as follows:[6]

'In 1877, Alexander III did not know what nerves meant. He was then a man of strong, if slow mental force, stolid, peremptory, reactionary, the possessor of a dull but firm resolution. He had a strong though clumsy seat on horseback, and was no infrequent rider. He had two ruling dislikes: one was war, and the other was officers of German extraction. The latter he got rid of; the former he regarded as a necessary evil of the hour. He longed for its ending, but while it lasted he did his sturdy and loyal best to wage it to the advantage of the Russian arms; and in this he succeeded, strenuously fulfilling the particular duty which was laid upon him, that of protecting the Russian left flank from the Danube to the foot-hills of the Balkans. He had good troops; the subordinate commands were fairly well filled, and his headquarters staff was efficient. General Dochtouroff, its *sous-chef*, was certainly the ablest staff-officer in the Russian army. But Alexander was no puppet of his staff; he understood his business as the Commander of the Army of the Lom, performed his functions in a firm, quiet fashion, and withal was the trusty and successful warden of the eastern marches.

'His force never amounted to 50,000 men, and his enemy was in considerably greater strength. He had successes, and he sustained reverses, but he was equal to either fortune - always resolute in his steadfast, dogged manner, and never whining for reinforcements when things went against him, but doing his best with the means to his hand. They used to speak of him in the principal headquarters as the only commander who never gave them any bother. So highly was he thought of there, that when, after the unsuccessful attempt on Plevna in the September of that war, the Guard-Corps was arriving from Russia, and there was the temporary intention to use it with our troops in an immediate offensive movement across the Balkans, he was named to take the command of the enterprise. But this intention having been presently departed from, and the reinforcements being ordered instead to the Plevna section of the theatre of war, the Tsarevitch retained his command on the left flank, and thus, in mid-December, had the opportunity of inflicting a severe defeat on Suleiman Pasha, just as in September he had worsted Mehemet Ali in the battle of Arkova....He never was a gracious, far less a lovable man....He was a brave man fifteen years ago.'

But whatever the degree of personal courage displayed by the Tsarevitch during the Turkish campaign, it had a great effect upon him all the same. For he returned home with a thorough horror and hatred of war and all its ways. He had got his baptism of fire, and he had no desire for total immersion. To the detestation of war which the Tsarevitch carried back with him from the Danube to the Neva may be ascribed that unfailing devotion to peace which characterised him during his reign as Tsar. It is true, he had not been able to make very much impression on the Turks. But Russia had still more terrible enemies than the Turks, in the shape of the corruption and peculation which were considered patriotic virtues by all the higher commanders in her army. Into the malpractices of these high-placed bloodsuckers, some of them members of the Imperial family itself, who had done more, perhaps, than the Remingtons of the Turks to impede the tide of Russian victory, a Commission, presided over by the Tsarevitch himself, was appointed to inquire after the war; and the result of this inquiry was so disgraceful to its chief objects, that for a long time afterwards the heir to the throne would not even speak to his uncle, the Grand Duke Nicholas, who had been the virtual commander of all the Russian armies in the field. The disclosures now made sickened the very heart of the future Emperor, and he registered a vow that, if ever he came to the throne, he would do his best to prove a Hercules in the work of cleansing the Augean stables of the Empire from the pollution and corruption everywhere prevailing. But he was not more enraged at the administrative rogueries which had been revealed by the war than disappointed and disgusted with its political results as embodied in the Treaty of Berlin, and his anti-German feelings now became intensified. With the signature of the Treaty of Berlin, the slumbering fires of Nihilism again leapt up into a threatening flame, and within the next two years several daring attempts were made to take the life of the Emperor. Among the Nihilists arrested were noblemen and ladies of good family. No circle was free from suspicion, and even some members of the Imperial family itself were the objects of police surveillance. The Emperor himself was at this time on anything but cordial terms with his heir, who had constituted himself, strange to say, the champion of reform. On the anniversary of his father's accession (March 2, 1879), the Tsarevitch headed a deputation to congratulate his Majesty, and said: 'We fervently wish and confidently hope that your Majesty, as ruler, may continue to carry out those wise resolutions which you have hitherto adopted.' To which the Emperor coldly and pointedly replied:

'My endeavour is that my heir shall find the Empire at the height of its prosperity and power, both internally and externally. We have» however, great tasks yet before us. Those immediately to be attended to are a reduction of expenses, a regulation of the currency, a further reconstruction of the army, the imperfections of whose administration have been recently laid bare, and improvement of the sanitary state of the country. There are other tasks to be seen after, but they must wait till the existing passions are appeased. If I do not live to see the time, my heir must undertake the improvement.'

It was added that the Tsarevitch retired in silence, and some little time after it was rumoured that he had been asked by his father to consider himself under arrest.[7] In any case, there were grave political differences between the two, and these were presently accentuated by the scandal to which the double marriage of Alexander II had given rise, and which wounded the strictly moral heir to the throne in his tenderest feelings. The haste with which the recently widowed Tsar espoused Princess Dolgorouki, who had borne him several children during the lifetime of his lawful consort, wounded the filial piety and mortified the self-love of the Tsarevitch. It was, according to Count Dmitry Tolstoy, gall and wormwood to him to be compelled to sit, with his own spouse, at the family table in Livadia, below Princess Yuriefski - the title conferred by the Tsar upon Princess Dolgorouki when he secretly married her, a short time before his death.

'Experiences of so staggering a nature,' said a writer on this period,[8] 'might have disturbed the balance of the strongest and most resolute character. But such a character the second son of Alexander II had never been, and could not have been under the given circumstances. Naturally severe and simple minded, the Tsarevitch, from his twentieth year, had stood under the weight of a task whose magnitude was above his powers and his education. He was torn hither and thither by impressions of the most contradictory kind. He was deceived in everything which he had accepted as fixed and authoritative. He was excluded from all participation in the business which should form the work of his life, and, from the nature of his position, he was prevented from sharing with trusted friends the burden imposed upon him. The consequence of all this was that he lost confidence in himself and in his powers. His grandfather had tried one system, his father the opposite, and both were baffled - both had found out that the instrument of war had failed at the critical moment, just as the painfully elaborated civil order had done, and that a desertion had followed the failure making the professions of the most loyal people on earth appear a mockery and a lie. Where should belief in the future and confidence in one's self be found, in the midst of a chaos which seemed incomparably worse than anything which had ever been experienced in the so-called 'pagan' lands of the West?'

But now the time was fast approaching when the Tsarevitch was to be relieved from the irksome *rôle* of a purely passive observer of events, and to be invested with the power of giving effect to those ideas of reform of which he had hitherto, as we have seen, been the ardent advocate.

NOTES

1. 'It is a melancholy circumstance,' wrote the Vienna correspondent of the *Standard* on the day after Alexander III died at Livadia (November 1, 1894), 'that, at the moment when the Tsar was breathing his last, another member of the Imperial House, the Grand Duke Alexis Michaelovitch, accompanied by his brother, Sergius Michaelovitch, was on his way to Vienna, *en route* for San Remo, suffering from tuberculosis.' At the same time the Tsar's second son, George, was believed to be dying of consumption.

2. *Aus der Petersburger Gesellschaft.* ('Distinguished Persons in Russian Society.')

3. Mr E.B. 'Lanin' (a pseudonymous and, according to some, a compound personality) in a most able and interesting article on 'The Tsar Alexander III,' in the *Contemporary Review* for January 1893.

4. My authority for the information conveyed in this paragraph was a writer in the *Standard* (November 2, 1894).

5. Of this union the issue was six children. The first five, namely Nicholas, born May 18, 1868; George, born May 9, 1871; Xenia, born April 18, 1875; Michael, born December 5, 1878; and Olga, born June 13, 1882, all lived to maturity. A second son, Alexander, was born on June 7, 1869, but succumbed to meningitis the following year at a little under eleven months.

6. *Contemporary Review* for February 1893. Mr 'Lanin's' article had appeared in the January number of the same magazine.

7. The following was the account of this incident, which met with no official contradiction: 'After a conversation of three quarters of an hour on March 4, the Tsarevitch left his father's palace in a highly excited state. The Tsar immediately summoned the Council of Ministers, and informed them that for the safety of the State it was necessary that his son should be kept in custody, and charged him with being in connivance with the most dangerous foes of Russia. Finally, Count Adlerberg was sent to the Tsarevitch to inform him that he must not leave his palace, and must consider himself a prisoner.'

8. 'Russia under Alexander III and in the Preceding Period.' By H. von Samson-Himmelstiema. Translated from the German by J. Morrison, M.A.

CHAPTER III

CIRCUMSTANCES OF HIS ACCESSION

March 13, 1881 - The Anitchkoff Palace - An Equerry's message - Assassination of Alexander II - Alexander III's Manifesto - Accession formalities - Imperial funeral - English sympathy - Nihilist ultimatum - National slip between cup and lip - Loris-Melikoff's Constitution - A tap-room Parliament - Reform or Reaction? - Despotism by Divine Right - The choice of Hercules-Alexander

ON Sunday, March 13, 1881, the Tsarevitch was sitting at lunch with his family in the Anitchkoff Palace on the Nevski Prospect, to which he had just returned from the Michael Riding School, where his father had been holding a review of the Marine Corps, when he was suddenly startled by a loud explosion that filled him with a strange foreboding. In a flash of retrospection he remembered how several attempts had already been made by the Nihilists to take his father's life - by pistol, bombs, poison - how the Imperial train had been nearly blown up near Moscow, and how an explosion at the Winter Palace the previous winter had all but attained its aim. Nay, on this very morning, the Tsarevitch and Count Loris-Melikoff, alarmed by certain threats and information which reached them, had earnestly entreated the Emperor not to expose his person by going to the parade; yet his Majesty had insisted on doing so, with an escort of but half a dozen Cossacks, saying, 'Only Providence can protect me, and when He no longer sees fit to do so, these Cossacks cannot possibly help.' It had always been the Tsar's custom after such Sunday inspections to drive to the Anitchkoff Palace to lunch with his heir and see his grandchildren, of whom he was very fond; but for some reason or other he did not do so to-day, and the Tsarevitch had returned home alone, leaving his father to pay some visits on his way back to the Winter Palace.

In a flash of retrospection, I say, the Tsarevitch remembered all this, and he had barely recovered from the shock of the explosion referred to when he was startled by another, and a louder one. In a few minutes more an Equerry of the Emperor came galloping furiously into the courtyard of the Palace, to anticipate whom both the Tsarevitch and his wife rushed downstairs, but it was some time before the messenger could speak. At last he stammered out: 'He is frightfully wounded,' and then hurriedly explained that, as the Tsar was driving home, he had been made the target of two petards, one of which had mutilated him in the most terrible manner, beyond all hope of recovery. Jumping into a sleigh, the agonised heir-apparent and his wife drove off at full speed to the Winter Palace, where they were the first to arrive after the Grand Duke Michael, and then they learned the awful truth.

While driving along the road between the wall of the Summer Garden and the Catherine Canal, a bomb had been hurled under the Imperial carriage, throwing down the two horses of the escort, tearing off the back of the carriage, wounding one of the Cossacks and a baker's boy, and doing other damage, but leaving the Tsar himself unhurt. The coachman was for driving off home, having received private instructions from the Emperor's family to waive all ceremony when deeming his master to be in danger; but his Majesty pulled the cord so hard that his driver at last stopped, and then the Tsar got out to inquire after the wounded. An officer ran towards him and asked whether he was hurt. The Tsar replied calmly: 'No, thank God, I am untouched. Don't disturb yourself. Let us see after the wounded.' The Emperor ordered that all attention should be given to the injured, and especially to the Cossack who had been seriously hurt. Then, turning round, he beheld the assassin a few paces from him, surrounded by a gathering crowd of people. A soldier of the Preobrajenski Regiment of the Guard held him fast by the arms. He had a revolver in one hand, and a dagger in the other. The Emperor approached the assassin with the utmost calmness, and ordered him to be removed.

Then his Majesty turned to go home, but he had only gone a few steps when a yoimg man threw another bomb at his feet A tremendous explosion followed, which was heard all over the city. When the smoke cleared away, the Emperor was seen lying on the ground in a pool of blood. Many other wounded persons were lying near him. The assassin himself fell to the ground, and he was instantly surrounded by a furious crowd, from which the police had great difficulty in protecting him. The Emperor, who was quite unconscious, was placed on the sleigh of the Chief of Police who took him in his arms, resting the head, which was covered with blood, on his breast.

The Emperor's helmet had been carried away by the explosion, and it was found that he was suffering from the most frightful wounds. One leg was shattered right up to the top of the thigh, and the other was severed at the knee. The abdomen was torn open, and the face was dreadfully disfigured. The right hand, which had been gloved, was much lacerated, his Majesty's wedding-ring being broken and the pieces driven into the flesh. On being asked by his brother, the Grand Duke Michael, who was driving behind him at the time of the explosion, whether he would like to be taken to the nearest house, the Emperor could only murmur, 'Quick home, carry to Palace, there die'; and while being carried home he repeatedly complained of the cold, and asked whether his heir apparent was alive. One of the doctors, who had been through the Crimean and Turkish wars, said he had never seen such awful wounds.

Arrived at the Palace, the mangled Emperor was laid on a couch in his study, and then it became apparent that he had only a short while to live. He must have bled to death sooner but for the cauterising effect of the explosion and the extreme cold; still, the snow outside and the staircase of the Palace were dyed with blood. The Grand Duke Constantine moved in and out of the room unable to bear the heartrending spectacle and all the others were distracted with grief. Instruments were fetched for the purpose of amputating the legs, which were only held on to the body by ligaments of flesh. It is doubtful whether the poor Emperor ever recovered consciousness after being laid on his couch. But at one time he *seemed* to have done so, and then the Holy Sacrament was administered. At about half-past three (the explosion had occurred after two) the murdered monarch breathed his last as the Archpriest was reciting the prayers for those *in extremis* while all present knelt, the spectacle being described as more than heartrending. A *post-mortem* examination proved that the heart and veins had been almost wholly drained of blood, though otherwise all the internal organs were found to be in a normal state.

The sinking of the imperial standard half-mast high had announced to the vast crowds, which had been quick to stream to the Winter Palace from all parts of the city, that the Tsar Emancipator had succumbed to the frightful wounds inflicted upon him by a Nihilist assassin, and the soldiers, in particular, by whom the Emperor was greatly beloved, were furious. 'I myself,' said the correspondent of an English paper, 'saw men and women some time after searching for relics, and rubbing their handkerchiefs in the blood-stained snow, some falling on their knees at the scene of the occurrence, weeping, crying, and crossing themselves.' More than twenty persons had been killed and wounded by the two bombs, which were found to have been filled with a preparation of nitro-glycerine that tore the flesh and clothes into mere shreds. All the windows in the neighbourhood had also been smashed by the force of the explosion.

The chief assassin had been captured, and he turned out to be one Nicolai Vanoff Russakoff, a dark, thick-set, short-necked, repulsive-looking man, nineteen years of age, hailing from Tikhovin, in the province of Novgorod. He had received his elementary education in two towns of his native province, whence, in 1879, he had come to the Institute of Mines in St Petersburg, of which he was a member at the moment of his crime.

From information yielded by this assassin the police, though meeting with a desperate resistance, made some important captures the following day; and then, too, it was discovered that the Nihilists had undermined a thoroughfare called Little Garden Street, leading to the Nevski Prospect, so as to blow up the Tsar had he taken this way home instead of the Catherine Canal route.

Humanly speaking, on that Sunday, the 13th of March, his Majesty was a doomed man - so firm and comprehensive had been the resolution of his foes. The choice of two deaths had been given him - death by hand-grenades or by underground explosion, and chance had caused him to select the former. And even on the banks of the Catherine Canal his murderers had taken the greatest precautions against his escape, several of them being posted along the road with a pre-arranged code of signalling and of action, so as to make sure of their imperial quarry should one or even two of their bombs miss their mark. In all history there is no mention of a more deliberately planned and desperately executed murder of a crowned head.

On the evening of the murder a Council of State was held at the Anitchkoff Palace by the new Tsar, Alexander III, who hastened to issue the following proclamation - the work, as afterwards appeared, of his old tutor, M. Pobedonostseff, now Procurator of the Holy Synod, just as the manifestoes of the Emperor Frederick of Germany had been similarly drafted for him by Dr Geffcken:

'We by the grace of God, Alexander III, Emperor and Autocrat of All the Russias, Tsar of Poland, Grand Duke of Finland, &c, hereby make known to all our faithful subjects that it has pleased the Almighty, in His inscrutable will, to visit Russia with heavy blows of fate, and to call her benefactor, the Emperor Alexander II, to Himself. He fell by the hands of impious murderers, who had repeatedly sought his gracious life, and made their attempts because they saw in him the protector of Russia, the foundation of her greatness, and the promoter of the welfare of the Russian people- Let us bow to the unfathomable will of Divine Providence, and offer up to the Almighty our prayers for the repose of the pure soul of our beloved father.

We ascend the throne, which we inherit from our forefathers, the throne of the Russian Empire, the Tsardom of Poland, and the Grand Dukedom of Finland, inseparably connected with it. We assume the heavy burden which God has imposed upon us with firm reliance upon His almighty help. May He bless our work to the welfare of our beloved fatherland, and may He guide our strength for the happiness of all our faithful subjects. In repeating before Almighty God the sacred vow made by our lather, to devote, according to the testament of our forefathers, the whole of our life to care for the welfare, power, and honour of Russia, we call upon all our faithful subjects to unite before the altar of the Almighty their prayers with ours, and command them to swear fidelity to us and to our successor, his Imperial Highness the Hereditary Grand Duke Nicolai Alexandrovitch. Given at St Petersburg in the year of our Lord 1881, and the first year of our reign.'

It was thought necessary to follow up this proclamation by a special ukase calling separately upon the peasants to join their allegiance with that of all other faithful subjects to the new Tsar and his heirs. In this document the loyal peasantry were reminded of the Government decree abolishing serfdom on February 19, 1861, and constituting them free owners and cultivators of the soil.

Next morning, after the issue of his proclamation, the new Emperor received the allegiance of the officers of the Guards, Court dignitaries, and officials in the Winter Palace. On the open space in front of the Palace large crowds watched the numerous officers and officials going to the ceremony. The large company assembled about noon in the various halls of die Palace through which Alexander III had to pass on his way to the chapel. Coming from the private apartments of his late father, where the remains of the latter were lying, his Majesty advanced, accompanied by the Empress, who wore a white satin robe with a broad crown of diamonds and the rest of his family. In passing through the Hall of St George, his Majesty, addressing the officers there assembled, said, with deep emotion: 'I know how much my father appreciated your fidelity and devotion. I count upon your fidelity to myself, and when I am no more, to my son, the Tsarevitch, Nicolai Alexandrovitch.' These words were greeted with tremendous applause, amid which the procession moved on to the chapel. The form of oath was then gone through by kissing the Bible and Cross, after which the new Tsar left to return to the Anitchkoff Palace, the crowds again cheering loudly as he passed. Throughout the day a large number of Cossacks kept patrolling the streets with lances couched.

For the next fortnight all St Petersburg, one may say all Russia, was nothing but a solemn, sorrow-stricken mortuary chamber. After lying in state for a week at the Winter Palace the remains of the murdered Tsar were removed with most impressive pomp to the Fortress Church, the funeral car being followed by all his sons, brothers, and nephews on foot, accompanied by a crowd of foreign princes. On Sunday, March 27, just fourteen days after the murder, the corpse, which had been gazed at by thousands upon thousands during the time of its lying in state, was finally placed beside that of his Majesty's late consort, in the presence of all the imperial family - the Duke and Duchess of Edinburgh, the Prince of Wales, the Crown Princes of Germany and Denmark - and a multitude of high dignitaries of State, all forming, in the circumstances, such a scene of funereal pomp and moving, mysterious interest as the century had never yet beheld. Before leaving St Petersburg the Prince of Wales, on behalf of his royal mother, ceremoniously invested the new Tsar with the Order of the Garter, recalling how it had been worn by his Majesty's illustrious father and grandfather before him. England, for the rest, had been foremost with her expression of pity and indignation at the murder of Alexander II, and in the House of Commons Mr Gladstone, in moving an address of sympathy to the Queen and the daughter of the assassinated Tsar, quoted, as appropriate to the occasion, the lines of Pope:

'Let tyrants govern with an iron rod,
Oppress, destroy, and be the scourge of God;
Since he, who like a father held his rein.
So soon forgot, so just and mild in vain,' &c.

What the character of the murdered Tsar had been was known to all; but now public interest began to be concentrated on the policy of his successor. What would he do? How would he rule his subjects? With the reforming sceptre of his father, or with a reactionary rod? He was known to have constituted himself the champion of certain Liberal reforms when heir to the crown. Now that it was on his head, would he remain true to the promise of his heir-apparency, or discard his old companions, as our own King Hal had done when he came to the throne? While as yet the corpse of his father was lying in state, the Russian Press openly advocated the granting of a Constitution, not in timid and ambiguous language as hitherto, but in plain, bold, and unequivocal terms. But more than this had reached the new Emperor's eye. For even before his murdered sire was entombed, the Executive Committee of the Nihilists had found means of transmitting to him an ultimatum, of which the following is the substance:

'Yes, your Majesty, do not be deceived by the words of flatterers and parasites. From such a position there are only two outlets - either the inevitable revolution, which cannot be obviated by capital punishments; or voluntary compliance with the will of the people on the part of the Government....Be sure, sire, that as soon as the supreme power ceases to act arbitrarily, and only thinks of yielding to the injunctions of conscience and recognising the rights of the people, you can safely dismiss the spies that do your Government harm, disband your personal escort, and burn your scaffolds. Then, also, would the Executive Committee of its own accord give over its activity, and disperse the forces gathered round it, to devote itself to the national welfare and progress....We forget that you are the representative of mere force, which has so often worked the nation woe, and we turn to you with the hope that feelings of personal bitterness in you will not quench the recognition of your duties and the desire of truth. The exasperation on our side is just as great. You have lost a father; but we have lost, not only fathers, but also brothers, wives, children, friends, and property. But we are ready to repress every personal feeling when the weal of Russia is at stake, and we expect the same of you.

We impose no conditions - those which are necessary to substitute peaceful labour for revolutionary agitation were created by history, not by us. We do not impose those conditions, we merely call them to mind, and, in our opinion, they are two: (1) A general amnesty of all previous political offenders, for they were no criminals, but mere executors of a hard civic duty; (2) the convocation of representatives of all the Russian people for a revision and reform of the private laws of the State, according to the will of the nation. We think it necessary, however, to remind you that the sanctioning of the supreme power by the popular will can only be rendered valid by thoroughly free elections in the following manner....and the Government, therefore, to grant as follows: full liberty of the Press, full freedom of speech, full right of public meeting, and full freedom of election programme.

'These are the only means of restoring Russia to the paths of peaceful progress. We, therefore, solemnly declare in the face of the Fatherland and the whole world, that our party will submit in all respects to the decisions of the National Assembly, if it be convoked under observance of the above conditions ; and, further, that we shall never be guilty of any act of violence against the measures of a Government created by this popular Parliament. So, therefore, your Majesty has to decide. You have two ways before you; it is for you to choose which you will take.'

It is not too much to say that this ultimatum proved the feather which finally determined the Emperor's mind, hitherto trembling between the scales of reform and reaction, in favour of the latter. Already guilty of a crime, the Nihilists had now committed a blunder. They had not read the character of the new Tsar with acuteness enough to perceive that he was a monarch whose mantle of autocracy might be wheedled off by the heat of the sun when it could not be wrenched away by a roaring, threatening wind. And yet, had they but held their peace, had they but allowed their pen to lie awhile, how different might have been the result! Little did the Nihilists and the nation just at this time know what a marvellous slip they had made between the cup and the lip. For, a few hours before Alexander II had been set upon by his Nihilist assassins, he had actually signed a decree conferring upon his people something like the beginnings of a parliamentary representation. It was actually in type when he drew his last breath, but at the last moment it was withheld.

This unpublished ukase had a very curious and a very dramatic history, and there can now be no doubt as to the main facts which M. Leroy-Beaulieu, from whom we mainly borrow their recital, received 'from a sure source, principally from one who was a Minister.' Count Loris-Melikoff was in power at the time, and he and several of his colleagues felt the necessity of at last doing something to give the nation a voice. It was not very easy to make the Emperor (Alexander II) himself accept the idea, but at last he gave way on its being shown to him that the proposed National Assembly would leave his autocratic power intact. For it would merely be a consultative, not a legislative, body, to begin with. It would be composed of delegates from the provincial and municipal assemblies, much in the same way as the first United Diet, or baby Parliament, granted by Frederick William IV of Prussia in 1847, and its sole function meanwhile would be to study and advise upon the projects of laws submitted to it.[1]

'Gentlemen,' said the Emperor, at a sitting of the Council, 'what they propose to us is the Assembly of Notables of Louis XVI. We must not forget what followed. Still, if you think it for the country's good, I will not oppose it.'

The thing was discussed at a council attended by several of the Grand Dukes, including the Tsarevitch, and after a long debate it was adopted in principle. Then a commission met at the Palace of the heir to the throne (whom Loris-Melikoff had sounded and won over beforehand) to elaborate the details of the measure. Thus the matter was settled and embodied in a kind of charter. But a strange kind of fatality hung over it. 'Inclined by nature to procrastination, absorbed at the time by the autumnal joys of his recent morganatic marriage, Alexander II put off for several weeks, till after Lent and the holidays, the promulgation of the act on which depended the future of the Empire and his own existence. He forgot that nobody commands the morrow.'

At last, on the day after the discovery of a new Nihilist plot, on Sunday morning, March 13, just before leaving to attend the parade, from which he was to be brought back a mangled mass of flesh and bones, he actually sent to the Minister of the Interior an order for announcing the important reform in which he intended to surprise and beatify his subjects. 'I have just signed a paper,' said the Tsar to his new consort; Princess Yuriefski, a few minutes before leaving the Winter Palace, 'which I hope will produce a good impression upon Russia, and show that I am ready to give her all that it is possible to give.' And then he added, crossing himself, as was his wont on solemn occasions, 'To-morrow it will be published; I have given the order.'

Alexander II drove forth and met his doom, and the promised charter remained a dead letter. In the confusion which followed the assassination, Loris-Melikoff went to the new Tsar, told him of the order which his father had given that morning, and asked if it should still be carried out. 'Change nothing in what my father ordered,' replied Alexander III; 'this shall be his bequest to his people.' 'Oh, that he had persisted in this resolution,' exclaims M. Leroy-Beaulieu,' and respected his predecessor's last will! By accepting this legacy, moist with the blood of the martyred Tsar, he would have escaped many perplexities and many dangers. Had he acted without delay, in the name of the assassinated Emperor, the new Sovereign would have met public opinion half-way, without seeming to yield to force and riot; he would at once have glorified his father's memory and restored the prestige of the Crown. Just imagine what would have been the feeling of the country and the confusion of the conspirators had Russia and Europe heard in the same breath of the Tsar's violent death and of the convocation by that cold and lifeless hand of a representative assembly! The modest posthumous charter would have received from these dramatic associations a sort of consecration.

'On that evening (March 13) the opportunity which had slipped from the hand of Alexander II was still in the grasp of Alexander III. It was one of those critical moments when on the fleeting hour hangs the whole future of the beginning reign. The point escaped him. Yielding to the impulse given by certain counsellors, the imperial pupil of Pobedondstseff went back on his first inspiration. The Minister of the Interior received a countermanding order in the middle of the night. The project did not appear in the *Official Messenger* on Monday. The new measure, they assured the young Sovereign, had not been sufficiently matured. Before taking such a step all consequences should be weighed. A few days later an extraordinary council, to which were invited several of the survivors from Nicholas's time and several declared apologists of the *status quo*, went over the whole matter in presence of the Emperor. This time stagnation had the day. The convocation of a National Congress was declared imprudent or premature. The question was adjourned - *i.e.* indefinitely, I believe. Eye-witnesses have assured me that, at the end of the sittings the Emperor was seized with a sort of faintness, as though, while taking this decision, he had a foreboding of what it portended.'

It was but a poor substitute for the National Assembly (with consultative powers) which the new Tsar had at first been willing to grant as a legacy from his father, that, in the autumn after his accession, he convoked a commission of thirty-two persons, mostly members of *zemstvos* and municipal councils, to consider the question of tap-rooms and that of peasant emigration. Among those delegates who bore the title 'experts,' there were marshals of the nobility and presidents of provincial assemblies, to whom was joined one peasant, a simple canton elder. But at the same time this commission was a distinct advance on anything of the kind that had ever been seen before, in that it did not include any element of *tchinovnism*, and that its discussions were conducted without the supervision of any government official. Again, its debates were not kept secret, but freely reported in the Press, which was thus for weeks deluged with dissertations on the use and abuse of *vodka*, the native equivalent of whisky. This was the most that ever came of the promised Constitution. Nevertheless, it marked a very slight advance towards popular representation, and it satisfied many. On the part of the Tsar, the tap-room congress was an experiment; on the part of his subjects, a source of amusement. Parliamentarism in Russia had begun with a fiasco, and ended with a farce.

The history of this transition of Alexander III from a constitutional to an autocratic frame of mind is otherwise related in an interesting account of Loris-Melikoff's constitution, of which the substance was first given to English readers in the *Daily Chronicle* (January 15, 1884). This history[2] claims to have been compiled from the papers of the deceased Loris-Melikoff himself - who died in Paris after virtually becoming an exile from the country which he had vainly sought to benefit with a parliamentary voice at least, if not a vote — and bears internal evidence of being pretty correct, at least as to its facts. According to this authority, Alexander III, a few days after the murder of his father, convened and presided over a special meeting of all the

Ministers and other high dignitaries of the State. At that meeting Count Loris-Melikoff* read the draft of a manifesto written by him in the name of the new Tsar, which was only a modification of the one adopted by his father. The new Tsar was already acquainted with it, and had written on its margin, 'Very well done.' The voting resulted in eight 'Ayes' (Loris-Melikoff, the Grand-Duke Vladimir, the Count Valoueff, Nabdkoff, Solsky, Miliutin, Sabouroff, Abaza) and five 'Noes' (the Count Strogonoff, Pobedonostseff, Makoff, Prince Liven, and Possiet). The Tsar himself seemed to be greatly pleased with the result, a joy which he several times manifested in the course of the afternoon, exclaiming; among other things: 'I feel as if a mountain had been taken off my shoulders.'

Loris-Melikoff, to whom the Grand Duke Vladimir communicated all this, came to the conclusion that his battle was won, and remained in St Petersburg without taking any further steps to strengthen his position, while the representatives of the reactionary party, and in the first place M Pobedonostseff (Procurator of the Holy Synod and late tutor to Alexander III) exerted themselves in Gatchina, where the new Tsar resided, to divert him from the adopted plan, and induce him to make up his mind for a reactionary step. On May 9, 1881, Alexander III, without acquainting Loris-Melikoff, ordered quite a different manifesto from the one adopted by him some forty days ago to be promulgated. On sending it to the Grand Duke Vladimir, he wrote -

'I send you, dear Vladimir, the project of the manifesto, approved by me, and I desire to have it promulgated on my arrival in the capital I am doing it after long consideration. The Ministers are talking about some measures they are going to take which would render a manifesto unnecessary. But I cannot get out of them any decisive step, while, on the other hand, a certain fermentation in the people's minds is going on, and they expect something unusual and extraordinary to occur. Therefore, I applied to K.P. Pobedonostseff. I entrusted him with drawing up the project of a manifesto in which it should be clearly set forth what direction I want to give to State affairs, and that I will never suffer autocracy to be limited, as I believe autocracy to be necessary and useful to Russia. The manifesto seems to be very well done. It was fully approved by the Count Strogonoff, who also believes such an act to be quite seasonable. To-day I have read the manifesto to A.V. Adlerberg, who fully approved of it Well, so be it, God helping.'

The manifesto, referred to by the Tsar in the above letter to his eldest and ablest brother, was issued on the 21st of May, after passing in review on the Champ de Mars of his capital about 50,000 of his finest troops, so as thus to emphasise the connection between his political power and military strength. It began by recalling to the Tsar's faithful subjects the martyrdom of his illustrious sire, who emancipated the serfs and instituted courts of justice and local government, and exhorted the prayers of Russia on his present Majesty's assumption of the sacred duties of autocracy. It then proceeded:

'In the midst of our great affliction, the voice of God commands us to discharge courageously the affairs of government, trusting in God's providence, with faith in the strength and justice of the autocratic power, which we have been called to support and preserve for the people's good from all impairment and injury. Therefore, let courage animate the troubled and terror-stricken hearts of our faithful subjects, of all lovers of the Fatherland, devoted from generation to generation to the hereditary imperial power. Under its shield, and in unbroken alliance with it, our land has more than once lived through great troubles, and has grown in strength and glory. Consecrating ourselves to our high service, we call upon all our loyal subjects to serve us and the State in truth and justice to the rooting out of the horrible seditions that dishonour the land of Russia, the strengthening of faith and morality, the good education of the young, the extermination of injustice and plunder, and to the introduction of order and justice in the operation of these institution presented to Russia by her benefactor, our beloved father.'

So thus, then, Hercules had made his choice. Alexander III had made his bed, and now he would have to lie upon it. 'The lightning,' wrote Mr 'Lanin,' in the article before referred to, 'which killed his comrade in the streets of the little German town, changed the wordly-minded Luther into a pious monk; and the blood-curdling scenes by the Catherine Canal, which culminated in the tragic death of his father, produced a somewhat similar effect upon the mystically inclined Grand Duke, Alexander Alexandrovitch. His frame of mind when he ascended the throne can scarcely be conceived. Ho was as bewildered and helpless as a man suddenly aroused from a profound slumber by a murderous onslaught of robbers. His advisers could offer him no help. They hopelessly contradicted each other and themselves. The one asked for a Constitution, another advocated the *status quo*; his own brother pleaded for a speedy return to the iron rule of his grandfather Nicholas. The air was saturated with treason; the very palace was believed to harbour an imperial protector of assassins. The Emperor found himself face to face with an awful invisible power of darkness, with no one to stand between him and it, or to stretch out a helping hand. To crown all, he had no motive power within himself, no stimulus to action, no goal, and no ideal. Not one of his advisers rose to the level of the occasion; not one had faith in himself, much less in his methods.

'It was under these conditions that his old teacher, M. Pobedonostseff, who had been freely inveighing against the Ministers as a band of 'idiots and fools,' on being called to the imperial presence, came prepared with a complete system of policy, a soothing religion, an inspiriting faith, and a glorious ideal. He played to perfection the part of Samuel to the Russian monarch. He proclaimed that everything had taken place in accordance with the inscrutable will of God, who had chosen the Tsar as his anointed servant to lead his favourite people out of the wilderness of sin and misery. The halcyon days of Nicholas's reign were to be brought back under infinitely more favourable conditions, religion was to be reinstated in her place, and the Lord was to be ruler in the land. In a word, God was God, and the Tsar was His prophet.'

NOTES

1. When applied to for his opinion in the matter, the German Emperor had, on the whole, advised his imperial nephew of Russia to grant his subjects a Constitution, but with the following safeguards: 'No universal suffrage; a Parliament of two Chambers, without power to overthrow Cabinets; triennial budgets; no substitution of a civil list for Crown-land revenues; freedom of worship, but not unlimited freedom of the Press and of education.'
2. 'Konstitoutsiya Grafa Loris-Melikova.' ('The Russian Constitution,' projected by Count Loris-Melikov.) (London: The Russian Free Press Fund.)

CHAPTER IV

THE LORD'S ANOINTED

Autocrat of All the Russias - Moscow - Triumphal entry - Oath to Imperial Standard - Prodamation *Urbi et Orbi* - Ambassadors of the Press - Church of the Assumption - Coronation Ceremony - Second burning of Moscow - The Kazan Cathedral

ALEXANDER III succeeded to the throne in March 1881, but it was not till more than two years later that His Majesty was crowned with unparalleled pomp; and on that occasion I had the honour to be the sole representative of the English Press who was admitted to the Church of the Assumption at Moscow to witness and describe for the *Times* the coronation ceremony.

In no circumstances could the 'Autocrat of All the Russias', as he is officially styled, afford to dispense with a ceremony intended to bring home to the minds of his subjects in the most vivid manner the Heaven-appointed nature of his high functions and inheritance; and the unusual length of the interval that was allowed to elapse between his accession and his coronation was only due to grief at the loss of his father, as well as to nervousness about the possibility of a similar fate for himself, should he expose his person too much. But in time the days of his mourning and moping passed away, and May 26, 1883, was fixed for his solemn coronation in the Cathedral Church of the Assumption, within the walls of the Kremlin, or Palatine Hill, so to speak, of the city of Moscow.

Every country has its coronation city, which does not invariably correspond with its present capital, as witness, for example, Drontheim, in Norway; Rheims, in France; Scone, in Scotland; and Königsberg, in Prussia. In the case of Russia this city is Moscow, the ancient cradle and seat of the Tsars. But where is Moscow? In Europe or in Asia? All the maps certainly assign it to Europe; but a walk through the streets of this ancient and enchanting city, this head-centre and stronghold of Panslavism, makes the visitor doubt whether he has not already crossed the Asiatic line. For Moscow carries the imagination far to the East, with its orientally-garbed inhabitants, its green and golden minarets and domes, its whitewashed stones, its emerald roofs, its embattled walls, its myriad temples, and its thousand towers.

This was the city into which Alexander III, coming from St Petersburg, made his triumphal entry a few days before the date of his coronation, and rarely or never, perhaps, in all history, had a more gorgeous open-air pageant been seen. The Field of the Cloth of Gold was nothing to it; and it was only rivalled, though not perhaps outshone, by Queen Victoria's jubilee procession to Westminster Abbey, with a crowd of monarchs, princes, and other magnates in her train.

The great White Tsar's retinue, too, was made up of all the rulers and governments of the civilised world, in the person of their special ambassadors, who were sent at very great expense to honour the coronation, the English mission alone, with all its housings and entertainments, costing as much as £6000. The *fêtes* themselves, and all the incidents of imperial hospitality, must have occasioned the Tsar himself an outlay of several million roubles, or as much as would have sufficed to clothe his army or save his people from famine.

But even more sumptuous and magnificent than the embassies of the Old and New worlds which figured in the triumphal entry of the great White Tsar were the deputies from the Asiatic tribes and peoples subject to his sway - Kalmucks, Khirghiz, Khivans, and the denizens of the Kizil Kum and the Kara Kum, dwellers on the banks of the Jaxartes and the Oxus, roaming warriors from the far Siberian steppes and the great Mongolian rivers - on they rode, in all the gorgeous variety of their picturesque costumes, before the mighty monarch whose sway extended from the amber-yielding shores of the Baltic to the ice-bound Straits of Behring.

On passed the procession amid a never-ceasing roar of cheers from the immense multitudes which lined the route, the booming of guns, and the deafening clangour of all the city bells - a most dazzling and kaleidoscopic cavalcade, relieved at intervals by the gorgeous state coaches of the Empress and the other ladies of the imperial family and Court, each drawn by beautiful and richly caparisoned cream-coloured steeds; and in the centre of all the mighty Tsar himself, tall, yet not terribly in shining panoply of war on a prancing battle charger, but meek and lowly-looking in his simple dark-green uniform and sheepskin cap, on a snow-white palfrey - the picture of Spenser's 'very perfect, gentle knight,' with a pleased and gracious smile on this, the proudest and most memorable day of his life.

The next day was devoted to the consecration of the imperial standard, prior to the Tsar swearing military allegiance thereto, in the trophy-room of the Kremlin Palace. The ceremony, which was attended by a brilliant throng of his Majesty's relations and guests, was performed by the metropolitan of Moscow, assisted by half a dozen of the higher clergy arrayed in all their sumptuous robes of office which made them look more like men of gold than men of clay. A gorgeous piece of variegated embroidery, the imperial standard, stood behind a reading-desk, in front of which was a reading-table supporting a golden vessel filled with consecrated water, a cross of gold, a gilt-bound folio Bible flanked by burning tapers. Terribly in earnest, the

Bishop's voice rang through the vaulted hall like a spirit-stirring trumpet, and when it lingered with deeply venerating emphasis on the name 'Alexander Alexandrovitch,' it could only be compared to the modulated roar of a lion. After the consecration, the imperial family filed before the altar, kissing the cross and the hands of the priest who bore it.

This was a private ceremony, but on the following morning the outer court of the Kremlin drew all the populace of Moscow to witness the solemn proclamation by cuirassier-escorted heralds and pursuivants, gorgeously arrayed in cavalier hats of crimson with variegated plumes, satin mantles of gold, slashed hose doeskin riding boots, and gilded spurs, living pictures of English Charles I and Rupert of the Rhine - the solemn proclamation, *urbi et orbi*, of the forthcoming coronation, 'to the end that on this auspicious day all the faithful subjects of his Majesty may send up to the King of Kings their most fervent prayers, and implore the Almighty One to extend the favour of His blessing to the reign of his Majesty, to the maintenance of peace and tranquillity, to the very great glory of His holy name, and to the unchanging weal of the Empire.' And what scrambling there was among the struggling throng to secure one of the beautifully printed vellum copies of this proclamation which the golden-mantled pursuivants flung fluttering among the crowd.

Outside the embattled walls of the Kremlin, richly hung with the coloured escutcheons of all the provinces of Russia, the proclamation ceremony was once more gone through; and away again for the purpose of repeating the dazzling pageant at some of the chief barriers, gates, and public places, moved the shining company of gigantic cuirassiers with their eagle-crested helms and dancing lance-pennons, looking for all the world like a departing train of crusading knights.

But what were all these preliminary pomps and pageants compared with the actual coronation ceremony itself in the Cathedral of the Assumption! The church is so small that it could only contain all that was representative in Moscow narrowed down to irreducible dimensions, including only one member of the Press of each country. Crowds of journalists had streamed to Moscow from every quarter of the globe, but the Anglo-Saxon world was only enabled to witness the actual crowning of the Tsar through the eyes of two observers, the correspondent of a New York newspaper and the present writer, who represented the leading journal of London. For Alexander III, though not as a rule particularly partial to the Press, had on this occasion frankly recognised its utility and power, and accorded its ambassadors place and precedence before his throne, beside the special envoys of mightiest monarchs.

Coated with gold and silver and precious stones - one emerald alone, in an image of the Virgin, being valued at £10,000 - rich in costly shrines, sanctified by the bones and ashes of the venerated dead, containing numerous Christian relics of awe-inspiring origin, rendered sacred by religious tradition, and endeared to the national heart by some of the most prominent incidents in Russian history, the Cathedral of the Assumption was well calculated to be the scene of the august ceremony by which, in the name of the King of Kings, Alexander of Russia with his Danish consort, Marie Feodorovna, received formal ratification of his claim to be sole and absolute ruler of more than 100,000,000 of his fellow-men.

The air was balmy with the breath of approaching summer, and his Majesty the sun, who had sulkily veiled his face almost ever since the Emperor made his triumphal entry into his ancient capital, now burst through the clouds, deluging the gilded walls, the frescoes, pillars, and the storied nave with a glorious flood of light. Glorious light, and glorious sound from the magnificent voices of the choristers, who take the place of organs in the Greek Church. But the chanting of their hymns was almost drowned by the billow-like murmurs of the vast crowds outside, for the courtyards of the Kremlin presented one surging sea of human beings who had come to catch a glimpse, if possible, of the new-crowned Tsar. And they had hours to wait, for the ceremony was long and elaborate.

How gorgeously picturesque looked the group of the imperial family and their illustrious guests as they stood ranked up near the throne - for no one may sit in the Greek Church. There, among others, stood the Duke of Edinburgh, the Tsar's brother-in-law; the tall and soldierly figure of Prince Albrecht, of Prussia, looking every inch of him a fighting son of the Hohenzollerns; the aristocratic-looking Duke of Aosta; the picturesque Highlander Prince of Montenegro, and the bearded Prince Alexander of Bulgaria, with a decided touch of the old Teutonic knight about him; there, also, Lord Wolseley, the recent capturer of Tel-el-Kebir; and not very far off, the handsome General Skobeleff, the hero of the Plevna and the Shipka Pass, the conqueror of Khiva.

The Empress was arrayed in a sweeping robe of silver, so heavy as to fatigue her, while the Emperor wore the dark-green and gold-embroidered uniform of a general, with riding boots, and the chain of St Andrew, the patron-saint alike of Scotland and of Russia, sparkled on his breast. Slightly bald, but taller by a good head than any of his great officers of State around him, was Alexander III, while his shoulders were broad, his chest deep, his limbs long, and he looked as if he could with ease bear heavy armour - altogether a most uncommon and impressive figure.

Scene the first of that solemn spectacle may be said to have been completed when their Imperial Majesties took their stand in front of the altar to await the approach of the servants of the Almighty. The blaze of gold and silver, the richness of the various uniforms, the sparkling of the gems, the clouds of floating incense, the assembled beauty, valour, rank, and station of all Russia and of all the chief States and countries of the world, all this made the scene at once most impressive and memorable. At the invitation of the Metropolitan of Novgorod, the Emperor recited the Orthodox Creed in a clear, firm voice, though not of that depth and sonorousness which one would have expected to come from so deep and broad a chest.

Assisted by his two brothers, the Grand Dukes Vladimir and Alexis, as well as by the Metropolitans of Kief and Novgorod, the Tsar now donned the gorgeous imperial mantle that was presented to him on two sumptuous cushions. Cloth of gold was the stuff of this majestic robe, with a border of ermine, and, after being arrayed in it, the imperial wearer bowed his head before one of the prelates, who crossed his hands in mystic rite upon his Majesty's head and uttered a fervent prayer.

From the hand of Monseigneur of Novgorod the Emperor now received his crown, which he himself - mark that! - placed upon his own head. Then, taking the sceptre in his right hand and the globe of empire in the left, he seated himself on his throne. It was a most impressive moment; the gazing assembly was hushed, and even the severe representatives of unostentatious republics could not but feel the sublime significance of the scene.

Invested with all the symbolism of his mighty power, there now sat the accredited master of so many millions of his fellow-creatures, and never was Solomon in all his glory more gorgeously arrayed. Of dazzling majesty was his crown of gold, enriched with pearls and diamonds, and surmounted by a very large ruby - a crown of flashing, sparkling light, worthy to be worn by the ruler whose dominions are spanned by half the circuit of the sun; and rarely has the sun lent its rays to such a gem as sparkled in the sceptre of Alexander III. The companion of the great Koh-i-Noor brilliant, now in the possession of Queen Victoria, this priceless jewel found its way, after strange vicissitudes, from the eye of a golden idol at Delhi into the sceptre of the Tsars.

After occupying his throne for a few seconds, the Emperor took off his crown, and touched with it the forehead of his consort, who knelt before him on a crimson velvet cushion; after which he placed upon her head her own crown, topped by a large and lovely sapphire. Then the Empress was arrayed in her own gorgeous mantle and with the collar of St Andrew, which completed the investiture of both their Majesties.

Meanwhile, the cannon and the bells without had been mingling their accents of announcement and felicitation, and the tedious hours wore on with their hymn-chantings, their performance of high mass, their prayers, and their anointing of their Majesties with the consecrated oil.

At last, arrayed in all their imperial pomp, their Majesties emerged from the cathedral by a door different from that by which they had entered, and passing along under a gorgeous canopy to another Church, Alexander III showed himself to a mighty concourse of his acclaiming subjects as their crowned and consecrated ruler. Emperor and Autocrat of All the Russias by inheritance, by divine right, and by heavenly unction.[1] The solemn strains of the national anthem, the joyful pealing of the bells, the thunder of the swiftly served cannon, the surging sea of spectators, and the loud and continued cheers, all produced a scene that can never be forgotten by those who witnessed it.

And again at night the city went almost mad with monarchical joy. Moscow burned again for the second time - burned as it had never done since the days of the first Napoleon; blazed with illuminations which made it look more like a city of variegated fire than a city of stone, and which could only have been described by a pen dipped in rainbow hues.

And then, what pen could have given an adequate notion of the *fêtes* and functions which followed? The sumptuous banquets in the halls of the Kremlin, the brilliant balls, the gala performances at the opera, one of the largest in Europe; the ambassadorial entertainments, the military spectacles, and, last of all, the vast popular *fête* on the plain of Petrovsky, where hundreds of thousands of the Tsar's poorest subjects were treated to *panem et circenses* - food, drink and frolic - on a scale that would probably have astonished the indulgent masters of imperial Rome.

But I think the prettiest and most touching scene of all was the last, when, after a long period of so much revelry and excitement, their imperial Majesties returned to St Petersburg, and at once repaired to the Kazan Cathedral to offer thanks to the Almighty for all the mercies accorded them in Moscow - to the Kazan Cathedral, of which the entrance was guarded, not by crowds of soldiery, but by a white-robed and silver-throated throng of schoolchildren.

From the Kazan Cathedral their Majesties drove to the island-fortress Church of Saints Peter and Paul to worship before the tomb of Alexander II, where burns perpetual taper-fire, and thence by water to Peterhof, their favourite suburban retreat, on the breezy shore of the Gulf of Finland, with enough to think about for many years to come.

NOTES

1. Alexander III's full title, as now proclaimed, was: Emperor and Autocrat of All the Russias, of Moscow, of Kieff, of Vladimir, of Novgorod; Czar of Kazan, of Astrakan, of Poland, of Siberia, of Kherson-Taurida, of Grousi; Gosoudar of Pskoff; Grand Duke of Smolensk, of Lithuania, of Volhynia, of Podolia, and of Finland; Prince of Esthonia, of Livonia, of Courland; of Semigalia, of the Samoyedes, of Bielostok, of Corelia, of Foer, of Ingor, of Perm, of Viatka, of Bulgaria, and of other countries; Master and Grand Duke of the Lower Countries in Novgorod, of Tchernigoff, of Riazan, of Polotsk, of Rotstoff, of Jaroslaff, of Bielosersk, of Oudork, of Obdorsk, of Kondisk, of Vitelsk, of Mstilaff, and of all the countries of the North; Master Absolute of Iversk, of Kastalnisk, of Kabardinsk, and of the territory of Armenia; Sovereign of Mountain Princes of Tcherkask; Master of Turkestan, Heir Presumptive of Norway, and Duke of

Sleswick Holstein, of Stormame, of Dithmarse, and of Oldenburg.

CHAPTER V

THE TSAR PEACE-KEEPER

Foreign Policy Circular - Imperial meeting at Dantzig - Its results - Skobeleff the Teutophobe - M. de Giers - His meetings with Bismarck - Mr Gladstone and the Tsar - Russo-German *rapprochement* - The Three Emperors at Skierniwiece - The Tsar and Francis Joseph – Germany's 'Hecuba' - Fresh Russo-German misunderstanding – The Tsar in Berlin - His interview with Bismarck - The Forged Despatches - Friends once more - Bismarck on the Tsar - 'Printer's Ink' - The Kaiser in St Petersburg - The Tsar in Berlin - 'Hurrah for the Russian Army!' - Results of the meeting - Russia's 'One Friend' - The 'Key of your House' - The Kaiser at Narva - The Tsar at Kiel - 'Long live the German Navy!' - *'Vive la Marine Française!'* - Beauty and the Beast - Franco-Russian relations - A Petersbourg! à Petersbourg! - The French at Cronstadt - 'For the sake of our dear France' - 'You *must* marry me' - The Russians at Toulon - Gold *versus Gloire* - *'Souvenirs de Sebastopol'* - Customs-War - *'La France, c'est l'Ennemi!'* - Russia in Central Asia - Skobeleff's prophecy - English 'Mervousness' again - *'Beati possidentes!'* - The Penjdeh Incident - *Si vis pacem, para bellum* - John Bull puts on his Boots - Arms or Arbitration? - The Russo-Afghan Frontier - Central Asian and Siberian Railways - The Black Sea Fleet - Masterful Declaration of the Tsar - Batoum *versus* Bulgaria

THREE days after the murder of Alexander II, M. de Giers, on behalf of the new Emperor, addressed the following circular to all the representatives of Russia abroad:

'His Majesty the Emperor, on ascending the throne of his ancestors, assumes as an inheritance the traditions consecrated by time, by the acts of his ancestors, and by the sacrifices and toil of generations - all of which has built up Russia in the past. In completely taking upon himself this inheritance, his Majesty makes it a sacred duty to deliver it inviolate to his successors. Like all other States, Russia, in constituting herself, had to sustain a struggle in which her strength and her national spirit became developed.

'Russia has now attained her full development, and feelings of jealousy or discontent are equally foreign to her. It only remains for Russia to secure her position, to protect herself from without, and to develop her forces, her wealth, and the well-being of her people. This is the aim which our august monarch has set before himself, with the firm resolve to pursue it without intermission. The Emperor will first give his attention to the internal development of the State, a question closely connected with the progress of civilisation, and with the social and economic questions which form the subject of special study on the part of all governments.

'The foreign policy of the Emperor will be entirely pacific, Russia will remain faithful to her friends, she will unchangeably preserve the sentiments consecrated by tradition, and will, at the same time, reciprocate the friendliness of all States by a similar attitude, while maintaining the position to which she is entitled among the Powers, and assuring the maintenance of the political equilibrium. In accordance with her interests, Russia will not deviate from her mission, in common with other governments, to protect the general peace based upon respect for right and treaties. Above all, Russia has to care for herself, and only the duty of protecting her honour or security may divert her attention from the work of material development. Our august monarch will endeavour to strengthen the power and advance the welfare of Russia, and secure her prosperity without detriment to others. These are the principles by which the foreign policy of the Emperor will invariably be guided.'

'The foreign policy of the Emperor will be entirely pacific' - consistent, of course, with the honour and the interests of Russia. Such, in brief, was the new Tsar's international programme. How did he proceed to carry it out?

In the first place, by hastening to make his peace with Germany, for which purpose he sought and obtained an interview with his grand-uncle, the old German Emperor William, at Dantzig, in the autumn of 1881, the year of his accession. This was now the second surprising somersault which Alexander III had cut since coming to the throne. As Tsarevitch he had allowed himself to be used by the Liberals, and posed as the champion of reform. But no sooner had he felt the weight of the Imperial crown upon his brow than he declared his 'unshaken faith in the strength and justice of the autocratic power....which we have been called to support and preserve for the people's good from all impairment and injury.' Again, as Tsarevitch, he was known to be bitterly anti-German, and now, to the intense surprise of the Panslavists, who had been looking forward to his reign as to the seventh heaven of their hopes, he was suddenly seen rushing into the arms of the German Emperor - verily, a man of contradictions from first to last.

But the fact was that Russia had already found in Germany a willing ally in the combating of their common foes - anarchy and revolution. By refusing to extradite Hartmann, the author of the attempt to blow up the train of Alexander II near Moscow, France had alienated the sympathies of Russia, causing the latter Power to draw closer to Germany; and when at last Alexander II fell a victim to those who had already made five different attempts to take his life, Prince Bismarck, by command of the Emperor, immediately took steps for combining the European Powers in common action against political crimes and international anarchy. One by one the other Powers had fallen away and left Germany and Russia to concert their own measures, which ultimately (January, 1885) found expression in the signature of a new and more vigorous Extradition Agreement. But I may now remark that it was this community of action between the two Empires - isolated, as they were, on this subject from the rest of Europe - which acted as a salve to the wounds inflicted on Russia at the Congress of, Berlin, and paved the way for the new Emperor's visit to Dantzig in September 1881. 'Socialism and Anarchy, which he always identified, constituted,' as was well said of him, 'the bugbear of his life. His burning desire to root out 'this cancer of modern society,' as he often termed it, drew him nearer to Prince Bismarck than any Western notions about the balance of power.'

With the German Emperor at Dantzig were the Crown Prince and Prince Bismarck; while the Tsar was attended, among others, by M. de Giers, the successor-designate of Prince Gortchakoff, who had now virtually resigned the management of affairs. If ever any poor mortal inherited a crown of thorns; it was surely Alexander III; and there is reason to believe that, apart from the wish to make his peace with Germany, and thus dispose at least of one of his troubles, his Majesty more especially desired to take the advice of one of the wisest statesmen of the age on the domestic ills that might well have perturbed a more perspicacious and resolute soul than his.

That, at least, the conversation at the Dantzig meeting turned less on international relations than on European anarchy would appear from the following telegram, addressed by the Austrian Ambassador at St Petersburg, Count Kalnoky, to Baron Haymerlé, his chief at Vienna:

'M. de Giers, whom I have just seen, is greatly pleased with the mutual impressions produced by the Dantzig interview. The Emperor Alexander has returned with an increased feeling of tranquillity and inner contentment. In particular, the wisdom and unexpected moderation of Prince Bismarck's language have made a good impression, no less on the Tsar than on de Giers, and convinced them that in no direction has he anything but peaceful intentions. There being in reality no disquieting question of foreign policy to be dealt with, the conversation mainly turned on the means of combating the revolutionary danger, and here also Prince Bismarck recommended great caution and moderation in the matter of international measures. M. de Giers said the most important aspect of the Dantzig meeting was this, that the Tsar had thus openly and unequivocally signified to all Russia his will to pursue a conservative and pacific policy.'

That such, indeed, was the Tsar's firm will could no longer be doubted when next year be at last formally relieved Prince Gortchakoff from his cares of office, and also accepted the resignation of Count Ignatieff who was the life and the hope of the anti-German war-party. Great was the jubilation in Germany at the removal of these two statesmen from the council-chamber of the Tsar, but not greater than the joy which greeted the imperial frown incurred by General Skobeleff on account of his anti-German speeches. With the laurels of Geok-Tepé still fresh upon his heroic brow, the great 'White General' of the great 'White Tsar' had, like another Peter the Hermit bearing a fiery cross, swept across Europe, preaching death and destruction to the hated Germans.

'We are not masters in our own house,' he cried; 'the foreigner is everywhere and everything in Russia, and from his baneful influence we can only be delivered by the sword. And shall I tell you the name of the intriguing intruder? - it is the German. I repeat it, and entreat you never to forget it - the German is the enemy. A struggle is inevitable between the Teuton and the Slav; it cannot be long deferred. It will be long, sanguinary, and terrible, but I hold the faith that it will terminate in favour of the Slav.'

Launched as they were at Paris, by such a man as one of the Tsar's greatest warriors, these fulminations could not fail to excite uneasiness in Berlin; but this uneasiness was quickly dispelled when the Russian Ambassador disavowed all connection of his Government with the tirades of Skobeleff; when the official *Gazette* of St Petersburg likewise not only published a disclaimer[1] but also an order forbidding the future delivery of all political speeches by military persons; and when Skobeleff himself was ordered to return home at once and rejoin his Corps - which he dutifully did, and died next year, Prince Gortchakoff following him to the tomb a twelvemonth later.

M. de Giers had taken the Prince's place - his place, but not his position; his task, but not his title. For Alexander III determined, like his grandfather, to be his own Chancellor, and thus save his Empire from the dangers to which his father's clever and ambitious Foreign Minister had frequently exposed it. Prince Gortchakoff, with his tendency to intrigue and initiative, had been an anomaly in an autocracy like Russia. All the new Tsar wanted was a chef-de-bureau, a silent and discreet man who would content himself with doing and saying what he was told, a passive penman, an unquestioning instrument of his imperious master's will - and such a man his Majesty found ready to hand in M. de Giers, a Swede or Finn by origin, though some averred him to be of German-Jewish extraction - Giers (so reasoned the philologers) being but the Finnish form of 'Hirsch.' It was one of the many inconsistencies of Alexander III, the uncompromising champion of 'Russia for the Russians,' that he should have chosen a Dr Hirsch (the name is German-Jewish) as his medical adviser, and a Herr von Giers as his ministerial assistant in the field of foreign affairs.

'By never anticipating the wishes of the Tsar,' wrote one who knew him well, 'and by always confining himself to the practical questions of the moment and their solution, Giers makes it possible for the Emperor to fed that be himself is the real leader of Russia's policy. Von Giers, who is of a retiring and taciturn nature, has never yet disclosed his views to anybody on the Slav or Eastern question; nor has it ever leaked out whether he has embraced the cause of France, or of the Powers of Central Europe; whether he strives after a permanent or a provisional condition of peace, or what he thinks of the future of Russia and Europe' - truly a man of maddening mystery for foreign diplomatists to deal with. 'He seems to have been so moulded by nature as to feel little desire to form definite opinions of his own; hence it may be easier for him simply to act as the docile executor of his monarch's orders, in which capacity he is ably assisted by the highly gifted Sinovieiff, a colleague of Ignatieff - the 'Father of Lies.'

The hearts of the Germans jumped with joy on their seeing that the Teutophile successor of the Teutophobe Prince Gortchakoff had not been long in office before he hastened to visit the lord of Varzin (November 1882). It was well understood that M. de Giers on this occasion carried with him a pretty luxuriant olive-branch, one twig of which he left at Varzin, another at Berlin, where he saw the Emperor, and another at Vienna, by way of which he returned home to Russia from Rome. And this pilgrimage of peace was repeated in the following year (November 1883), when M. de Giers was again found with the German Chancellor at Friedrichsruh - a year that had otherwise been rich in tokens of reconciliation between the two Empires.

It is true that no slight sensation was caused in Germany when the Tsar's most peaceful assurances, on the occasion of his coronation at Moscow (in May 1883), were followed by his casual meeting at Copenhagen (September) with the English statesman who was perhaps more of a bugbear to the apprehensive Germans than ever Prince Gortchakoff had been. Indeed, the sudden appearance of Mr Gladstone at the side of the Tsar in Copenhagen - the greatest democrat and the greatest despot of the time - filled the Gentian Press with something like the panic once inspired by the ghost of Hamlet's father in the castle sentinels at Elsinore. The public writers of Berlin at once clutched up their partisans; but, the English apparition being so majestical, Bismarck would not have them offer it the show of violence. 'Fear not,' the Chancellor was reported to have said: 'Gladstone is a man of cool blood and sound understanding, and I am convinced that he has exhibited both these qualities even in the highly dangerous atmosphere of Hamlet.'[2]

It was said (and with an appearance of truth) that the Tsar, on his way home from Copenhagen, wished again to meet the German Emperor at some Baltic port, but that Bismarck prevented the realisation of this plan so as thus to deprive Russia of the credit accruing from the semblance of perfect amity with Germany, while the distribution of her army on the western frontier was still far from reassuring to the General Staff at Berlin. But if this was still a source of disquietude to the German Government, it was soon thereafter removed by the gradual retirement of the threatening masses of Russian cavalry more towards the interior, as well as by the altered tone of the Moscow Press, which now declared that 'a war between Russia and Germany would be the most absurd of all absurdities.'

It was about this time, too, that M. de Giers made his second pilgrimage of peace to Berlin and Friedrichsruh (November 1883); and when, shortly afterwards a Russian squadron, by special command of the Tsar, repaired to Genoa to salute the German ironclads that were to convey the Crown Prince to Spain; when Prince Orloff, a *persona gratissima* to Prince Bismarck, was transferred from the Russian Embassy at Paris to Berlin; and when, above all things, a Russian gold-loan was brought out at Berlin under the direct auspices of the Prussian Government - and subscribed for more than ten times over (April 1884) - there could no longer be any doubt that Russia had at last honestly resolved to walk with her immediate neighbours in the paths of peace.

This conviction was only strengthened next year (September 1884), when Europe was presented with the spectacle of the three Emperors, who were accompanied by their respective Chancellors, again embracing in effusive friendship at the little Polish town of Skiemievice.

Hitherto the newspaper Press had never found much favour with autocrats, but now representatives of the leading journals of Europe were encouraged to dwell within the precincts of the park at Castle Skiernievice, and to acquaint the world with all but the secret conversations of this fraternal meeting; to telegraph how their Majesties were photographed in one group, and their Chancellors in another; to record how the Emperors William and Francis Joseph, in Russian uniforms, led splendid battalions that bore their name past their devoted friend the Tsar; to tell how, when their Majesties went out to slaughter partridges, their Ministers met in serious confabulation; how lofty decorations and compliments were exchanged; how flattering toasts crowned the banquet, and how even the Tsar drank to the personal health of Bismarck; how the little theatre looked gorgeous with its parterre of Emperors; with what nice gradation of esteem the Tsar distinguished the German and the Austrian Chancellors; and how the former was honoured with the life-size portraits of the Emperors Alexander and Francis Joseph, as souvenirs of the golden days of Skiernievice - of which the general result was summed up by one of the three Emperors themselves when he said that 'for a further period there was now a fair prospect of peace, of undisturbed labour, and of augmented general prosperity.' But there was no question among the three Emperors of their recurring to the old *Drei-Kaiser-Bund*. This had now been effectually replaced by the Triple Alliance; still, it was always something that the three most powerful military rulers in

Europe should thus have met to embrace and avouch their love of peace while discussing the best means of coping with the common danger - social revolution.

The following year (August 1885) Alexander III paid Francis Joseph a visit at Kremsier, in Moravia, where the Archbishop of Olmütz, Cardinal von Fürstenberg had a spacious summer-palace, which he lent for the purpose of the imperial meeting. Both Emperors were accompanied by their respective consorts, their ministers, their heirs-apparent, and by other members of their families. It was a gay time of banquets, theatrical performances, shooting parties, and political conferences. Old Kaiser Wilhelm telegraphed to his brother Sovereigns to assure them that he was with them in spirit; while they, on their part, flashed to Berlin a common message of fraternal greeting. At Kremsier the chief topic of conversation had been Bulgarian affairs, which were now in a very tangled and dangerous condition; and there can be little doubt that the Tsar returned home with the assurance from Francis Joseph that Russia was quite entitled to pursue a freehand policy in the Balkans within the limits of the predominating influence accorded her there by the Treaty of Berlin.

Bismarck himself had repeatedly sent assurances of the same kind to St Petersburg, saying, in effect, that the Tsar might do whatever he liked in Bulgaria, as far as Germany was concerned. But the German public were not aware of this, or had forgotten all about the Congress of Berlin, where Bismarck claimed to have acted, in spite of the recriminations of the Russian Press, as the 'fourth plenipotentiary of the Tsar.' The German public, I say, had forgotten all this; so that when at last the *Prinzenraub* was perpetrated at Sofia (of which more anon), and the German Government failed to do so much as lift its little finger on behalf of the 'German Prince' who had been so barbarously treated in Bulgaria at the hands of Russian agents, the whole nation burst out, so to speak, into a storm of pity and indignation, denouncing Bismarck, in effect, as the passive coadjutor of the rancorous Ruler of All the Russias. But Bismarck lauded to scorn such an idea, saying that he ought to have been arraigned for high treason had he complied with the counsel of such soft-hearted fools. All the blubbering and sentimental declamation of the German Press at that time forcibly reminded him of the player in 'Hamlet,' who shed real tears for the fate of Hecuba.

'For what is Bulgaria to us? It is a matter of perfect indifference to us who rules in Bulgaria, or what becomes of it altogether. I repeat that, and I also repeat everything which I formerly conveyed by my much-abused and hackneyed phrase about the bones of a Pomeranian grenadier - namely, that for us the whole Eastern Question is not a question of war. On its account we shall let no one throw a rope round our necks in order to embroil us with Russia. Our friendship with Russia is much more important to us than that of Bulgaria and that of all Bulgaria's friends whom we have among us here.'

What Bismarck declared to his countrymen in open Parliament, he had also previously conveyed to the Tsar (of this there can be no doubt) through the lips of the German ambassador in St Petersburg so that the impression thus produced upon the mind of his Majesty was just as clear and comforting as it could possibly be. This impression was further deepened when Germany, in deference to the views of the Russian Government, abstained from recognising Prince Ferdinand, the 'Coburger,' who had been chosen by the Bulgarian Chamber to succeed the 'Battenberger.' Not for all the world would Germany do anything to incur the displeasure of Russia in a matter which did not closely concern her, and yet the statesmen of Berlin began to feel that they were gradually losing ground in the estimation of the powers that be at St Petersburg. Once more the Russian Press, the semi-official portion in particular, broke out into the bitterest diatribes against Germany, declaiming against her perfidy and duplicity; and M. Katkoff, who died shortly afterwards at Moscow, burst forth into a swan-song of vehement vituperation. About this time, also, M. Deroulède, the French apostle of revenge, rushed away to Russia to preach death and destruction to the hated Teuton, the common foe of the Republic and the Empire, and was welcomed as if he had been a political Messiah.

So far the displeasure of the Russians had vented itself in words. But now these were followed by acts in the shape of a series of stringent anti-German measures - a prohibitive raising of the iron duties, a more rigorous Russification of the Baltic Provinces, imperial edicts aimed at alien holders of real property, and, worse than all, another threatening concentration of the Russian army towards the Western frontier. What, in the name of wonder or of reason, was the meaning of it all? Why these ugly frowns on the brow of the Tsar? Bismarck was destined soon to know - and from the lips of his offended Majesty himself.

The Tsar and his family, as usual, had spent the autumn (of 1887) in Denmark, and a variety of causes had rendered it necessary for him to return home through Germany. In these circumstances, the laws of courtesy made it imperative on him to take Berlin on his way, however averse he might otherwise have been from claiming hospitable attentions there at a time when there was so much bad blood between the two nations; in addition to which, he could not very well have abstained from paying what was as much a call of condolence as of courtesy, seeing that the German Crown Prince had but lately been pronounced to be suffering from an incurable disease.

Accordingly, as I have written elsewhere, the Tsar and his consort came to Berlin from Copenhagen to visit the old and failing Emperor, by whom their Russian Majesties were received with all due pomp and honour, the festivities including a grand banquet in the Schloss. But previous to that banquet, on the day of his arrival, the Tsar had granted a long audience at the Russian

Embassy to the German Chancellor, which was one of the most sensational incidents of modern times. It was clear from the Tsar's manner that he was suffering from irritation and displeasure of some kind, and his visitor made bold to inquire the reason thereof.

His Russian Majesty, with perfect frankness and courage, at once referred to Bulgaria, and to the double part which Germany had been playing in the politics of the Principality, running with the hare, in fact, and hunting with the hounds. Bismarck protested that the policy of the Empire towards the Bulgarian question had been consistent throughout and free from guile, and that his Majesty must have been grossly misinformed if he thought otherwise. The Tsar replied that his sources of information were precise and absolute - correspondence, in fact, which had come to his knowledge between Prince Ferdinand of Bulgaria and the Countess of Flanders, as well as between Prince Ferdinand and Prince Reuss, German Ambassador at Vienna, proving conclusively that the German Government, false to its official declarations, was secretly encouraging the new Prince of Bulgaria with hopes of support. Was that not enough to provoke the anger of any confiding Tsar?

Bismarck was stupefied, and could only avow again with all the emphasis of truth that the Emperor had been cruelly imposed upon. 'But there are the documents!' argued his Majesty, in a tone which seemed to admit of no more discussion. 'The documents may be there,' replied the Chancellor, 'but I solemnly declare them to be a bold and impudent forgery, committed for the purpose of sowing distrust and enmity between two friendly nations.' It was now the Tsar's turn to feel thunderstruck; but Bismarck had little difficulty in proving to his Majesty that he had, indeed, been made the credulous victim of a vile conspiracy, and that there was not one single word of truth in the charges of duplicity against German policy in which he had thus been craftily led to believe.

The threatening storm-clouds which had of late been gathering round the relations of Russia and Germany at once dispersed, and that same night, at the State banquet in the Schloss, the Tsar made a point of raising his glass and drinking a renewed lease of confidence in the much maligned and misrepresented German Chancellor, as well as in the latter's continued claim to the title of 'honest broker.' A few weeks later the forged despatches were officially given to the world, and, though the name of their nefarious author was mercifully withheld, it was declared that they emanated from the camp of the Orleanists (to whom the Prince of Bulgaria, by his mother, was nearly allied), who thus hoped, by setting two Empires by the ears, to precipitate a European conflict which might enable them to make one last desperate push for their fading heritage.

Since the early days of the Franco-German War, when Bismarck struck a heavy blow at the French Government by the publication of the Emperor Napoleon's proposals for a partition of Belgium, no more sensational incident had occurred in the field of European politics than this startling disclosure that an attempt had been made to embroil Russia and Germany by forged documents misrepresenting the policy of the latter Power; and what rendered the conspiracy all the more dangerous was that it was contemporaneous with an odious attempt on the part of a small Court clique in Berlin itself to inspire the Tsar with the erroneous belief that, in his foreign policy, the Chancellor was not acting in complete harmony with the views of his own imperial master.

In view of all these astonishing things it was little wonder that Russia had again begun to mass threatening numbers of troops on her Western frontier, and that the European situation grew so strained and alarming that it could only be relieved by the publication, in February 1888, of the text of the Austro-German Treaty of Defensive Alliance - to which Italy was also known to be party, though this was no news to Russia, who had been officially informed of the fact in the friendliest manner when the Treaty was first concluded in 1879. Speaking a week or two later in the Reichstag, in support of a new Army Bill, Bismarck said:

'The Emperor Alexander III has the courage of his convictions, and if he contemplated unfriendly relations with Germany he is the first who would say so, and let it be understood. Every one can repose confidence in him who has had the honour of coming; in contact with him....We shall have no disputes with Russia unless we go to Bulgaria to seek them.

'We live in the same friendly relationship with Russia as under the late Emperor, and this relationship will not be disturbed on our side. What interest have we in seeking disputes with Russia? I challenge any one to show me any. Mere braggadocio cannot possibly cause us to seek a quarrel with a neighbour who does not attack us. German Governments and German political views are not susceptible to such a barbaric instinct. For our part, I repeat, we shall not disturb the peace with Russia; and I do not believe that we shall be attacked by Russia. Nor do I believe that Russia seeks alliances for the purpose of attacking us in association with others, or that advantage would be taken of the difficulties which we might have elsewhere in order that we might be attacked with ease.'

A little later still, when it was pointed out to him that, in spite of the pacific assurances of the Tsar himself, the Russian Press still continued its bitter attacks on Germany, Bismarck said:

'As for the Russian Press, he was not of the opinion that it meant more than it did in France. In both cases the Press, for him, was only printer's ink on paper, to which he attached no importance. Behind every article in the Press there was only an individual, who wielded the pen in order to launch an article into the world. The pen which in an independent Russian paper wrote an anti-German article had no one behind it other than he who held it in his hand. In general, any protector of a Russian newspaper was a superior State official, but both were as light as a feather in comparison with the authority of the Emperor. In Russia a paper had not the same influence on public opinion as in France, and in contrast to the voices of the Russian Press he had the testimony of the Emperor Alexander himself, having lately had the honour of being received in audience by his Majesty the Tsar. He had convinced himself that the Emperor of Russia cherished no bellicose designs against Germany. He heeded not the Russian Press, but he placed absolute belief and confidence in the words of the Emperor Alexander. On both being placed in the scales before him, the Russian Press, with its hatred of Germany, would mount up like a feather, and the word of the Tsar would make the balance kick the beam.'

About a month later the old Emperor William died, enjoining his grandson, with his latest breath, to be ever considerate towards Russia; nor had William II been long upon the throne (the wreaths upon his father's tomb had scarcely time to wither) before he rushed away to St Petersburg (July 1888) to make his first 'duty call.' His German Majesty was, of course, received with magnificent hospitality by the Russian Court, and no pains were spared to gratify his well-known passion for show parades. So much is certain. What was not so certain was the kind of personal impression which the youthful and impulsive Kaiser left behind him; but there were rumours, at least, that this might have been a little more favourable. It is, indeed, impossible to conceive that the two Emperors should ever have fallen into a state of mutual admiration. Their characters were much too diverse for that. But they had at least two things in common - devotion to peace and the doctrine of divine right, and this double bond was quite sufficient to give them the semblance of being united by the ties of personal attachment. 'His first favourable estimate of the present German Emperor,' wrote a close and acute observer of the Tsar, 'was recorded after that monarch's discourse on the divine right of kings.'

Next year (October 1889) Alexander III returned the visit of William II by going to Berlin, where no little surprise was felt that he had deferred the payment of this debt of courtesy so long. And even now the Tsar had not come straight to Berlin from Russia, but merely taken it on his way home from Denmark, where, as usual, he had been spending the autumn, 'out of prison.' The lateness of his call was all the more marked as the Sovereigns of Italy and Austria, who bad been visited by the new German Emperor *after* his return from Russia in the previous year, had hastened to return the compliment before the Tsar. In consequence of this and other considerations, the popular reception of the Tsar in Berlin was of a very cool kind - all the more so by contrast with the enthusiastic demonstrations which had made the arrival of King Humbert and the Emperor Francis Joseph resemble triumphal entries. But these two Sovereigns were the solid 'allies' of the German Emperor, whereas Alexander III was but his sentimental 'friend.' Those 'allies' had been the guests of his German Majesty, and were quartered at the Schloss; whereas the Tsar, following the example of his grandfather and father, preferred to lodge at his own Embassy, on Russian soil, so to speak, thus maintaining the high and stiff reserve which made the Western nations feel that they were being kept at their distance.

I was a witness of most of the ceremonies and banquets connected with this Imperial meeting, and I thought that I had never seen anything more artificial and constrained. The Tsar seemed to suffer throughout from a suppressed feeling of boredom; while the Emperor, on his part, was never free from an appearance of *gêne*. At the grand State banquet in the White Saloon of the Schloss, of which I was a spectator, there was practically no conversation between the two Sovereigns. The difference between their two characters was never better displayed than when the time came for the usual interchange of toasts. The Kaiser was all enthusiasm and hospitable zeal. 'I drink,' said he in German, 'to the health of my honoured friend and guest, His Majesty the Emperor of Russia, and to the continuance of the friendship which has existed between our Houses for more than a century, and which I am resolved to cultivate as a legacy derived from my ancestors.' The Emperor concluded with a few Russian words in compliment to his guest, and led off with a hearty '*Hoch!*' which was thrice repeated by the company, while the band played the Russian anthem. After touching glasses with their German Majesties, the Tsar turned to the Emperor and, speaking in a rather low voice, *in French*, replied:

'*Je remercie votre Majesté de vos bonnes paroles, et je partage entièrement les sentiments que vous venez d'exprimer. A la santé de sa Majesté l'Empereur et Roi!*'

Saying which the Tsar raised high his glass, and, turning to the brilliant company, led off the cheering with one abrupt "Hurrah!' which rang out sharp as a musket-shot - an exclamation which, though not quite so familiar to German as to English ears, is said to be of Slavonic origin, so that it was thus peculiarly appropriate on the lips of the Tsar. But, sharp and almost electrifying as was his utterance of this exclamation, it produced less effect perhaps than did the extreme brevity of his speech and its entire lack of anything bearing the faintest resemblance to a political hue. The toast of the German Emperor contained allusions which found no direct echo in the reply of the Tsar, and those who listened to this passage of sentiment between the two monarchs must have felt that it formed a striking contrast to the speeches which were made in the same place when the rulers of Italy and Austria were respectively the guests of the Emperor William.

After the banquet the Court went to the Opera, where the most brilliant house I remember to have ever seen there for a long time bad assembled by special invitation in honour of the Emperor's august visitor. In one box sat the representatives of all the Great Powers, while even Prince Bismarck showed himself - a thing he had not done within the memory of the younger generation. The Court occupied the grand central box, the Tsar again sitting between their German Majesties. The appearance of the house did not certainly come up to that presented by the same theatre on the occasion of the Shah's summer visit to it, but it was a brilliant and memorable scene all the same.

Another notable incident of this meeting was a sumptuous luncheon that was offered to the Tsar by the officers of his 'Own,' or Kaiser Alexander Regiment of the Guards. After an inspection and march past of the regiment, its richly decorated mess-room became brilliant with a festive gathering of all the military magnates of this military capital, with the two Emperors in their midst. After the band had discoursed a selection of music associated with Russia, in which Glinka's 'Life for the Tsar' held a prominent place, the colonel of the regiment proposed the health of the Tsar in most ardent and devoted terms, after which his Majesty - speaking in Russian this time, which the Emperor William appeared to understand - called for a bumper in honour of his German entertainer. Then the Emperor William clinked his glass (as signalising his desire for silence), and in words of fiery and captivating enthusiasm thus toasted the Russian army:

'At a festival like this, concerning as it does a regiment which can look back on a long and glorious history, and which, at the same time, enjoys the honour of seeing its Imperial Chief in its midst, recollection naturally plays a great part. It is this recollection which carries me back to the time when my deceased grandfather, as yet a young officer, received the Cross of St George for valour displayed before the foe, and by his deportment in the bullet rain acquired the chiefship of the Kaluga Regiment. That is an incident which I recall in order to drink to the glorious common traditions and memories of the Russian and the Prussian armies. I drink to the memory of those who, in heroic defence of their Fatherland, fell at Borodino, and who, in union with us, bled in victorious battle at Arcis-sur-Aube and Brienne. I drink to the brave defenders of Sebastopol and to the valiant combatants of Plevna. Gentlemen, I call upon you to drain your glasses with me to the health of our comrades of the Russian army. Hurrah! hurrah! Hurrah!'

But nothing could move the stolid chief of the regiment to a corresponding reply, which simply took the form of a cold and curt 'To the health of my brave Grenadier Regiment.' When the imperial chief of this regiment left the barracks, 'there disappeared also the only single person who was noticeable as a spectator of all this military stir on the roofs of adjacent houses - namely, a policeman in uniform' - a reference to the extraordinary precautions which had been taken by the police in connection with the Tsar's visit. Of this visit, the general opinion in Germany, as expressed by one of its leading organs) was that it had 'rendered more cordial the mutual sentiments of regard entertained by the two monarchs, but that it had changed nothing in the political relations of the two countries.' On the other hand, the *Novoe Vremya*, voicing the sentiment of St Petersburg, said:

'The time when Alexander I. sentimentally swore before the tomb of Frederick II, Russia's bitterest foe, to support various Prussian schemes having nothing in common with the real interests of the Russian State has passed away never to return. So also has passed away for ever the time when we permitted Denmark, the guardian of the Baltic, to be dismembered, and the European equilibrium to be disturbed by the defeat of France and Austria, receiving in return for our generosity nothing but a platonic right to keep a few ironclads in the Black Sea.'

Before leaving Berlin, the Tsar was again closeted for more than an hour with Bismarck, to whom he finally said: 'Prince, I have every confidence in *you*, but do you yourself think that you are likely to remain in office?' To which the Chancellor replied that he would retain his position until his death; and on this the Tsar went home assured and happy, comparatively speaking. For, shortly before coming to Berlin, had he not toasted the Prince of Montenegro - whose daughter, Princess Militza, had been married to the Grand Duke Peter - as 'Russia's only true and sincere friend'? Nevertheless, he had left Berlin with the conviction that he could also now rely on Bismarck, the 'honest broker,' the man who claimed to have acted at the Berlin Congress as the 'fourth plenipotentiary of Russia.' But what was the Tsar's disappointment and surprise, in the following spring, on finding that the young Emperor had suddenly 'dropped his pilot,' dismissed his Iron Chancellor, who had given his Russian Majesty such comforting assurances when in Berlin?

It is not too much to say that, of all who deplored Bismarck's retirement from office, none regretted this more sincerely than Alexander III; and the Prince himself afterwards confessed that the bitterest thing of all which he had to bear in connection with his dismissal was that it had belied his words to the Tsar, and made him look so foolish in the eyes of his Majesty. It was this, perhaps, more than anything else, which roused his resentment against his young master, his '*neue Herr*,' and made his recriminations take the form of an endeavour to sow distrust between him and the Emperor of Russia.

After taking leave of his Russian visitor at Berlin, in October 1889, the Emperor William had rushed to Athens to see his sister married, and then to Constantinople to see the Sultan; and Bismarck, after his dismissal, made no secret of the fact that his Majesty had done this against his advice, as being a visit that would be likely to excite suspicion in St Petersburg. Moreover, he indulged in remarks to newspaper interviewers tending to show that be was the best friend Russia had ever had, and that Count Caprivi, his successor, was doing all he could, in conjunction with his thoughtless master, to worsen the good relations which had always subsisted between the two countries. He even held out to Russia a kind of encouragement to take Constantinople as the 'key of your house.' To the correspondent of the *Novoe Vremya* (and his words must have been read by the Tsar) the ex-Chancellor said:

'If the German Press lately declared war against you, and injured Russia, and even my own organs joined in the campaign, it took place against my will. I have always been against war with Russia. If any one thinks that fighting with Russia would not be terrible, he is very much mistaken. If Russia were to invade Germany it would be different. The severe winter, and the great distances in Russia, would be terrible weapons against an attacking force. Finally, what do we want from Russia, or she from us? We should receive no milliards from you, nor you from us. It would be a crime of Germany to endeavour to extend her frontiers beyond Memel, for the Baltic provinces without Poland would be of no value, and the annexation of Poland, with its nine millions of Catholic Poles, would raise the number of Catholics in Germany to one-half the population, and would be a misfortune for Germany, just as the acquisition of East Prussia would be unprofitable to Russia. A war with Russia is, therefore, almost impossible.'

It was doubtless to correct the impression which must have been made upon his Russian Majesty's mind by these and other remarks of the ex-Chancellor - all tending to sow distrust between the Courts of Berlin and St Petersburg - that the Emperor William, in August 1890, paid a second visit to Russia. On taking leave of his German entertainer at Berlin in the previous October, the Tsar, with the customary parlance of parting friends, had expressed the hope that the Kaiser would favour him with another visit next year, and the Kaiser took him at his word.

With his new Chancellor, among others, in his train, his Majesty set sail for Reval, where he was met by the Grand Duke Vladimir and conducted to Narva to witness the sham-fighting which had been planned for his delectation on an unusually grand scale. The Kaiser in person even led a cavalry charge, which was, of course, no less brilliant than successful. It was at Narva, as I need not remind my readers, that Charles XII of Sweden achieved such a crushing victory over the half-disciplined hordes of Peter the Great; and it was also at Narva where William II of Prussia equally hoped to conquer the hearts of the modem Muscovites. So, at least, Bismarck remarked of this visit 'The Emperor,' he said, 'fancied that he would be able to 'manage' the Russians, politically speaking, by means of his own great personal amiability. Even, however, when in St Petersburg, there had reached his Majesty's ears from the entourage of the Tsar remarks about himself which left no doubt that his visit had been unproductive of any political result' - with other bitter criticisms on the policy of the 'new course,' all intended to show the Tsar that the real man to have cultivated friendly relations with Russia was himself, and not Count Caprivi or the Kaiser either.

This second visit of the German Emperor to Russia was only returned about two years later (June 1892), when the Tsar dropped anchor at Kiel on his way from Copenhagen, where he had been attending the golden wedding of his Danish parents-in-law. That the German Emperor was content to receive this return visit at Kiel, whither he had to make a day's journey for the purpose, instead of remaining in Berlin, was considered by many of his Chauvinistic subjects to be a strange derogation of his dignity; and they scrupled not to indulge in most unsavoury comparisons between Mahomet and the mountain, arguing that the German Kaiser was the mountain, which ought on no account to move in order to meet the convenience and caprice of the Russian prophet.

The Tsar did not stay the night, but left again after attending a grand banquet in his honour in the ancient Schloss of Kiel, which, curiously enough, might be considered as the cradle of his race, seeing that it had been the birthplace of Karl Friedrich, Duke of Holstein-Gottorp, whose son ascended the Russian throne as Peter III, and who was thus the founder of the present line of Romanoffs. But Alexander III was the first of this line who had ever broken bread under the roof-tree of this seat of his German ancestor. At dinner, the German Emperor rose and said: 'I drink to the health of the Russian Emperor whom I have now enrolled, with his high permission, as Admiral *à la suite* of my navy!' To which the Tsar replied: 'I am delighted with this distinction, as well as with the reception accorded to me here, and I drink to the health of my dear friend and cousin. Long live the German Emperor and the German navy!' The same night the 'Pole Star' steamed away out again into the Baltic amid a tremendous outburst of jubilant music, cannonading, and fireworks from the German warships and batteries in the Kieler Bucht. It seems to me that one of the smartest things the German Emperor ever did was, in present circumstances to send away home the Autocrat of All the Russias in the character of an Admiral of the German Fleet - a delicious bit of courteous irony.

'Long live the German navy!' the Tsar had cried. But there was now another navy which Alexander III had toasted in still more ostentatious (I will not say enthusiastic) terms, and that was the Fleet of the French Republic, which had caused such a tremendous fuss to be made about itself at Cronstadt in the previous year. And that was, doubtless, the real reason why the Tsar, for common decency's sake, had not in that year (1891) returned the Emperor's second visit of 1889. For how can any man turn all at once from a table flowing with French champagne to a festive board foaming with German beer?

Of all the shams and insanities in which the century has abounded, none was ever more grotesque and ridiculous than this episode of the so-called Franco-Russian Alliance - this unnatural and impossible union between Beauty and the Beast, between Democracy and Despotism. Any friendship that ever existed between France and Russia had been of the most flimsy and artificial kind. Alexander I and Napoleon had formed an alliance for the purpose of common conquest, but this was soon converted into the inevitable blood-feud which ultimately disrupts all gangs of robbers. With the English the French fought shoulder to shoulder against Russia in the Crimean War, and in 1863 they attempted to intervene in the affairs of Poland until scared away with an emphatic 'Hands off!' from Alexander II. In 1866, Napoleon would have been much more imperious with his demands on Prussia had he not been aware that this latter Power enjoyed the sympathy of Russia; and even M. Flourens,[3] 'speaking dispassionately,' had to admit that 'the attitude maintained by Russia throughout the war of 1870-71 rendered possible the crushing triumph of the German Army, by restraining Austria from indulging her desire to rise and rush to the assistance of the French.

On the other hand, France affected to believe that it was solely due to the 'magnanimous intervention' of Alexander II on her behalf that she was saved from attack and dismemberment by Germany in 1875 - the year of the famous 'war-scare' produced by the *Krieg in Sicht* article of the Berlin *Post* as supplemented by a Paris letter to the *Times*. Now, subsequent revelations of diplomatic documents conclusively proved that this war-scare was nothing but the product of interested and unscrupulous alarmists; that the German Emperor and his responsible Ministers never entertained the least design of falling upon France; that the French allowed themselves to become the victims of one of the most extraordinary hallucinations recorded in all history; and that Alexander II did not, and could not, save them from assault and battery, for the very simple and sufficient reason that Germany did not meditate then, as she has never in one single instance done since the great war, a wanton attack on her Western neighbours. Nevertheless, hallucinations, like lies, continue to live and act as motive-powers in history; and now there was introduced into French international politics an extravagant feeling of gratitude towards Russia, founded on absolute ignorance or misconstruction of facts, and fed by a feeling of implacable hostility to France's hereditary foes - England and Germany; or, perhaps, it would be more correct to say that it is France who is the hereditary and implacable foe of those two Powers.

This spurious sense of undeserved gratitude became all the more intense when France realised that her hopes of revenge on Germany had been utterly baulked by the conclusion of the Triple Alliance, which check-mated her on every side, and that Bismarck's policy of isolating her from the rest of Europe had succeeded to perfection. But Bismarck had done more than isolate France. He had also helped to prevent the recurrence of France to a monarchical régime - one of his most masterly and far-sighted strokes of policy - as arguing that a Republic was the form of government best calculated to make the French stew in their own juice, and, above all things, render them '*bündnissunfähig*,' or incapable of forming alliances with any of the monarchical Powers. Events proved Bismarck to have been absolutely right in his forecast, though that his calculations were not belied was certainly not for want of excessively hard trying on the part of France.

In 1889 the Tsar had plaintively confessed that Russia had 'only one true and sincere friend' among the nations - the Prince of little Montenegro; and the sad avowal seems to have touched the sensitive hearts of the French. For straightway, with one accord, they rose up (forgetful of the maxim, *benefida non obtruduntur*) and hurled themselves, so to speak, at the head of the Tsar. The friendlessness from which Russia was suffering was, at least, a failing which they could remedy, if the Tsar would only let them. Surely Russia, they argued, was not more friendless than France. For Russia had at least *one* friend; but who and where was the friend of France? It was as clear as day that the French and the Russians were born to be allies. Brothers in isolation and calamity, they must be friends. Here was the German Emperor already currying favour with his mother's people, swopping islands with them in token of his amity, as bride and bridegroom exchange wedding rings, becoming an Admiral of the English Fleet, and expending all his powers of honest admiration on the magnificence of the British navy as the supreme arbiter of the seas. Were they, the French, to sit still with folded hands, and behold all this without making a bid for the favour of Russia, with the view of re-establishing the balance of power which had lately been so much deranged to their common detriment? *'Allons, enfants de la patrie!'* and presently the Boulevards which had erstwhile (in the mad July days of 1870) resounded with furious cries of *'à Berlin! à Berlin!'* now equally began to ring with exultant shouts of *'à Petersbourg! à Petersbourg!'*

Towards the close of the reign of Alexander II, France had deeply wounded the Russian Government by refusing to extradite Hartmann, the Nihilist, who had been concerned in the attempt to blow up the Imperial train at Moscow. But the times were now vastly changed; and France, at the wish of Alexander III, would have hastened to render up a hundred thousand Hartmanns without asking any questions. France had no more Hartmanns to offer, but she had money - which opens a road into the most reluctant hearts; so that when the Russian Government failed to raise a loan in Berlin, and appealed to Paris, its request was at once responded to with the offer of a three per cent gold-loan of four hundred million roubles! Was that not an act of sincere and unmistakable friendship on the part of France for friendless Russia? 'Go to,' now cried the patriots of Paris, 'let us at once despatch an imposing fleet into Russian waters to show the Tsar what a magnificent and 'alliance-capable' people we are, and thus cement the union between the two countries which has now been initiated by this golden bridge.'

Accordingly, in the autumn of 1891, Admiral Gervais duly appeared in the Gulf of Cronstadt at the head of a gallant squadron of Gallic ironclads; and just about the time when the German Emperor was being acclaimed by enthusiastic crowds on his State passage from Buckingham Palace to the Guildhall, the Gulf of Finland formed the scene of such festive sound and confraternal show as it had never yet beheld. A Russian squadron accompanied by hundreds of private steamers, all gaily dressed, and crowded with subjects of the Tsar shouting '*Vive la France!*' came out to meet and greet the French flotilla, and the waters of Cronstadt were wrapt in the smoke of saluting guns.

For more than a week Admiral Gervais and his officers were *fêted* and petted to more than their hearts' content. One day the Tsar, surrounded by all the Grand Dukes and Duchesses of his family, reviewed the French fleet, went on board its flagship, the 'Marengo,' and then entertained the commanding officers of both squadrons on board his own yacht, the 'Derjava,' when he toasted the President of the French Republic; while, at a subsequent banquet at the Naval Club in Cronstadt, Admiral Gervais said: 'Since yesterday I seem to have been living in an enchanted world, so convincing are the proofs of sympathy which meet us on all hands - and all for the sake of our dear France.' In his seaside palace, at Peterhof, the Tsar gave another grand banquet, when he again drank the health of M. Carnot, and stood up with the rest of the company while the 'Marseillaise' was being played. At a dinner given him and his officers by the Artillery Corps of St Petersburg, Admiral Gervais toasted the Russian army, which he hoped, and was sure, would reap new laurels should God ever again call it to defend its fatherland'. Each of the French vessels received from the city of St Petersburg the present of a silver goblet, as 'a souvenir of this rapprochement between the two great nations.' After being nearly killed with kindness at St. Petersburg, Admiral Gervais and his officers repaired to Moscow, where similar ovations awaited them. Here General Tchernaieff, in toasting the Frenchmen, said that, 'taught by misfortune, France was now collecting her strength, and that, strong in her unity and in the friendship of Russia, she might now look to the future with a calm confidence.' To crown all, the Tsar and M. Carnot exchanged telegrams. Said the Emperor to the President:

'The presence of the splendid French squadron now at anchor off Cronstadt is a new proof of the deep sympathies which unite France with Russia. It gives me pleasure to convey to you my lively satisfaction, and to thank you for the real pleasure I feel in thus receiving the visit of your gallant sailors.'

To which M. Carnot replied:

'I am deeply touched by the sentiments which your Majesty has been graciously pleased to express with regard to our squadron. Our gallant sailors will not forget the reception of which they have been the object I thank your Majesty for that reception. I am happy to recognise in it an eloquent proof of the deep sympathies uniting France and Russia.'

After the exchange of these identic notes there only remained the signature of a formal treaty of alliance between the two countries; and, sure enough, the tongue of rumour would presently have it that Admiral Gervais had steamed away home with the duplicate of such an instrument in his pocket. But this was the purest fiction that was ever launched into an ill-informed and credulous world. The treaty relations between France and Russia remained precisely what they were before the Cronstadt visit - and for the simple reason that, in the eyes of the Tsar, Republican France was still in a deplorable state of what Bismarck called '*bündnissunfähigkeit*' - a total unfitness for international marriage. The truth is that Alexander III, however fond he might be of Frenchmen personally, distrusted and even detested them as a nation given over to democratic rule, and containing so many dangerous elements of irreligion and anarchy. From an alliance with such a people, thought the Tsar, no good could possibly come.

A creditor had come to pay him a visit, and been treated with exquisite courtesy and kindness - that was all. The isolation of France was just as great as ever. Dr Geffcken pretty well expressed the truth on the subject when he wrote as follows, and I know that his views were shared by the Foreign Office in Berlin.

'Alexander III was never in favour of the French alliance, and the visit of Admiral Gervais to Cronstadt, which he could not very well refuse, was painful to him, and he was glad when it was over. On the other hand, he assured the German Emperor, on his visit to Kiel (in the following year), that he would never give marching orders to a single soldier in order that France might re-conquer Alsace-Lorraine. His Ambassador at Paris had strict orders to keep the Toulon and Paris festivities within certain bounds. Briefly, he treated the French advances, in the words of a witty English diplomatist, like a man who carelessly suffers the caresses of a girl throwing herself at his neck, but who, at the same time, does not want to have anything to do with her.'

Russia did not withdraw her cheek; but France did all the kissing. Europe, in fact, was treated to the spectacle of the French maiden with the Phrygian cap teaching the ladies of the Boulevards a lesson in the art of solicitation. It was not so much, 'Will you marry me?' as 'You *must* marry me!' But the Tsar would none of it. The Russian Joseph was proof to the enticements of the Gallic Mrs Potiphar, although it suited the purposes of the French patriots to insinuate, nay, to assert, that her charms had proved victorious over the object of her passion.

The same comedy, though on a more colossal scale, was witnessed a couple of years later (1893), when a Russian squadron, under Admiral Avellan, as in courtesy bound, came to Toulon to return the visit of Admiral Gervais - came to Toulon and landed its officers and men to be *fêted* and lionised, both there and at Paris, in a manner which caused many to fear that the French had, at least, taken absolute leave of their senses. Perched upon the head of the Bear, the Eagle screamed and flapped its wings at such a rate that the poor bewildered brute scarcely knew where it was, so that at last it began to feel like Bottom when addressed by Quince: 'Bless thee, Bottom! bless thee! thou art translated!'

The incidents of that insane time are of too recent occurrence to require minute recall. *Te Deums* were chanted in the churches on the arrival of the Russians; they were *fêted* by the great heads of State, from the President downwards; the provincial municipalities sent delegates; the people everywhere turned out in enormous, cheering, weeping; worshipping crowds to acclaim their Russian guests, their very deliverers, upon whom gifts of all kinds kept pouring in - Paris alone showering upon them presents valued at £100,000, while the whole nation abandoned itself to unparalleled transports of joy. French officers carried their Russian comrades shoulder high, and French ladies pressed forward with hysterical emotion to offer their sweet lips to the rough exotic sailors, redolent of garlic and vodka. Not with a deeper sense of relief had the ever-dwindling and ever more despairing garrison of Lucknow hailed the final coming of Sir Colin and his kilted men than France now seemed to experience at the sight of Admiral Avellan and his gallant blue-jackets. And when the two forces, the relieving and the relieved, had long enough mingled their tears of joy, the following exchange of compliments took place between their respective chiefs (one of them with the tongue slightly in his cheek) -

The Emperor to the President:

'At the moment when the Russian fleet is leaving France, it is my ardent wish to express to you how I am touched by, and grateful for, the chivalrous and splendid reception which my sailors have everywhere experienced on French soil. The expressions of warm sympathy which have been manifested once again with so much eloquence will add a fresh link to those which unite the two countries, and will, I trust, contribute to strengthen the general peace, which is the object of our most constant efforts and desires.'

The President to the Tsar:

'The telegram, for which I thank your Majesty, reached me when on the point of leaving Toulon to return to Paris.

'The magnificent fleet on which I had the great satisfaction of saluting the Russian pennant in French waters, the cordial and spontaneous reception which your brave sailors have everywhere received in France, prove gloriously once again the sincere sympathies which unite our two countries. They show at the sometime a deep faith in the beneficent influence which may weld together two great nations devoted to the cause of peace.'

It was no wonder that, on a calm survey of all the circumstances connected with this international fraternisation at Cronstadt and Toulon, Count Tolstoi[4] was moved to pour out upon it all the phials of his scathing satire, describing the whole thing as a farce and a fraud from beginning to end. And the Count was not very far wrong. On the part of France, it was a farce - all this protestation of love for Russia; while, on the part of Russia, it was a fraud. What the French wanted was *gloire*; what the Russians aimed at was gold - and the attainment of the latter end was pretty well the only solid outcome of the comedy. As a German officer wrote:[5] 'As regards the rapprochement with France, it is not Russia but France who will have to pay the piper. Neither nation has any solid bond of union - except, perhaps, hatred of Germany. On the other hand, Russia needs gold, much gold. The Tsar gained the goodwill of France in order to dip his hands in her well-filled coffers. Russia, on her side, will take good care not to venture too much for France. The Tsar's policy will remain unchanged: cautious, reserved, he will ever keep exclusively before his eyes the well-being of his own land.'

It is more than strange that a people so highly gifted as the French, so clear-sighted and so acute as reasoners, should at the same time be so prone to become the victims of the grossest self-deception and illusion. When Alexander III lay down to die, they began to weep and wail as for the light and lode-star of their national life which were about to be eclipsed. The Tsar was France's dearest friend, her warmest admirer, her noblest champion, her loyalest ally, her Heaven knows all what. Just consider what had not his Majesty done to bring about a closer union between the two nations. Had he not, among other things, caused to be rendered into French the 'Souvenirs de Sebastopol,' collected and edited by his Imperial self from the original manuscripts preserved in the Historical Museum in the Crimea?[6] And was it not the aim of the Emperor, in undertaking this task: first, to provide an imperishable record of the 'glory' of the contending parties in the war, in which, as General Saussier put it, 'there were neither victors nor vanquished'; and, second, to cement a political alliance with the French, *'the only men capable of disputing victory with the Russians!'* 'It may be added,' said the French translator, 'that two armies which love each other, admire each other, and fight together, are henceforth invincible.'

With a malicious pleasure the French had watched the progress of the *Zollkrieg*, or 'Customs War,' which had broken out between Germany and Russia during the course of this year, and threatened to end in a conflict of a more terrible kind. But what was their surprise, their secret mortification, to find that the Tsar seemed to set still higher store by his friendship with Germany than by his 'alliance' with France, as evidenced by his personal intervention to put an end to the destructive war of tariffs? Very much more of a 'written alliance' was now concluded between the two Empires than existed between France and Russia; for not one single scrap of treaty paper had been the outcome of all the Toulon and Paris inanities. Nevertheless, had all these demonstrations not served the cause of European peace by showing that 'two armies which loved each other, admired each other, and had fought against each other, would henceforth, if combined, prove invincible?'

From the French point of view no one, of course, could doubt that all these demonstrations were directed much more even against England than Germany, as a kind of warning of what she might possibly have to expect in the way of a coalition against her in certain eventualities. *'Man schlägt den Sack und meint den Esel,'* as the Germans say - 'He thumps away at the sack, but what he really aims at is the donkey's ribs.' For England had by this time taken the place of Germany as the main object of French hatred and resentment. Effectually blocked and barred on every side by the bulwark of the Triple Alliance, France had become condemned to absolute and hopeless inaction in Europe, and there was no possible outlet for her energies, her restlessness, and her ambition as a 'grand nation' marching at the head of civilisation – 'the first nation of the universe,' in fact - except a policy of spite and contradiction to 'perfidious Albion' wherever their paths ran parallel or crossed beyond the seas. What France had ever been to patient and pacific Germany before her final unification - domineering, insolent, quarrelsome and interfering - she had now become to England in connection with our task of empire-building. For several years back Anglophobia has been the dominant note of French statesmanship. On the part of France, Cronstadt and Toulon were demonstrations against England much more than against Germany. *'La France, c'est l'ennemi!'* There is no use blinking the fact, however much it may be ignored by the short-sighted advocates of a peace-at-any-price and impossible understanding with our jealous and obstructive neighbours.

In comparison with Russia, at least, this is certainly true. For during the reign of Alexander III we never had half so much trouble with Russia as with France. Several times during this short period we were on the apparent brink of war with France, but only once with Russia. This was in 1885, when the question of the Afghan frontier had become acute by the Russian annexation of Merv. Ever since the wings of Russian ambition in the East of Europe had been so cruelly clipped by the Congress of Berlin, her statesmen had schemed to obviate the recurrence of such a diplomatic disaster as that which resulted from the war of 1877. To this disaster, it is but just to say, England had contributed more, perhaps, than any of the other Powers. For at Constantinople she had at last put her naval foot down with an imperious 'Thus far and no farther!' or rather, 'Not so far as this!', and at Berlin she had also helped to curtail the luxuriance of Prince Gortchakoff's San-Stefano laurels in a most woeful manner.

Nothing, therefore, was more natural than that Russia should take steps to create some means of countervailing England in the event of her attempting a similar policy of obstruction in the future - and the creation of this means was possible in Central Asia. The nearer Russia got to our Indian frontier, the greater the preventive pressure she could bring to bear upon us in Europe. If threatened with an invasion of India, England could not afford to obstruct the policy of Russia in the Balkans. The Russians never dreamt of *conquering* India, knowing this to be beyond their utmost powers. But an *invasion* of India would be a very different thing, by way of a diversion. Calcutta would be a line of attack on Constantinople; the Ganges a mere channel to obtain a footing on the Golden Horn. As Skobeleff wrote in 1881:

'To my mind the whole Central Asian Question is as clear as daylight. If it does not enable us in a comparatively short time to take seriously in hand the Eastern Question - in other words, to dominate the Bosphorus - the hide is not worth the tanning. Sooner or later Russian statesmen will have to recognise the fact that Russia must rule the Bosphorus....Without a serious demonstration in the direction of India, in all probability on the side of Candahar, a war for the Balkan peninsula is not to be thought of. It is indispensable to maintain in Central Asia, at the gates of the corresponding theatre of war, a powerful body of troops fully equipped and seriously mobilised.'

It was, then, in pursuance of this far-sighted policy that the Russians, after the Congress of Berlin, began to push their Central Asian frontier ever nearer the borders of Afghanistan, till at last Englishmen were one fine morning startled with the news that Merv (which the Russians repeatedly avowed, in the most solemn manner, they did not mean to take) had at last been occupied by them in the spring of 1884. And then the English were seized with another violent fit of that 'mervousness' from which they had intermittently suffered for years back - a fit for which the political doctors, as well on the Thames as on the Neva, could only prescribe a dose of Delimitation Commission.

It was natural that, in such circumstances, the Tsar should have been suspected, and indeed roundly accused, of perfidy; but as Mr Curzon justly remarks, in his otherwise somewhat long-winded and big-worded book about 'Russia and Central Asia,' 'it is scarcely possible to over-estimate the degree in which the extension of Russian dominion, particularly in Central Asia, has been due to the rash personal ambition of individuals acting in rash independence of orders from home.' And again, 'the Russian Government has often been as surprised at its own successes as rival States have been alarmed, and there is reason to believe that the Kushk episode in 1885, far from being, as was supposed in England, part of a deep-laid design, was an impromptu on the part of Komaroff and Alikhanoff that burst with as much novelty upon the Foreign Office of St Petersburg as it did upon that of Whitehall.' At the same time it must not be forgotten that it had ever been the policy of the Tsars to ratify and reward these irresponsible acts of their over-zealous agents, when successful, with swords of honour, and to disavow and even punish them if it suited them to do so.

The Delimitation Commissions (Sir Peter Lumsden as chief of the English one) finally repaired to the debateable ground in Central Asia, and now there arose the burning question - was Penj-deh within or without the Afghan frontier? The English, supported by the Afghans, who were in possession of the place, emphatically said 'Yes;' the Russians just as doggedly said 'No'; so that meanwhile it was agreed, pending the settlement of the dispute, that the Russian and the Afghan forces should remain 'as they were.' But one day the Russians, under General Komaroff, arguing that they had been provoked thereto by the Afghans, delivered a violent assault upon the latter in Penj-deh, driving them headlong out of the position, with a loss of 500 men, besides all their camps and stores, and mingling paeans of victory with the exultant shout of the unscrupulous land-grabber: *Beati passidentes!*

On hearing of this scandalous breach of agreement, all England burst out into flames of revengeful wrath, and even the millennially minded Mr Gladstone, who was then in power, hastened to address the Commons: 'The House will not be surprised when I say, speaking with measured words in circumstances of great gravity, that to us, upon the statements I have recited, this attack bears the appearance of an unprovoked aggression.' The *Times* insisted on justice being done to the national honour, while even the *Daily News* said that 'war could only now be avoided by prompt disavowal on the part of Russia of the action of her commanders,' &c. At the same time the spirit of the Jingoes, rose to a most unparalleled pitch, and the National Anthem was again replaced for the time being by the immortal ballad of the great Macdermot, which declared that -

'We've got the ships, we've got the men, we've got the money too.'

The ships - many of them, at least - were forthcoming in the shape of fast cruisers, selected from the finest vessels of the merchant service, which were chartered by the Government and armed with one or two heavy guns to harass the 'enemy's' trade; while the reserves were called out, and troops who had been despatched to Egypt for operations in the Soudan were stopped at Suakim or elsewhere on the main road from India. Our arsenals began to work night and day in the preparation of arms and ammunition; and, to crown all, Mr Gladstone ultimately called for, and got, a credit of eleven millions sterling, whereof 'six and a half would be devoted to' - he did not mention our quarrel with Russia, but the people knew what he meant and lauded his meaning to the echo. *Si vis pacem, para bellum.*

It can well be imagined that a fine flutter had meanwhile been caused in St Petersburg by the news of all these bellicose preparations, this stem and resolute appearance of at last putting on his boots by the long-suffering John

Bull, whom it took such a deal of provocation to rouse out of his pacific torpor; and Europe began to gather in its amphitheatre, as 'twere, to watch the course of the conflict, long deferred but now at last come which Bismarck had once said could only resemble a combat between an elephant and a whale. But what was the disappointment of the Jingoes, and of those who had been looking forward with an eager interest to the spectacle of this amphibious duel, when Lord Granville announced at the Academy Dinner (May 2), in the presence of the Russian Ambassador, his firm belief that the peace of Europe would, after all, not have to be disturbed. His lordship had spoken on the strength of a telegram just received from St Petersburg. For on this very same day a Council of State, presided over by the Tsar himself, had been held at Gatchina, when it was decided to accept, in some form or other, the principle of arbitration which had been suggested by the British Cabinet as the best channel of escape from war - horrid war. There was reason to believe that this conciliatory spirit of the Tsar had been to a great extent brought about by the representations of the Berlin Court, acting at the instance of the Queen, who was residing in Germany during the crisis.

As a matter of fact, the arbitration proposed never came to anything, though the King of Denmark was spoken of as the judge; and meanwhile the Tsar hastened to present General Komaroff, the captor of Penj-deh (which remained for the present in the hands of the Russians), with a golden sword studded with diamonds, 'in recognition of the excellent measures taken by him as commander of the troops of the Murghab division, of the equal foresight and decision exhibited by him in the action against the Afghans, and of the courage and valour he had shown in the affair at Dash Kepri' - which was a pregnant enough reply to the original demand of the English for the virtual trial of Komaroff. Komaroff remained cock of the walk, and had the satisfaction of seeing the recall of honest Sir Peter Lumsden, who had given the strongest evidence against him all along. It was felt by the Government that the delimitation work would proceed better, after all that had happened, if entrusted to others; and, to make a long story short, this work was completed next year, or rather in 1887, by the final marking out of the Russo-Afghan frontier between the Hari Rud and the Amu Darya.

Russia had now got as near to India as it was possible for her to get without annexing the 'buffer State,' Afghanistan; and, if for nothing else, the reign of Alexander III will always be memorable for the accomplishment of this great and long-desired result. Besides, by the employment of other methods, the Tsar did more, perhaps, than any of his predecessors to revolutionise the relations between England and Russia in Central Asia; and the opening of the railway line from the Caspian to Samarkand, with branches to other strategic points on the landward route to India, will rank as one of the most important and abiding monuments of the reign of Alexander III; though even this vast undertaking will be dwarfed by the completion of the great Siberian Railway, begun in 1886 at Samara, and intended to connect by rail St Petersburg and Vladivostock, a distance of 6666 miles. For the rest, let me quote the words of Alexander III to Colonel Grambcheffsky before he set out on one of his Central Asian journeys of exploration:

'The Tsar, before giving me permission to go, distinctly impressed upon me - and these are almost the identical words of his Imperial Majesty - 'to avoid anything that would give England the least ground of complaint, otherwise I will not let you go. I do not wish for more territory. My late father has left me quite sufficient. All I wish is to keep what I have and to develop its resources.'[7]

In the matter of Penj-deh, which was ultimately assigned to the Russians, the Tsar had shown himself pacific, if firm. But, in the following year, he committed himself to a line of action which was firm without being over-pacific. Having prepared the way for countervailing in Central Asia the antagonism of England in Europe, he now began to shake himself free from those trammels which had been imposed upon him by this oppugnancy at the Congress of Berlin.

During the spring of 1886 there was an Imperial progress in the southern districts of Russia. The Tsar was received with the usual manifestations of official enthusiasm, accompanied by arrests of Nihilists, and on arriving at Sebastopol he issued (May 19) a proclamation to the Black Sea fleet, which caused no little stir in the European capitals. Alluding to the reconstruction of the fleet, as evinced by the launching of several new war-vessels, the Tsar said that, though he had done his utmost 'to promote the pacific development of the Russian people,' circumstances might compel him 'to defend by force of arms the dignity of the Empire. You will, with me, uphold it with devotion, and you will show the same firmness as that of which your fathers gave proof, in response to my grandfather's appeal, in a manner which gained the admiration of all their contemporaries. I call upon you in turn to watch over those waters which have witnessed in past time Russian heroism, and to your care I confidently commit the honour and security of Russia.'

On arriving at Moscow (May 25), his Majesty reviewed the troops, and then received the Mayor at the head of the municipal authorities, who, in his address, remarked that the Tsar had now 'restored life to the Black Sea,' thereby strengthening the belief and hope of Moscow that 'the Cross of Christ would yet shine on Saint Sofia.'

Presently the meaning of all this became alarmingly clear, when, towards the end of June, the Tsar solemnly declared that it was his intention to terminate the arrangement embodied in Article 59 of the Treaty of Berlin, constituting Batoum a free port. This declaration strikingly resembled that made by Russia during the Franco-German war in regard to the Black Sea articles of the Treaty of Paris; and Lord Rosebery, in two 'vigorous despatches,' protested against this new disregard of treaties on the strength of the protocol of the Black Sea Conference of 1871, recognising that 'it is an essential principle of the law of nations that no Power can liberate itself from the engagements of a treaty, or modify the stipulations thereof, unless with the consent of the contracting Powers by means of an amicable arrangement.'

None of the other Powers, however, made bold to back up England in her protest against the conduct of the Tsar's Government, while M. de Giers repelled, 'with all the strength of his convictions,' the charge that Russia had violated the faith of treaties, and adhered to the opinion 'that the spontaneous declaration of the intention of the Emperor to make Batoum a free port did not constitute an obligation, and that consequently the modification of that intention, which circumstances require, could not be considered as a departure from engagements which did not exist.' The despatch concluded with a hint that the Berlin Treaty had already been violated in the case of Bulgaria (union of Eastern Roumelia with it, for example), in spite of the efforts of the Russian Government to maintain it, and an assurance 'that the Imperial Cabinet are still anxious to contribute to the consolidation of the general peace, in the hope that the Powers which have fixed and guaranteed its bases will themselves respect them.'

So this, then, was the end of Batoum, which Russia - who had solemnly agreed to regard it as a free port - was now at liberty to convert into a war-harbour - another link in the chain of her military preparedness stretching from Penj-deh to the Bosphorus, a chain which she had further sought to lengthen, but meanwhile without success, by repeatedly seeking to obtain free passage for her ships-of-war through the Turkish Straits. It is not to be doubted that the attitude of England with respect to Bulgaria had irritated Alexander III, and caused him to retaliate by thus repudiating the Batoum clause of the Treaty of Berlin. He had kept the peace with other Powers, but it was England who now kept the peace with him. He was, however, as near as possible breaking that European peace by his conduct towards his Battenberg cousin of Bulgaria; though the story of the Tsar's relations to Prince Alexander forms a tragedy which deserves a chapter all to itself.

NOTES

1. In a note in the official *Gazette* it was declared that private utterances by persons having no authority from their Government to make them can naturally have no influence upon the general course of our foreign policy, nor can they affect our good relations with neighbouring States, which are based not only upon ties of friendship existing between crowned heads and their clear perception of the interests of their people, but also upon the strict and mutual observance of existing treaties.'

2. The Tsar was at Copenhagen when Mr Gladstone and Lord Tennyson reached that port on a voyage of pleasure. He showed a touching courtesy towards both the illustrious Englishmen. There is a pretty story of the artifices he used to induce Lord Tennyson to read one of his poems. It is worth mentioning that during Mr Gladstone's blindness after the operation for cataract, one of the most sympathetic inquirers was the Tsar. His message considerably moved Mr Gladstone, who caused his thanks to be conveyed to the Emperor.

3. 'The Relations between France and Russia since 1871' in the *New Review* for August 1889.

4. His reflections on the subject, embodied in a work entitled 'Patriotism and Christianity,' were first presented to English readers in the pages of the *Daily Chronicle* of July 7, 9 and 10, 1894.

5. *Neue Militärische Blätter* for March 1892.

6. 'Souvenirs de Sebastopol,' recueillis et rédigés, par S.M.I. Alexandre III, Empereur de Russie - traduction de M Nicolas Notovitch - d'après les originaux conservés au Musée Historique de Sebastopol.' Paris: Ollendorff, 1894.

7. Colonel Grambcheffsky was here speaking to the St Petersburg correspondent of the *Daily Chronicle*, who gave an account of his interview in the *Asiatic Quarterly Review* for November 1891.

Alexander II, Tsar of Russia

Marie Alexandrovna, Tsarina of Russia

Grand Duke Nicholas, Tsarevitch of Russia, and Grand Duke Alexander, c.1863

Grand Duke Alexander, Tsarevitch of Russia, and Princess Dagmar of Denmark, at the time of their engagement, 1866

Alexander II and Marie Alexandrovna, Tsar and Tsarina of Russia, 1866

Alexander II and Marie Alexandrovna, Tsar and Tsarina of Russia, with Alexander and Marie Feodorovna, Tsarevitch and Tsarevna, 1866

Alexander II, Tsar of Russia, with his children, Grand Dukes Paul and Sergei, Grand Duchess Marie (later Duchess of Edinburgh), Grand Duke Alexis, Tsarevitch Alexander, and Grand Duke Vladimir, with the Tsarevna and her eldest child, Grand Duke Nicholas, later Tsar Nicholas II, seated on her lap, c.1870

Alexander, Tsarevitch of Russia, with Tsar Alexander II, and Alfred and Marie, Duke and Duchess of Edinburgh

The Winter Palace, St Petersburg

Alexander and Marie Feodorovna, Tsarevitch and Tsarevna, and their three elder surviving children, Grand Dukes Nicholas and George, and Grand Duchess Xenia, c.1878

A contemporary impression of the assassination of Tsar Alexander II, St Petersburg, 13 March 1881

Tsar Alexander III rouble, 1883

Constantin Pobedonostseff, Procurator of the Holy Synod and tutor to Alexander III when Tsarevitch

Prince Alexander of Battenberg, Sovereign Prince of Bulgaria

Gatchina Palace and Park, near St Petersburg. Tsar Alexander III and his family spent most of their time here, as it was deemed safer to live in than the Winter Palace

The imperial train at Borki after the crash, 29 October 1888

Tsar Alexander III, Tsarina Marie Feodorovna, and her sister Alexandra, Princess of Wales

Alexander III and Marie Feodorovna, Tsar and Tsarina of Russia and family, c.1888. From left to right: Grand Duke George; Grand Duke Nicholas, Tsarevitch and later Tsar Nicholas II; Grand Duchess Olga (in front of Empress Marie); Grand Duchess Xenia; Grand Duke Michael

Tsar Alexander III and Tsarina Marie Feodorovna of Russia, c.1890

Tsar Alexander III of Russia and Princess Marie of Greece and Denmark

Livadia Palace, the imperial summer retreat at the Crimea, where Tsar Alexander III died in 1894

The funeral procession of Tsar Alexander III, November 1894

A contemporary impression of Tsar Alexander III of Russia and the Tsarevitch, later Tsar Nicholas II, at the former's deathbed at Livadia, from Le Petit Journal

CHAPTER VI

THE TWO ALEXANDERS

The two cousins - Prince Alexander of Battenberg - A glimpse of him at Bucharest - Prince of Bulgaria Elect - Explosion at the Winter Palace - The Tsar says, 'Do your best!' - Muscovite art of managing men - A Russian Satrapy - The Prince and his Nessus-shirt – 'Good, as long as it lasts' - *Pour décourager les autres* - Fat on the Russian fire - Kaulbars and Soboleff -Tactics of the Duumvirs - 'Cowardly King Milan' - 'Power into Russian hands' - Prince Alexander at Moscow - Turning of the Russian tide - The two deputations - 'Not at home!' - *'Aut Caesar, aut nullus!'* - M. Jonin bullies the Battenberger - The Prince takes the trick - *'Je suis heureux et tranquillisé'* - 'Swine, rascals, perjured rabble!' - 'The Tsar is not Russia' - Military quarrels - The Prince dances with Madame Jonin - The Prince in England and Austria - His confidences to Herr von Huhn - The Tsar cannot stand liars - A thunderbolt from Russia - The Servians rush to arms - But have to reel back on their pig-styes and their Russian patrons - The two Bulgarias - Climax and anti-climax - *La Russie boude* - Conspiracies to 'remove' the Prince - 'Beware of the Struma regiment!' - The *Prinzenraub* - 'Here may you see a traitor!'- Muscovite 'stoutbrief and hamesucken' - An exchange of telegrams - 'Farewell to Bulgaria!' - The Prince's Seven Years' War - Worried to death - A thunder-loud 'No!'

ALEXANDER III of Russia, and Alexander, first ruler of the Bulgaria created by the Russo-Turkish war and the Treaty of Berlin, were full cousins. The mother of the former - a Princess of Hesse-Darmstadt - and the father of the latter had been brother and sister. The Prince's mother had been a Countess von Hauke, daughter of a Polish ex-Minister of War (some said there was a strain of Jewish blood in the family), who was raised to the rank of Princess on her morganatic marriage with Prince Alexander of Hesse. The Tsar was the senior of his Battenberg cousin by twelve years, the latter having been born in 1857. He received a careful education at Darmstadt, at Schnepfenthal near Gotha, and afterwards at the Military Academy in Dresden, where he remained until he was ripe for a commission in a regiment of Hessian dragoons. Subsequently he received the grade of an officer on the super-numerary list of a Russian cavalry regiment, and when the Russo-Turkish war broke out he was provided with staff employment at the headquarters of his imperial uncle. He was then in his twentieth year, full of military ardour and the spirit of action. He was present at the siege of Plevna, and afterwards crossed the Balkans with General Gourko.

Take the following glimpse that is afforded us of the Prince at this time by Count Pfeil, in his 'Experiences of a Prussian Officer in the Russian Service':

'In the hotel (at Bucharest) I made the acquaintance of Prince Alexander of Battenberg, afterwards Prince of Bulgaria, who was having some stomachic complaint attended to. He had only just returned from the seat of war (September), and expressed his great dissatisfaction with the leading of the Russian troops, especially of the cavalry; for, although there were sixteen cavalry regiments on the road from Plevna to Lovcha, the Turks were able to send many hundred waggons full of provisions to the besieged city along this very road. I drove with Prince Battenberg to Herr von Alvensleben's, at that time German Consul in Bucharest, where we dined. It was mentioned there that the Russians would gladly make the Prince the future Prince of Bulgaria; but the young Prince strenuously opposed the idea, and declared that he would never accept the position. When subsequent events falsified those words, I remarked to myself that the young man, who then appeared so innocent, possessed, at any rate, so much aptitude for diplomacy that he knew how to employ language in order to conceal his thoughts.'

But it was only after the war, when the sword of the soldier gave place to the pen of the diplomatist, that the young Battenberg Prince began to be publicly heard of. The sword of the Tsar, supplemented by a European Board of Green Cloth at Berlin, had carved a Bulgarian State out of the decrepit body of the Turkish Empire, and this State required a Prince to rule over it. After all the immense sacrifices in men and money made by the Tsar in the creation of this Bulgarian State it naturally fell to him to suggest the name of its first ruler, and his choice fell on his German nephew, Prince Alexander of Battenberg, who by this time had exchanged into the Prussian army and was serving at Potsdam as a Lieutenant in the Gardes du Corps.

When the news of his election by the Bulgarian Assembly at Tirnova (April 29, 1879) reached the Prince, he was helping to celebrate the birthday of his imperial uncle at a dinner given by the Russian Ambassador in Berlin. But it was only after an internal struggle that he declared his readiness to proceed to Livadia, and accept the proffered crown. 'Pleasant reminiscence' (*schöne Erinnerung*) forsooth! 'even if you don't remain there long.' As a matter of fact, these much-quoted words were addressed by Bismarck, not to Prince Alexander at all, but to Prince Charles of Hohenzollern when offered the crown of Roumania; and, in any case, they would have been singularly misapplied, as it afterwards turned out, had they been used by the Chancellor to Prince Alexander as an encouragement for him to proceed to Sofia.

Arrived at Livadia, he there explained that he had not yet received his father's consent to accept the Bulgarian throne, on account of the absurdly free Constitution which had been given the Bulgarians. But the Tsar urgently begged his nephew not to cast a slur upon the name of Russia by refusing, speaking to him in a warm, paternal manner, saying that he loved him as his own son, and that he would aid him in every difficulty to which the working of the Constitution might give rise. Thereupon the Prince yielded, declaring, as the Tsar embraced him, that he would ever strive to justify the confidence which his Majesty had reposed in him.

The next meeting between the two was marked by an incident of a most extraordinary kind. It was the winter (January) of 1880, when Prince Alexander, after having become formally installed at Sofia, had journeyed to St Petersburg to be present at the celebration of the Emperor's jubilee of rule, the twenty-fifth anniversary of his accession to the throne. The Bulgarian Prince was received like a son by his imperial uncle. On Sunday evening, February 17, the Prince's father was expected to arrive from Darmstadt, and in order to include him in the family dinner-circle, the meal, of which the usual hour was half-past six, had been postponed till seven. Accompanied by his son, Prince Alexander of Hesse was just in the act of ascending the grand staircase, at the top of which stood his imperial brother-in-law to welcome him, when he was startled by a roar like thunder, followed by sudden darkness, and a shower of stones, lime, and wooden splinters.

The Tsar knew very well what this meant, but he thanked God that the late arrival of his German brother-in-law had caused him to be on the grand staircase instead of, as usual, in the dining-room at the time of the explosion. This dining-room was just over the guard-room on the ground-floor, which at this time contained about sixty soldiers of the Finland Regiment; while underneath this guard-room was a vaulted basement, where carpenters and other workmen had been having free access of late for the purpose of repairs. It was here where the dynamite had been laid and fired at the moment when the Imperial family was assumed to be already at the table above, according to wont. The explosion killed and wounded a great many of the soldiers in the guard-room and split asunder the floor of the imperial dining-room, besides totally wrecking the Prince of Bulgaria's bedchamber. The Tsar had caused an elaborate Constitution to be granted to the Bulgarians, but had, nevertheless, continued to refuse one to his own subjects; and this, then, was the protest of the Nihilists against this strange act of political inconsistency.

The Russians, it was argued, were not yet ripe for a Constitution, and after the excitement and confusion caused by the Nihilist explosion in the Winter Palace had subsided. Prince Alexander took occasion to point out that his own subjects were just as immature in this respect as the Russians. In fact, the Tirnova Constitution, he said, was a decided hindrance to his rule, and, indeed, unless it underwent great changes, he knew not what would come of it all. The Tsar called a council of his wise men, when the War Minister,

General Milutin, argued that the constitution had not yet been long enough on its trial, and that the Prince would meanwhile do well to try and govern with the help of the Liberals. This plan met with the approval of the Tsar, who congratulated the Prince on having displayed so much firmness and patience, saying, 'If you act with moderation, and, should it be necessary, energetically exercise your lawful powers, you will succeed in winning esteem and affection for yourself. I rely on your personal qualities. The art of managing men is a thing that may be acquired, and you will gain experience in it day by day.'

How the Russians themselves exercised this art of managing men in Bulgaria may be inferred from the following anecdote. Among the crowd of Muscovites who surrounded the Prince at Sofia, intriguing against him because he was a German, and determined that he should be a mere puppet in their hands, was one well-meaning person, Davidoff, the diplomatic agent. Now this Davidoff was a truth-speaking man, and sent veracious reports of things to St Petersburg; whereas Parenzoff, the Bulgarian Minister of War appointed by the Tsar, was a pupil, no less in theory than in practice, of General Ignatieff, the celebrated 'Father of Lies.' Parenzoff had taken very good care that the reports of Davidoff to the Tsar should never reach their destination; but his heart sank within him, and even his knees began to knock together, on discovering that Davidoff was to accompany Prince Alexander to St Petersburg on the occasion already referred to, and that he was actually going to take with him the drafts of his reports to the Emperor and the Foreign Office, who might thus, after all, be put into possession of the truth. But Parenzoff was equal to the occasion:[1]

'When the Prince,' wrote Pastor Koch, his court chaplain, 'left his room at five o'clock on the morning of his departure, to repair to the carriage that was in waiting for him, the Minister of War (Parenzoff), who appeared in full dress, announced that four horses were still wanting at every (post) station, and therefore the luggage would have to be sent on after him. I was standing near the Prince, and I still see the little man, who, with his heron's feather on the kalpak, just reached up to the Prince's nose, making this unpleasant announcement with a military salute; I still see the dark shadows that crossed the Prince's face at the news. The Prince, however, issued an order that each of the three carriages was to have three horses put to instead of four, in order that the luggage-cart should be sent on at once. This order was not executed, the luggage was not despatched for some hours later, and so Davidoff's trunk (containing all the drafts of his veracious reports) was lost. Parenzoff afterwards gave himself all possible trouble to discover the trunk; he sent off an officer *attaché* to the War Office for 'special missions;' but this gentleman naturally found nothing, as he himself best knew where it was.'

On the representations of the Prince, the Tsar replaced Parenzoff by an honest Finlander, General Ernroth, as Bulgarian Minister of War, and for some time after things went on a little better. Acting on Milutin's advice, the Prince had made an honest trial to rule with the aid of the Liberals, but the result was most disheartening, and again he appealed to the Tsar by letter, setting forth the unsatisfactory nature of his position. Thereupon M. de Giers sent fresh instructions to his diplomatic agent at Sofia, according to which the Prince was to be left absolutely free to take his own course. But again the Prince had to complain of the tactics of the diplomatic intriguer; and once more the Tsar, yielding to the appeal of his half-distracted nephew, sent to Sofia a more straightforward and congenial representative. Alexander II, it must be allowed, behaved towards the Prince with the utmost fairness, but he was served by agents who were far more Russian than their Imperial master himself, and aimed at nothing short of converting the Principality into a mere satrapy of the Empire, a stepping-stone to Constantinople. At the end of 1880 the Prince said:

'I have borne everything, and am ready to bear still further, but I do not see how I am to comply with Russia's demands and wishes in the face of the anti-Russian current in my nation and the army, especially as, in addition to this, a Russian party of underground intriguers is hidden behind the opposition that I encounter, which pursues the sole aim of making my position untenable by raising strife betwixt Russia and myself.'

The spring of 1881 came, and with it the assassination of the Tsar Liberator (of Bulgaria as well as of the serfs), and Prince Alexander hurried to St Petersburg to attend the obsequies of his murdered uncle. It was known that the new Tsar was anti-German in his feelings, and it was feared that the Prince's position would now become infinitely worse. Yet his first conversation with his cousin, Alexander III, certainly reassured the Prince to some extent. His Majesty promised to maintain all the obligations which his deceased father had undertaken towards him (the Prince), to be ready to support him in the same manner as the late Tsar had done. More than this, he expressed himself against the Bulgarian Constitution on principle, though there was yet no question of altering or abrogating it.

But within two months of this time this Constitution had gone by the board. The Prince had found it to be a mere Nessus-shirt, and, on mature reflection, he pulled it off and threw it away, saying in his proclamation to his people:

'I have determined to convene the Grand National Assembly, the highest exponent of the people's will, in order to replace my crown and the destiny of Bulgaria in its hands. In the event of the Assembly approving the conditions, to be more accurately indicated later, which I consider indispensable for the government, and the want of which is the fundamental evil of our present state, then, and only then, can I continue to wear the crown of Bulgaria and discharge my heavy responsibilities in the sight of God and posterity. Should it not do so, I am prepared to renounce the throne with regret certainly, but with the consciousness that I have fulfilled my duty to the end.'

The Prince had taken the bull by the horns, but now he had to explain himself to the bear. 'In the event of your Majesty not approving my proceedings,' he wrote to his Imperial cousin, 'a word will suffice to determine me to leave the country;' while at the same time he caused an inventory of his goods and chattels to be made, with a view to depart. The Liberals began to stir up the people against the Prince, and his dethronement was openly discussed. But presently there came a telegram from St Petersburg, which the Russian agent, Hitrovo, caused to be placarded about. 'The Tsar's Government,' it ran, 'wishes that the Bulgarian people should remain indissolubly united with their Prince, and withstand all the lures of the traitors who are working against him.' *Cela va bien pourvu que cela dure* – i.e. very good as long as it lasts.

Prince Alexander's journey throughout his realm now proved a triumphal procession, and the horses were taken out of his carriage in Rustchuk and other towns. The Opposition appealed for help to 'the most liberal men in Europe,' to Gladstone and Gambetta, the latter of whom had just reached the summit of power. On the other hand, Zankoff, a rank and pestilent intriguer, wrote to the Tsar's agent: 'We will accept neither the honey nor the sting from Russia.' By an overwhelming majority the elections invested the Prince with the absolute power which he had demanded, and the hall of parliamentary session was changed into a banqueting and ball room, in which both Prince and people danced the national *choro*.

But in the midst of all this saltatorial jubilation it was an ominous circumstance that honest General Ernroth, Minister of War, left Bulgaria because he had found it impossible to get on with his diplomatic Colleague, M. Hitrovo - mark the name! It was mainly on Ernroth's advice that the Prince had quashed the preposterous constitution which hampered his every act, and now he looked as if he had suddenly been left in the lurch. All the same, the courageous and much-enduring Prince kept on his course amid such a welter of heart-breaking intrigues and make-shift ministries as was never heard of.

So far the Russian party had been riding roughshod over him. But now, at last, he determined to put his foot down and make an example *pour décourager les autres*. At Shumla there was a cavalry regiment officered by Russians, against whom very grave charges of peculation and mismanagement had reached the Prince's ears. He therefore summoned it to Sofia for inspection, and soon convinced himself of the truth of the accusations that had been brought against its officers. For the moment he said nothing. But presently there came pouring into Sofia delegates from the Shumla villages adjacent to the cavalry camp, with complaints that their farmsteads had been harried night after night by the men of the regiment in question, and that all their hay and oats had been stolen.

Then the Prince called the non-commissioned officers out of the ranks and asked them if this was true. They denied not that it was true, but pleaded that they had merely acted in compliance with the will of their majors. The majors in turn threw the blame on their colonel, who was treasurer of the regiment, and had paid them out no forage coin for a considerable time. Now, conduct of this kind, though deemed a military virtue in Russia, was held to be a heinous offence in Bulgaria, and so the Prince at once cashiered the delinquent officers of the Shumla horse regiment without fear or favour. At the same time he dismissed the Russian chief of the Engineers for peculation, and also sent about their business Kryloff, his War Minister, and Popoff, his assistant, for intriguing against his person and authority. In place of Kryloff he appointed General Lesovoji notwithstanding the vehement protest of Hitrovo (diplomatic agent) that such an appointment rested with the Tsar.

The fat was now on the fire in the military world of Russia, which viewed all these degradations and dismissals at Sofia as a studied insult to the army of the Tsar. But still the Emperor himself made a show of standing loyally by the Prince. The latter hurried off to St Petersburg to lay his hard case before his Imperial cousin, and found him leading the life of a terror-haunted prisoner at Peterhof. The Prince requested the recall of Hitrovo and the decoration of Lesovoy, in order that 'his authority should be upheld, and that it should clearly be shown he was right in his appointment of Lesovoy.' The Tsar granted both requests. In order to put a stop to all further intriguing on the part of the Russian officers in Bulgaria, the Prince further requested his cousin to give his consent to a general order, in which it was stated that he would look upon every misdeed or mutiny against the Prince as an offence against himself. Again the Tsar agreed to this, and the Prince wrote out the order in his Majesty's room. But a few months later the order was repudiated, and Lesovoy, who had read it out to the officers, was dismissed. Finally, the Prince begged the Tsar to let him have General Kaulbars, of whom he had been led to entertain a favourable opinion, as his Minister of War; and Kaulbars, in turn, was commissioned to look out for a colleague of the Interior. This colleague he found in General Soboleff, 'the husband of a lady friend' of his, and declared that he would either go with him or not at all to Bulgaria.

So far the Tsar had certainly not shown anything like his father's attachment to the Prince, yet he had given a benevolent support to the latter's plans. But now his attitude to the ruler of the Bulgarians began to change rapidly for the worse under the influence of Hitrovo, who had returned from

Sofia, and of Messrs Kaulbars and Soboleff, who had gone thither. Essentially a truth-loving and truth-telling man himself, no one was ever made the victim of so many lies and misrepresentations as Alexander III. About this time the Panslavist movement began to be very strong in Russia, and Soboleff was its fiery Teutophobe apostle. Another of these propagandists was General Obrutscheff, Chief of the General Staff, who was incensed against Prince Alexander for his cashiering of Russian officers in Bulgaria. Bulgaria he looked upon as the glacis of fortified Russia, and Generals Kaulbars and Soboleff as the pioneers charged with the task of clearing this glacis of all obstructions.

This worthy couple were not long in throwing off the mask, and in openly stirring up the Bulgarians into opposition to their lawful Prince. In their insidious reports to St. Petersburg they aimed at showing how pernicious for Russia was the Prince's line of conduct; how his professions of attachment to that great country were pure hypocrisy; how he misused the name of the Tsar and the Russian people in order to turn the hearts of the Bulgarians against their liberators from the Turkish yoke; how discontent and Nihilism in Russia must steadily increase with the loss of Bulgaria; and, above all things, how insulting it was to powerful Russia to have one after another of its agents at Sofia dismissed as useless and dangerous.

To Soboleff, the stupidest of the two, fell the task of undermining the Prince's authority over his subjects, while Kaulbars, on the other hand, set himself to take the army out of the Prince's hands so as to be able to use it against him, if need be. The Prince himself had honestly believed that he was acting in the interest of Russia when developing Bulgaria's own resources and civilisation to the utmost, and promoting the welfare of its army. 'But that,' says Pastor Koch, 'was a misconception. Alexander II was dead, and the new Russia wanted no developed Bulgaria. It wanted a weak one, in order to be able to control it more easily. It wanted no federation with the West, to which the Prince's efforts were directed. Bulgaria was to be isolated by a Chinese wall, and content itself with the crumbs of culture that fell from Holy Moscow's meagrely furnished table.'

As to the minds and methods of the two Generals let one anecdote suffice. The Prince had visited his neighbour King Milan, and by all the laws of courtesy was entitled to a return call. This was made at Rustchuk, in October 1882, but Soboleff went about proclaiming that the meeting was a gross blunder, and that 'Milan was coming as the ambassador of Austria.' The Prince had requested both Generals to attend the interview, and with some unwilling looks they did so. Kaulbars, however, who was naturally arrayed in all his showiest war paint, took care to fasten on his breast his Servian order (Commander's Cross of the Takova) below all his other decorations, in token of his 'thorough contempt' for this 'short-sighted and cowardly King Milan.' As a matter of fact, this contempt was afterwards to be more than justified by events still in the womb of time; but such a manifestation of scorn was clearly out of place on such an occasion as this, and Prince Alexander commanded Kaulbars either to fasten his Servian decoration above the others or to keep away from table. When the 'cowardly' Milan proceeded to distribute orders among the Prince's suite, the two Russian Generals were the first to beg the Prince to obtain for them a Gold Cross.

These Generals openly began to agitate against the Prince, his Ministry was divided against itself, while the Chamber was continually declaring that Bulgaria should be for the Bulgarians. The Prince's position was the most difficult that could be imagined. He had to treat Russia with consideration, and at the same time be the champion of his country's truest interests. He lived in a continual chaos of contradictions. Nothing that he did was right in the eyes of the Russians; nothing that they did commanded his approval. The sacrifices of *amour propre* and principle were always on his side. It was not enough that he should seek to prove considerate and complaisant to Russia. What was wanted of him was complete submission to her will in all things; and how thoroughly Messrs Soboleff and Kaulbars had done their work may be judged from the fact that the former General was able to write in the spring of 1883: 'The crisis of March 13 had the most decisive influence on the position of Bulgaria. The power passed into Russian hands.'

Bulgarian affairs - just think! - were in charge of the *Asiatic* Department of the Foreign Office at St Petersburg, and thus the Bulgarians learned that they must expect treatment like the Khivans or the Turcomans of Merv! Two things had helped to seal the Prince's doom at St Petersburg. One of these was his arrest and deportation of the Metropolitan of Sofia in strict conformity with the law of the State, which was construed on the Neva by M. Pobedonostseff and others as a gross outrage on the Orthodox Church, of which the Tsar was the blind champion. But, worse than all, the Prince had ordered his delegate, at the so-called Quadruple Conference in Vienna relative to the International Orient Railway, to sign the treaty which Soboleff protested against as being more favourable to Austria than to Russia; and this was the beginning of the end.

Soon after this Prince Alexander went to Moscow to attend the coronation of the Tsar, and then it was that he was made to feel that he had deeply offended the Autocrat of All the Russias. In 1879 I had the honour of a chat with the Prince at Potsdam just before he left for Livadia, and I thought I had never seen a finer-looking man, frank, fresh, unassuming, yet princely. The next time I saw him was in the grand state ball-room of the Kremlin at Moscow, on the occasion of his cousin's coronation (1883), and even in that large and brilliant assemblage of the great White Tsar, the Prince of Bulgaria stood out among his fellow-guests like Saul among the people - his countenance, with its dark and almost Oriental cast, having more affinity with the warlike visages of the picturesque Turanian chiefs from the Kizil

Kum and the Kara Kum than with that of flaxen-haired soldiers of the type of Skobeleff. But by this time a shade of deep seriousness had clothed the features of the handsome Bulgarian Prince; for the iron of his destiny had already begun to penetrate his soul, and he was now conscious of being the object of his Imperial cousin's deep dislike and distrust.

This displeasure was not long in manifesting itself. The Bulgarian Chamber had sent from its midst a deputation to Moscow to congratulate the Tsar and present him, as a national offering, with a model, in pure gold, of the cottage which had been tenanted by his Majesty, when Tsarevitch, during the Russo-Turkish campaign. But now the Prince - who had not come straight from Sofia but from Darmstadt - found to his great surprise that a second deputation was in waiting for admission to the presence of the Tsar. This was one which had, in the meanwhile, been sharked up by the scheming Soboleff himself, and brought to Moscow as representatives of the 'down-trodden Bulgarian people.'

Naturally enough the Prince would not recognise this factitious corporation of his corrupted countrymen. But what was his surprise, not to say his indignation, when the Tsar signified his desire to receive the 'down-trodden' delegates at the same time as the golden bearers of the 'national offering'; and accordingly the two rival deputations tramped together into the Imperial presence under the eyes of the dumfounded Prince.

This was the doing of the crafty Soboleff, and it was supplemented by the action of Kaulbars who had remained behind to pull the strings at Sofia. While the deputation of the 'down-trodden' was gaping about in Moscow, and feasting on the crumbs that fell from the Emperor's table, Kaulbars kept flooding the Tsar with a stream of congratulatory telegrams and addresses, all tending to show how the loyal Bulgarian people - for so Soboleff termed the Opposition - had on their knees, before the Russian Consulate at Sofia, implored blessings on his Russian Majesty; how indescribable rejoicing reigned throughout the Principality; and how universal was the hope that the Tsar would restore Bulgaria to the position of a constitutional State.

Another circumstance, trivial in itself, tended to estrange the Tsar from his cousin. His Majesty drove to see Prince Alexander at his residence in the Kremlin, and found him, really and truly, 'not at home.' But of course there were some, Soboleff among the number, who strove to give the incident a more serious interpretation; and the mind of the Tsar, like all such minds, was a ready soil for suspicion. *Per contra*, when the coronation festivities were over, Prince Alexander received no invitation to accompany the Tsar to St. Petersburg, though Prince Waddemar of Denmark, by way of pointed contrast, was asked to do so. When first the Prince, during the early days of his stay in Moscow, had sounded his cousin as to replacing Messrs Kaulbars and Soboleff with honest General Emroth, the Tsar had seemed to acquiesce in the proposal. But now he doubted the propriety of doing so, and soon after the Prince returned to Sofia he received a rather cold letter from the Tsar saying that, instead of Emroth, he would send Councillor of State Jonin to study and report upon the situation.

Meanwhile the Prince, on returning home, had hastened to annul or reverse all the arbitrary acts which had been done by the Russian party in his absence, and - what was more - to summon the Chamber for the 4th of September. Yet that this energetic campaign against the over-zealous and intriguing minions of the Tsar at Sofia did not imply any hostility on the part of the Prince to Russia herself may be gathered from what he said at this time to Pastor Koch: 'Should a Russo-German war break out' (and it looked very much like it just then), 'I should place myself, without hesitation, though against my will, on the side of Russia. I regard that as my duty in any circumstances. As Prince of Bulgaria I must overlook Russia's hatred to my person, and must only consider what my people owes to Russia.'

But even this was not enough for the Tsar. *Aut Caesar, aut nullus* was clearly what he wanted to be in Bulgaria, and M. Jonin was to be the mouthpiece of his imperious will. Said the Prince to the Pastor:

'I awaited Jonin's arrival with a full confidence in the Tsar's word that his ambassador was coming on a friendly errand. He arrived yesterday, and has handed me a fresh communication, in which I am told that Jonin is commissioned to inform the Tsar as to the situation, and *d'user s'il y a lieu, d'efforts pour aplenir les difficultés*, and I am requested to give him a kindly support in the execution of a commission which is as difficult as it is delicate. But that was not all. Jonin explained that, in addition to this, he was commissioned by the Tsar to make a communication to me by word of mouth. I at once answered, 'I am at your service,' and took him into my study. There he began to point out to me, in an imperious and disrespectful tone, that the Tsar was much displeased with my proceedings after my return from Moscow, and that he looked upon the summoning of the Chamber for September 4 as an act of open hostility against Russia, and a direct insult to his person: for he knew only too well that the Chamber was only summoned to provoke ill-feeling towards Russia, therefore *the Tsar requested and ordered me* to dissolve the Chamber, to keep the Generals (Soboleff and Kaulbars) for at least two years longer, to separate myself from the clique with which I terrorised over the land, and to replace my absolute powers in the hands of the country. 'For' - these are Jonin's very words - 'the Tsar gave you absolute powers, and he now takes them back from you because you have made a bad use of them' (*un mauvais et méchant emploi*). Jonin made insolent and impertinent answers to all my objections, and when I reprimanded him for all this unseemly behaviour, he remarked, 'As Herr Jonin, I ask your pardon for the expressions I have used ; but as his Majesty's envoy I am forced to repeat them, for I have received orders from the Tsar to use this language.'

'This, then, is my recompense for my obedience towards Russia for four years! On all occasions I have defended and protected the interests of Russia in

Bulgaria with boundless devotion, nor have I hesitated in a thousand instances to suffer myself, in order to do what was pleasing to Russia. I have had enough of it now. It is impossible for me to embark in warfare with the Tsar of Russia; I will resign. I request you to go to Darmstadt and acquaint my parents with events here and explain to them the position, and tell them I have made up my mind to resign.'

But, after all, he did not do so; and, meanwhile, M. Jonin made a 'stormy demand' for another audience, saying that he had received orders from the Tsar to be *'plus énergique'* in his dealings with the Prince in the event of his not giving an answer. The Prince did answer, but not in a compliant sense, and then he was threatened with deposition if he did not accept the following conditions:

1. The Generals (Soboleff and Kaulbars) to remain at their posts for a further period of two years.
2. The Chamber to be dissolved.
3. The Prince to accept unconditionally all measures that the Generals may propose.
4. To relinquish his absolute powers.
5. To separate himself definitely from the clique that surrounds him.
6. To accept a fresh Constitution.

The poor Prince knew not what to do. Some of his native counsellors urged him to hold out, while others advised him to give in. He appealed to the diplomatic agents of the Powers, and either got no answer at all, or an equivocal one. The Austrian, with a shrug of the shoulders, spoke of the 'legitimate influence of Russia.' The Englishman said he could very well understand that the Prince should feel no inclination to prolong his stay in Bulgaria. The German had a diplomatic illness and could not be consulted at all, for was not Bulgaria 'Hecuba' to his master? While the only member of the whole corps who ventured to give Prince Alexander positive advice was the Frenchman. This splendidly courageous Gaul counselled the Prince to end the whole business by laying the Russian Generals by the heels and packing them across the frontier.

As a matter of fact, what the Prince did do, after another insulting interview with Jonin - who, true to his imperial master's behests, comported himself with 'more energy' than ever - was to issue a manifesto promising a new Constitution, to be submitted for approval to a Grand National Assembly. This manifesto had been extorted from him by the Russians, much in the same way as her abdication was from Mary Queen of Scots, and he only signed it under protest, as he telegraphed to the Tsar, who was then romping with his children on the lawns of Denmark. *'Je suis heureux et tranquillisé,'* wired back his Majesty to the Prince, who was now in a very opposite frame of mind and body. 'I came here a strong and healthy man,' he said to his sympathising chaplain, 'and now I am wearied out and broken down by all the excitement I have had to pass through.' But he was not altogether without his sources of consolation. The army was still with him. Hearing at this time that Kaulbars had been essaying to stir up a revolt among the troops, he determined to go to the camp; and, on seeing the approach of their deeply-wronged Prince, they broke from their ranks, in spite of their officers, and ran towards him with loud cheers. On his leaving the camp, the soldiers surrounded his horse and accompanied him in vast numbers to the palace.

The Chamber met, and Kaulbars and Soboleff attended to reap the triumph of the intrigues with which they had meanwhile been plying the Liberals. But what was their astonishment and rage when the committee entrusted with the task of drawing up a loyal address to the throne begged the Prince to restore the Constitution of Tirnova, and, at the same time, specify the alterations in it which he would like to have made. There was a dead silence, and all eyes were turned on the Generals, who were fidgeting in their seats, white and speechless with anger. But when, to complete their discomfiture, Zankoff (whom they thought they had got 'on toast') rose and expressed his approval of the address, they both sprang up and vanished from the hall - Kaulbars, even without his cap, exclaiming, 'Swine! Rascals! perjured rabble!' accompanied by shouts of triumph from the Chamber. After this the obnoxious Generals found it impossible to remain at their posts, and the mayor of Sofia, who owed his position to Soboleff, sped the parting guests at a dinner debited to the Russian Consulate, which entered the item as 'cost of illumination on the occasion of the festivities given on the Tsar's birthday!' 'My honourable lord, we will most humbly take our leave of you,' said Soboleff and Kaulbars to Prince Alexander on quitting Sofia. 'You cannot, sirs,' returned the Prince, as in Hamlet, 'take anything that I will more willingly part withal.'

About this time the Tsar was said to have written a letter to the Princess of Wales, in which occurred the phrase: *Les Bulgares ne veulent plus de lui,* 'the Bulgarians do not want to have anything more to do with him.' But now when the Prince had outwitted Russia by restoring the constitution of Tirnova, he was never more popular with his subjects. The Tsar was in a towering rage, and his agent, Jonin, cast about to take his revenge. Meanwhile, the tables had been turned on him, and he could no longer bully and insult the Prince as he had done on first arriving. The Prince simply listened to what he had to say, and then dismissed him. But sometimes Jonin would flare up.

He had heard that the Prince meant to appoint General Lesovoy, the oldest Russian officer in the Bulgarian Army, War Minister *pro tem*: as he had done twice already, and hastened to declare that, in the name of the Tsar, he forbade the General to accept the position. 'Reasons, reasons?' asked the

Prince in effect, and received for answer that 'the Emperor would never leave the army in the hands of a man who listens to you more than to us.' On the Prince remarking that he must construe these words as a personal insult, Jonin, rejoined: 'Go on, it is in my power to bring about a quarrel, and,' with a laugh, 'it is certainly not we who are afraid of it.' 'God is my witness,' replied the Prince, 'that I certainly do not want to provoke a quarrel, but if Russia means to do so, I do not fear the consequences either.'

It seemed that Russia certainly meant to do so. In any case M. Jonin went about boasting that he 'meant to take his revenge,' and this he prepared to do by telegraphing and writing the grossest lies to St Petersburg. 'The Tsar is not Russia!' Jonin had insolently replied to the saying of some one that the Prince had always been on the best of terms with the Tsar up to the coming of Kaulbars and Soboleff) and there was much truth in the remark. But the Tsar was himself and Russia too in the matter of the military quarrel which now broke out between him and the Prince. In order to put an end to the insufferable interference of the Russian officers with the affairs of the army, the Chamber had resolved to sever its command from the Ministry of War, and to restrict the activity of the latter to mere questions of administration. The chief command of the forces was to be held by the Prince alone, who was to appoint a General Staff to assist him, while the War Minister must be a Bulgarian, and all foreign officers serving in Bulgaria should take the oath of fidelity to the Prince. For these innovations there was both constitutional law and reason; but the news of them threw the Tsar into a towering rage, and he at once telegraphed to his cousin commanding him to allow no change in the status quo of the army till the arrival of the aide-de-camp whom he would despatch to inquire into the matter.

The Prince promised to do this, but meanwhile sent off to the Tsar an elaborate justification of the contemplated changes. But what was his surprise when his own aide-de-camp, Lieutenant Polzikoff, was commanded to report himself at once in St Petersburg on pain of being treated as a deserter. The Prince was beside himself.

'I cannot,' he said, 'pocket this direct personal insult of having my aide-de-camp recalled without first hearing what I have to say on the subject....I am bound to vindicate my adjutant's honour as well as my own - my adjutant's, for what would respectable Russian society think of me if I quietly put up with such a provocation; my own, for if I am to fall I prefer to fall fighting. I am quite convinced that my resolve will involve a breach with Russia, but I must run the risk. The Tsar requested me, eight days ago, to maintain, intact the status quo of the army until the arrival of his aide-de-camp; and now he himself violates this *status quo* in so marked a manner. I have therefore telegraphed to him, 'On account of the proceedings against my adjutant, I consider myself released from the engagement, taken with your Majesty, to maintain intact the *status quo* of the army."

At the same time a Ministerial Council resolved: 1. That the Russian members of the Prince's suite should be discharged; 3. That the Bulgarian officers serving in Russia should be recalled; and, 4. That the acting War Minister (a Russian) should be dismissed. It was no wonder that the Prince was terribly agitated during these days. 'If such attacks become frequent,' he said, 'I shall certainly collapse. My nervous system is strained to the last degree.' The Prince's open telegram to the Tsar was said to have roused the wrath of his Majesty to an extraordinary pitch, and Prince Waldemar of Denmark was already spoken of as the new candidate for the Bulgarian Throne. But ultimately his reason got the better of his wrath, and he sent Colonel Nikolai Kaulbars, a brother of the redoubtable General of this name, to conclude a military convention with Bulgaria; and, after much wrangling and wriggling, a kind of *modus vivendi* in this respect was established.

Meanwhile the course of domestic events, with their coalition and Karaveloff Ministries, their native cabals and Russian intrigues, was preparing a fine kettle of fish for the distracted ruler of the Bulgarians. The Tsar was deriving all his information about the march of things in Sofia from Kaulbars the Second, who was a very fine person indeed to make objective and impartial reports to his master. 'The world,' said Kaulbars, 'is for me a huge sausage. What does not concern me is of no account to me. I am a most decided egotist.' Nevertheless, during his stay in Bulgaria, he was the means of rather improving than otherwise the relations between Prince and Tsar, and Sofia was treated to the astonishing spectacle of the Prince attending a ball given by M. Jonin, and even dancing and chatting gaily with Madam. The Prince himself also gave entertainments, and invited his subjects to meet and confer with their Russian benefactors. One night at a Court ball a deputy felt so much at home that he took off his shoes and wandered about the palace-halls of his Sovereign in his stocking-soles until a friend suggested to him that he was not in a mosque - which will give an idea of the kind of people whom Prince Alexander had been called upon to rule over.

In the autumn of 1885 the Prince came over to England to attend the wedding of his brother, Prince Henry, to one of the daughters of Queen Victoria, and on his way home he went to Vienna. For he was sick and tired of all these brabbles and bickerings with the Russians, and was willing to make any sacrifice almost, consistent with his self-respect, and his duty to his subjects, to become reconciled to his Imperial cousin. Bismarck had found means of hinting to him that he should regard himself as the 'vicegerent of Russia,' to which the Prince had returned that he had always been ready to listen to the advice of his Muscovite patrons, and would even now do everything consonant with their interests, provided it did not injure those of his own subjects. He, therefore, recognised the wisdom of drawing nearer to Russia, and so in Vienna he begged Count Kalnoky to pave the way for a reconciliation. The Austrian Emperor invited him to the manoeuvres at Pilsen, after which the ground being meanwhile smoothed - he repaired to Franzensbad where M. de Giers was taking the waters. This diplomatist promised that he would do all he could to promote the wished-for *redintegratio amoris*, but presently there happened something which widened the breach between the two cousins to an irreparable extent.

On leaving Franzensbad, Prince Alexander went to reside at Varna, and here there presently came to him two secret emissaries from Philippopolis, the capital of Eastern Roumelia, with the announcement that the revolution which had long been in secret preparation throughout that Turkish province was now on the point of breaking out - its object being 'personal union' with Bulgaria. What was the Prince to do in view of this prospect? For had he not, when in Franzensbad, given M. de Giers the most explicit assurances that he would do nothing to promote the union of the two Bulgarias? The Prince himself said to his confidant, Herr von Huhn, correspondent of the *Cologne Gazette*:

'Amongst other things he (M. de Giers) told me that the policy of Russia and the Northern Powers at the moment was based on maintaining the existing state of things in the East, and that, therefore, every movement tending to further the unification of Bulgaria and Eastern Roumelia would be opposed in the most energetic manner. I was able to assure M. de Giers, honestly and conscientiously, that, although I was naturally aware how universally this unification was desired by the people, yet I did not believe that the movement was at all likely to break out within a measurable space of time....At Varna, to my inexpressible surprise, I received notice of the plan, only three days before the revolt broke out, and I lost no time in despatching a confidential envoy to Philippopolis to dissuade the people most urgently from their intentions. I sent word to the conspirators that at this moment, immediately after my interview with Giers, there could, less than at any other time, be no question of bringing about the union - in short, I used every argument to dissuade them from the rash step. However, it came about differently, for, before my messenger had reached Philippopolis, I received a telegram which informed me of the revolt, and of the arrest of Gavril Pasha, and calling upon me to assume the government, and to place myself at the head of the movement.

'What was I to do? For two hours I thought it over; then my resolve was taken. He who is called upon to exercise political functions of a higher kind, no less than the general in the field, is often forced to make up his mind rapidly. I said to myself that, if I refused, there would be nothing left for me but to renounce my crown and to leave the country immediately, for it was inconceivable that I could remain Prince of Bulgaria after a refusal; I should, therefore, have fallen, and not precisely with much glory. On the other hand, I could not disguise from myself that I should also run a serious risk of losing my crown in case I accepted, and that, in fact, the prospects on both sides were decidedly unfavourable. However, it was of paramount importance that I should come to some decision immediately, and, in accepting, I was in great part influenced by the following considerations. I knew my country, and knew that there was the greatest possible danger of the movement degenerating in the most awful manner. Notwithstanding all my exertions, the hatred of nationalities is not yet stifled, and I foresaw that, in addition to the revolt, there would be a civil war between Bulgarians and Mahomedans. I alone was in a position to keep the movement within peaceful bounds, and to prevent it from leading to excesses. Without me anarchy would be rampant; with me peace and order were assured. That is why I accepted.'

But the Tsar was by no means satisfied with these reasons, which had been adduced to show how groundless were the accusations urged in Russia against the Prince of being deceitful and unreliable, and declared that he had been intentionally duped by Prince Alexander; that, in fact, the latter had told him a deliberate lie. 'The fact is,' said one of his Majesty's eulogists, or at least apologists (Mr Stead), 'that the Emperor regards such conduct as Prince Alexander's as men in society regard cheating at cards, as a kind of sin against the Holy Ghost, which, once committed, can never be forgiven or atoned for, either in this world or in that which is to come.'

But if the Tsar was deliberately duped by any one, it was more by his own agents than by Prince Alexander. His Majesty professed to be very much taken aback by the East Roumelian revolution. But what was the fact? Why, that his Consul-General and military attaché were both present at the decisive sitting of the Secret Committee when the day was fixed for the outbreak of the revolution, and that they repeatedly assured the Prince that they had sent report after report on the subject to St. Petersburg. The truth is that the revolution was condemned by the Tsar because it did not have the effect of removing the Prince, for it was his person, much more than his principality, that formed the object of Russian solicitude. It was in this respect that the Tsar was so grievously disappointed. Far from removing the Prince, the revolution only had the effect of carrying him on, as on the crest of a mountain-high wave of popularity, to a seat on an enlarged throne based on the reverence and affection of the united Bulgarian people.

The Tsar was not long in revealing his deep displeasure, and sent word that all Russian officers should at once retire from the Bulgarian army. The Chamber telegraphed to his Majesty begging him to rescind the order, but he was inexorable; and this order he by-and-by supplemented by a decree erasing the name of 'Prince Alexander of Bulgaria, Russian General and honorary Colonel of the 13th Rifle Battalion, from the lists of the Russian army.' This thunderbolt fell on the very eve of the Servian invasion of Bulgaria, when its author doubtless calculated that it would have the effect of degrading Prince Alexander in the eyes of his people, and thus paralysing his military power. But its effect was just the very opposite of this. Instead of moving the

Bulgarians to contempt, it only aroused their indignation. 'Rather Turkish than Russian!' they began to exclaim after this incredible display of Imperial spite, which, as afterwards appeared, had been indulged in against the advice of the Tsar's Ministers, especially of M. de Giers.

Prince Alexander himself remained perfectly calm under the blow, nor would he listen to proposals of retaliation in any form. Some urged him to issue a manifesto; others, to order the discontinuance of the prayers for the Tsar which were offered up every Sunday in all Bulgarian churches; while others, again, counselled him to return all his Russian decorations. But the Prince would not hearken to such counsellors. Remembering the very kind and fatherly way in which he had always been treated by Alexander II, he felt this rancorous treatment by his son most keenly, and, if he allowed the insult to pass without a reply, this was because he placed the interest of his adopted country higher than his personal feelings, and did not wish to give the Tsar any pretext for an armed intervention. It was, however, a source of great satisfaction to him that both the Emperors of Germany and Austria declined a proposal on the part of the Tsar to erase the Prince's name in a similar manner from their army lists, and, above all things, that the Bulgarians stood firmly by him in the hour of his insults and their country's danger.

King Milan had seized upon the union of the two Bulgarias - which seemed to him to threaten the balance of power in the Balkans - as a pretext for declaring war on Prince Alexander's unified people. But there were other old grudges to pay off, and even the Prince himself admitted (in a letter to his father) that his subjects had been very bad neighbours indeed to the Servians. Still there can be little doubt that King Milan, in thus rushing to arms, also looked upon himself as the informal executioner of the will of the Tsar - for he was ever an obsequious and knee-crooking knave - and already looked forward to the time when the Saint George's Cross would be sent him from St Petersburg for putting an end, violent and complete, to the pestilent and deceitful Prince of Bulgaria.

But the 'best laid schemes of mice and men' never went worse 'agley' than they did in the case of this wanton assault by the Servians on the national existence of their neighbours. The Russians, of course, would only have been too delighted to see the new Bulgarian army, with the Prince at its head, rolled into irretrievable wreck and ruin by this paltry nation of uniformed pig-drivers. But the wreck and ruin, to the bitter disappointment of the Muscovites, were just all the other way about. For on the fields of Slivnitza and Pirot, Prince Alexander, in the most brilliant and heroic manner, cemented the union of his people with the blood of their jealous and meddling Slavonic brethren across the Servian border, and sent them packing back to their pig-styes and their Russian patrons. Then Austria came forward with an imperious 'Thus far and no further!' to the conquering Bulgarians and their Prince, robbing them of the fruits of their victories, and earning the everlasting gratitude of the delighted Tsar, to whom it had been the bitterest of all pills that his hated cousin had thus crowned himself with glory without the assistance of the Russian officers who had been recalled.

'Money the Servians have none,' said a leading statesman of Bulgaria, 'consequently they will not be able to give us any. But pigs are to be found in plenty, and it would only be just if they were to hand us over at least two millions of these national animals as a war indemnity.' But the victors got no such compensation for the sacrifices they had made - nothing but the recognition by the Porte and the Powers of the personal union of the two Bulgarias; though even now the Tsar could not refrain from showing his bitter animus towards his cousin by insisting that Prince Alexander's *name* should be erased from the Treaty and replaced by that of the 'Prince of Bulgaria,' who would henceforth be 'Governor-General,' as for the Sultan, of Eastern Roumelia. On December 26 (1885) Prince Alexander made his triumphal entry into Sofia at the head of his victorious troops, frantically cheered by his exultant subjects and overwhelmed with laurel-wreaths and flowers.

This was the climax, and now for the anti-climax. While as yet the three days' battle at Slivnitza was in progress, Zankoff, a Bulgarian intriguer of the rankest kind, had entered into negotiations with the Russian Consul of Sofia for the 'removal' of the obnoxious Prince, who so manfully declined to be the mere tool of Russia. Repeated attempts had already been made to effect this 'removal.' Messrs Soboleff and Kaulbars had done their best to do so, but in vain. One night these 'duumvirs' had entered the Palace and requested to be taken to the Prince. But the officer on duty (Lieutenant Marinoff, who afterwards fell at Slivnitza) liked not the look of it and refused to comply, in spite of explicit orders from his immediate chief, the War Minister. On their attempting to force their way he made a stout and successful resistance, and reported the incident to the Prince. The neighbourhood of the Palace was then hurriedly examined, and what was found? Several carriages ready horsed, and a printed proclamation which set forth how the good people of Bulgaria, tired of the Prince's misrule, had made him a prisoner and transported him across the frontier; while a provisional Government had been established under Generals Soboleff and Kaulbars!

Later on, a similar and equally unsuccessful attempt was made to capture the Prince near Burgas. But the Russians are a dogged people, and, when once they have set their hearts on a thing; it is by no means easy to move them from their purpose. In war they never fly, preferring, if they cannot force their way like lions, to be slaughtered like oxen. And did not M. Stambuloff afterwards say of Alexander III (with what taste and discretion I will not stop to inquire) that he was 'the prototype of a Russian moujik - upright, Orthodox, of no resources, stubborn as an ox, a blockhead who would never change?' He had set his heart on the annihilation of his noble cousin, and destroyed he would have to be. That was what his agents at Sofia knew full well. But it is not necessary to assume that the Tsar sent explicit instructions to these agents to dispose of the hated Prince. For -

> 'It is the curse of kings to be attended
> By slaves that take their humours for a warrant
> To break within the bloody house of life,
> And on the winking of authority
> To understand a law, to know the meaning
> Of dangerous majesty, when perchance it frowns
> More upon humour than advised respect.'[2]

But if the Tsar did not, in set terms, convey to his slaves and partisans at Sofia the clear expression of his will, it is at least certain that he must have been aware what these obsequious agents of his were scheming to accomplish. If he did not expressly order the 'removal' of Prince Alexander, then never were the name and authority of any master more grossly abused. But, then, had M. Jonin not boasted that 'The Tsar was not Russia'? There were two Bulgarian officers, Dimitrieff and Bendereff, who thought they had not been sufficiently rewarded for their services in the war with Servia; and in the hearts of these two malcontents the Russian military *attaché* found the seed-ground he was searching for. This *attaché*, Sacharoff by name, represented to these two officers that he had been commissioned by the Tsar to induce them to expel the Prince, offering them certain inducements to comply, and these representations were backed up by money supplied from the Russian Consulate. Afterwards a Russian ambassador, Nelidoff, was reported on good authority to have said that the removal of Prince Alexander had been very cheap, as it had only cost 300,000 francs!

Whether any of this cash went into the pockets of the Prince's own Ministers is not so clear; but it is certain, at least, that the question of deposing the Prince, in compliance with the known wishes of the Tsar, had occupied the attention of the Cabinet. It is a mournful thought, as Pastor Koch remarks, that not one of these Ministers had the courage to tell the Prince frankly how matters stood. The Prince himself had written to his sister shortly before:

'As things are at present, it is difficult to see how, led by Russia, the struggle to expel me will end. Ninety-nine per cent of the Bulgarians are for me; but whether the remaining one per cent will, thanks to foreign help, be successful, depends on events over which I have no control.... Before autumn my throne will resemble a mine charged with dynamite. Be that as it may, I will in any case fall fighting, and should the Bulgarians, after all, prefer foreign rule to an honest-minded Prince, that is their affair. I shall be spared the trouble of shedding a tear for them....There will be many bullets flying, perhaps even one from behind -

who knows?'

'Beware of the Struma regiment! It will surprise you to-night in bed, and put you to death' - such was the warning that reached Prince Alexander on August 20. But he heeded not the warning, holding it, as Richard did, to be 'a thing devised by the enemy,' and went to bed as usual. In a few more hours he was a half-clad prisoner in the hands of an insulting, half-drunken mob of Bulgarian officers and men, who had forced him to sign his abdication, and hurried him off like a condemned criminal to execution, or, at least, to exile. At the same time, Bogdanoff, the Russian Consul, harangued a crowd of kneeling peasants and gipsies from the balcony of his house, declaring 'that, the Tsar would willingly again vouchsafe his protection to Bulgaria, which he had always loved, and loved still, but only the true, old Bulgarian people, and he would certainly now send them a new and better Prince.'

It does not fall within my scope to detail all the revolting brutalities of this nineteenth century *Prinzenraub*, which recalled the days of Kunz von Kaufungen. The kidnappers had at first thought of murdering their victim, and once Prince Alexander shuddered on seeing his captors halt in a forest, through which they were hurrying him towards the Danube, and look about as if for some fitting place of execution. But their courage failed them to do this dastardly deed, and on again they hustled him towards the Danube, down the river, ever nearer to Russia as to the country where his person, his head, thought the barbarous conspirators, would most be valued. At last the party reached Reni, and the Prince learned that he would not be received there, 'as there were no instructions of any kind from St Petersburg.' The fact is, that by this time such a storm of moral indignation (the electric wires took care of that) had swept across Europe, blowing in even through the bars of the Tsar's own palace-prison, that his Majesty began to feel uneasy and irresolute. The Prince could not land at Reni, and therefore he had to remain on board his steamer.

'Next morning,' he said, 'a Lieut-Colonel of Police came and showed me a telegram from Obrutscheff (Chief of the General Staff), which stated that the authorities at Reni were to receive the *Prince of Battenberg*, and conduct him safely by the shortest route to the frontier; that the police authorities should be responsible for the safety of the Prince, as *his life was in danger in Russia*. At my request, the officer telegraphed to St Petersburg to know whether I should be allowed to travel via Galats, and cross over on to Roumanian soil. This would have been the shortest way; but the answer was that the Prince was only to travel by Volocsyska or Varschau. About ten o'clock I set foot on Russian soil....unfortunately I was not yet free; two mounted police stood before the house door, and three sentries were posted in the yard, at night a captain of the mounted police slept before my door, &c. &c. Our train left. In the adjoining compartment sat a Prefect of Police and three gendarmes. Wherever we stopped, two gendarmes invariably stood at the doors on either side.....At last I arrived at the Austrian frontier, and was greeted with enthusiasm.'

The public heart of Europe glowed with indignation at the unspeakable indignities and insults of which the Prince was made the object in his criminal-like passage through the south-west corner of the Tsar's dominions - indignities which could not have been worse had the Prince been put into a cage and underwrit: 'Here may you see a traitor!' Nowhere had this indignation blazed up more fiercely than in Bulgaria itself, of which the people hastened to show that they must not be identified with ninety of their treacherous officers, and nearly a fourth part of their army - that army which Prince Alexander had led to such glorious victory. At Lemberg, where the Prince entered Austrian territory, the heart of Europe had gone out to him in the frantic cheering with which he was received by the sympathetic multitudes of that city; and on hearing that his own subjects were begging, praying, clamouring for his return, he allowed himself to be persuaded, against his better judgment, to go back.

At all the stopping-places in Galicia, Bukowina, and Roumania, he was overwhelmed with ovations. At Bucharest he was greeted by the Prime Minister in the name of the King, for the Hohenzollerns are not men to be afraid of Romanoff frowns. The Roumanians had stormed the Gravitza redoubt at Plevna for the Russians, and now in turn their own hearts had been stormed by the sufferings of the Prince to which conquered Plevna was subject. The Danube was wrapped in fluttering flags and the smoke of saluting cannon, while its banks were lined with gazing, weeping, acclaiming crowds. On the landing-stage at **Rustchuk** stood the Bishop, the chief authorities, the consuls - even the Russian one - all in gala dress, to welcome back the Prince who had been so barbarously made the victim of Muscovite 'stouthrief and hamesucken.' Stambuloff, Bulgaria's 'strong man' that was to be greeted the returning **Prince** with burning words of loyalty, saying that the whole country from the Danube to the Black Sea was ringing with the cry: 'We must, we must, we must see our Prince once more!' The people,' he added, 'are with you; they love you, they are ready to die for you.' Then the officers standing by shouldered high the Prince, and bore up into his Palace, where he issued a proclamation, and penned the following telegram to the Tsar:

'Sire, - Having resumed the government of my country, I venture to express my thanks to your Majesty for the attitude of your representative at Rustchuk. He has shown the Bulgarian people, by his official presence at the reception accorded to me, that the Imperial Government cannot approve the revolutionary act directed against my person.

'At the same time, I must ask your Majesty's permission to express my sincere thanks for the despatch of General Dolgoruki to Bulgaria. In resuming legal power in my own hands, my first act is to express to your Majesty my firm intention of making all necessary sacrifices to further the generous intentions of your Majesty to deliver Bulgaria from the serious crisis through which she is at present passing. I beg your Majesty to authorise General Dolgoruki to communicate directly and as soon as possible with myself. I shall be happy to offer your Majesty a definite pledge of the unalterable devotion with which I am animated towards your august person. Monarchical principles compel me to re-establish law and order in Bulgaria and Roumelia. Russia having bestowed my crown upon me» it is into the hands of her Sovereign that I am ready to resign it.

'ALEXANDER.'

Meanwhile the Prince undertook a triumphal progress through the country, and at Philippopolis (where the revolution, which was the head and front of his offending, had broken out) he received the following answer from his Imperial cousin:

'I have received your Highness's telegram. I cannot approve your return to Bulgaria in view of the disastrous consequences which it may entail upon the country, already so severely tried. It will not be advisable to despatch Dolgoruki; I shall refrain from doing so during the unhappy condition to which Bulgaria is reduced as long as you remain there.

'Your Highness will understand what devolves upon you. I reserve judgment on the course that I am bidden to take by the honoured memory of my Father, the interest of Russia, and the tranquillity of the East.

'ALEXANDER.'

What added to the unbearable bitterness of this reply was that it had been made public, as the Prince found on returning to Sofia, before he himself had received it, and then his courage utterly collapsed. As the poor Prince was 'Hecuba' to Bismarck, so he was also meat and drink to the personal rancour of the Tsar. Down upon his very knees, figuratively speaking, went the Prince to his Imperial cousin on being prevailed upon to return to Bulgaria; but his astonishingly submissive telegram - his *pater peccavi*, so to speak - at once drew down upon him an answer which had the same effect upon him as the vicious blow of a steel gauntlet would upon the lips of a contrite suppliant And now this knocked the very heart out of the long-enduring Prince; for he threw down his crown and fled from the ungrateful land which his heroism had done so much to benefit.

By many the Prince's submissive telegram to the Tsar was deemed to be quite unworthy of his past. But it must be remembered that at this time his nervous constitution had been shattered by the worries and excitements through which he had just passed; that the presence of the Russian consul at

Rustchuk had betrayed him into the belief (as it was, perhaps, intended to do) that there was still a possibility of reconciliation ; and that he was willing to make almost any sacrifice of his *amour propre* in order to appease the offended Tsar.

Prince Alexander's Seven Years' War with the foes of Bulgaria over, he now began a conflict, which was to last just as long, with his own memories and his own heart. But the spirit of romance still clung to him in all he did. Disappointed - but was he disappointed? - will be asked by some who knew more of the secrets of the time than could be gathered from newspaper gossip - in his hopes of gaining the hand of one of the Emperor Frederick's daughters, the Prince went and married beneath him, burying himself from association with the bitter past. One of the consolations which shed their cheering influence on his blasted life was the hope that, as a General in the Austrian army, he might one day yet be in a position to cross swords with the unspeakable authors of all his woe. But this hope, too, was doomed to disappointment, and he died, the spirit of tragic romance still attending him, on the very anniversary of the glorious day which had been the culminating point of his strangely chequered and pathetic career.

The deep personal hatred which the Tsar had felt towards his Battenberg cousin in life did not abate even with the latter's death at Gratz (November 1893), where he held a Brigade command in the Austrian army. The widow of Count Hartenau, the name the Prince had adopted on marrying an actress, received telegrams of condolence from all the chief Sovereigns of Europe, including Queen Victoria and the Emperors of Austria and Germany, who likewise sent special representatives to the funeral. But in the midst of all these signs of sorrow and sympathy the Autocrat of All the Russias remained as cold and silent as the grave into which his heroic but unfortunate cousin was presently lowered - a victim to Imperial persecution and spite. For it cannot be doubted that the seeds of the illness to which Prince Alexander ultimately succumbed were sown at Sofia, where he had been worried to death – *'todt-geärgert,'* the Germans call it - by the intrigues and attacks of his Russian foes.

One thing more. The union of the two Bulgarias had caused the Tsar to turn away the light of his countenance, completely and for ever, from his princely cousin, whom he accused of having deliberately deceived him, of having, in fact, told him a wilful lie. If he did so, it was a grievous fault, and grievously did Alexander answer for it. But if there was deceitfulness on one side, was there not also gross and scandalous breach of promise on the other? For did Prince Alexander not declare to his people that he had only resolved to resign his crown after receiving assurances from the Government of the Emperor of Russia that the independence and privileges of our State would remain uninfringed, and that no one would intermeddle in the internal affairs of the country? Whether the Tsar was true to this solemn promise, on the strength of which his cousin resigned his crown, is a question which the subsequent history of Bulgaria can only answer with a trumpet-tongued, a thunder-loud 'No!' And for the rest, the simple chronicle of the facts recorded in this chapter must carry with it its own commentary on the character of Alexander III, as revealed in his relations to his Battenberg cousin.

NOTES

1. Prince Alexander of Battenberg: Reminiscences of his Reign in Bulgaria, from Authentic Sources.' By A. Koch, Court-Chaplain to his Royal Highness. (London: Whittaker, 1887.)
2. Shakespeare, *The life and death of King John*, Act IV, Scene II.

CHAPTER VII

THE TSAR PANSLAVIST

The 'Father of Lies' - Shuffling of the pack - Domestic policy – Ignatieff's circular - The Tsar bad at figures - His sovereign responsibility - 'One King, one Faith, one Law' - 'Russia for the Russians' - Character of Finland and the Finns - The hall-mark of Muscovy - 'Violation of Finnish rights' - The Baltic Provinces - 'A bear's skin on the Teutonic bird - German 'a foreign language' - Vladimir at Dorpat - Anti-German edicts - Panslavism in Poland - High-handed measures - The Tsar 'the best cosmopolite' - Ignorance the pillar of Autocracy - The Tsar as Press Censor - His second sceptre a blacking-brush - The demoralisation of Russia - Famine, fetters and finance - *C'est à prendre, ou à laisser!* - 'The Russian army' - Duelling decree - Another ukase

WE saw that, on his coming to the throne, Alexander III's first act was to withhold from his subjects the quasi-constitution which his father, on the advice of his Minister of the Interior, Count **Loris-Melikoff**, had at last resolved to confer upon his subjects. Enraged and disgusted at the spirit of reaction which animated the new Tsar, **Loris-Melikoff** at once left Russia, and never returned. His place was taken by General Ignatieff, who had become known as the 'Father of Lies.' 'Don't go to St Petersburg,' he said to me at Moscow during the coronation time, 'for there they will tell you nothing but lies!' - a piece of advice which made me think of Tourgenieff's remark in his 'Virgin Soil.' 'It is a well-known, if not quite intelligible fact,' says that writer, who ought to know, 'that Russians lie more than any nation in the world. But, on the other hand, there is nothing they esteem so much as truth, nothing for which they have so much sympathy.'

Well, the 'Father of Lies' now became Minister of the Interior (though he only remained so for about a year). But, *per contra*, some of the principal sires of sin were hunted from their posts. Chief among these were the new Tsar's uncles, Grand-Dukes Nicholas and Constantine. The former had completely done for himself in the eyes of his nephew by his peculations while acting as Commander-in-Chief of the Balkan armies during the Turkish war, and now he hastened to resign all his offices and go abroad 'for the good of his health,' which had suddenly lapsed into a very serious state. His brother Constantine, who stood at the head of the Navy, was similarly relieved of his command

and replaced by the Grand Duke Alexis, second brother of the Tsar; while Constantine junior had actually been under arrest on suspicion of being mixed up in the Nihilist plot which ended in the murder of the Tsar Emancipator. Otherwise, the Ministerial pack was shuffled by the new Emperor in a manner which thrilled with joy the hearts of M. Katkoff, the powerful Moscow editor, and other 'Old Russians' who began to prostrate themselves before the rising sun of Panslavism, long prayed for but come at last.[1]

They looked to St Petersburg for a sign, and this was presently forthcoming in the shape of the circular which Ignatieff, on taking office, hastened to address to all the provincial governors, explaining the principles set forth in the Imperial manifesto, and announcing the views of the Government on the internal condition of the country. It referred to the dark sides of the present state of society, such as the irreligious education of youth, the inactivity of the authorities, the indifference of the holders of many public offices to the general welfare, and their avaricious management of the property of the State; and then proceeded:

'Herein is to be found the explanation of the painful fact that the various reforms introduced by the last Government did not yield the full benefit which the deceased Emperor had a right to expect. None but an autocrat, strong in the attachment and unbounded love of a great people, even with the enlightened co-operation of the best sons of the Fatherland, can successfully remove the great evils from which Russia is suffering.

'The first task to be accomplished is the extirpation of the spirit of rebellion, which society must counteract of its own initiative. The persecution of the Jews in Southern Russia shows how people, otherwise devoted to the Throne, yield to the influence of evil-disposed persons, and unsuspectingly serve their rebellious plans.

'The second task is to strengthen faith and morals. The Government will take especial care to introduce order and justice into the institutions created by the late Emperor. If there be cordial co-operation between society and the Government, the present difficulties will soon disappear.

'The nobility, who always listen to the voice of truth and honour, will indubitably contribute to that result. They and all other classes must have the certainty that all their rights will remain untouched.

'The peasantry may be sure that the Government will not only maintain all the rights accorded them, but also take care to relieve the people as much as possible of the burdens of taxation and improve their material condition.

'At the same time the Government will, without delay, take measures to establish a system for securing the participation of the local authorities in the execution of the Emperor's plans.'

Those were the words of Count Ignatieff, but they were the thoughts of the Tsar, who was really his own Minister in most things, except, perhaps, finance, the mysteries and methods of which he never could fully comprehend. Once, soon after his accession, it was reported to him that the paper-rouble was going down in value. 'What is that to me?' he replied, 'I am not gambling on the Stock Exchange.' After the retirement of Count Loris-Melikoff, the Minister of Finance, M. Bunge, also expressed a wish to resign. 'You forget,' said the Tsar, 'that in an unlimited monarchy Ministers are appointed and dismissed; they do not resign whenever it pleases them.' The Council of Ministers might consult on any measure they pleased; but the only way of carrying it was to submit it personally to the Emperor, who never attended a Council, but received his Ministers separately. In other words, the Russian Ministers were little more than Under-Secretaries, the real Minister being the Autocrat; so that he thus assumed direct responsibility for every act of policy devised for the good of his subjects.

It is well to remember this, because it is frequently urged by the apologists of despotism that the absolute ruler of a hundred millions of his fellow-men cannot reasonably be made accountable for all the wrongs that are perpetrated in his name. But this is logic of a most incoherent and unsatisfactory kind. For there is no reason why, if wrongs are committed, the truth about them should not at least reach the ears of the ruler, to the end that they may be punished and redressed; and if a ruler does not make sure of this, by one means or other, he must be prepared to hear that the principles of human justice make no difference in a case of this kind between the sins of omission and of commission, and that ignorance is no excuse. If an absolute ruler claims credit for all the right that is done within his dominions, he must also accept responsibility for all the unremedied wrong. What? Would the Autocrat of All the Russias belie the belief about himself that is so firmly rooted in the hearts of his own Moujiks? For what says even 'Stepniak' on this subject? 'The people repose implicit confidence in the Tsar's wisdom and justice. He is absolute master of the life and property of every man within his dominions, and no exception may be taken to his orders. The occasional blunders made by the Tsar, however heavy they may be, must be borne with patience, as they can only be temporary; the Tsar will redress the evil as soon as he is better informed on the matter.'

The Tsar's circular to the provincial governors, through the pen of Count Ignatieff, touching the condition of his subjects, was not altogether free from ambiguity. What did it really mean? In what direction would the Emperor's domestic policy move? It was known that he was by far the most ardent champion in all Russia of the three Slavophil principles of Autocracy, Eastern Orthodoxy, and Nationality – 'one king, one faith, one law' - and it soon became apparent that he had set his heart on carrying all these principles into practice in the most energetic and uncompromising form.

He had three alternatives before him: either to maintain the *status quo*; or to move in the same direction as Austria – *i.e.*, towards decentralisation; or, finally, to endeavour to nationalise the Empire at the expense of the subject races and in favour of the most important - the 'Great Russians.' He chose the third of these, and his watchword became 'Russia for the Russians.' Whoever stood in the way of the fulfilment of this design, whether Jew, German, or Swedish Finlander, must go to the wall. To carry out this policy, however, time was required, for, should war break out, and an enemy gain foot on Russian soil, a revolution might possibly ensue, and this would not only endanger the process of union, but might even imperil the cohesion of the State. It was therefore essential to the new Tsar's policy that there should be peace, so as to afford leisure for the innovations which he contemplated at home; and if Alexander III gained so much credit for keeping the peace of Russia abroad, it was only at the cost of the civil strife into which he now prepared to plunge a large portion of his own people.

Lack of space debars me from describing in detail the carrying out of this Panslavist policy - this deliberate attempt to root out of the Empire proper every non-Russian element, and at the same time reduce the homogeneous nation thus produced to a more absolute state of subjection to the will of one man than it had almost ever known before. I can only quote several typical instances of the way in which these principles of Alexander III were applied in the purely political domain, reserving for a separate chapter the subject of his more atrocious persecutions in the overlapping fields of race and religion.

Let us begin with the Finns, formerly the subjects of Sweden, who finally became annexed to Russia in 1809. Alexander I solemnly swore for himself, *and his successors*, to preserve intact and respect the ancient constitution of the country, which included a very large measure of autonomy, a free Press, and other privileges. Alexander II, on the whole, respected all these liberties, the consequence being that he had no more devoted subjects throughout his vast domains than the Finns. They were his best subjects, and his best soldiers. What the Scottish men-at-arms were to Louis XI, the Finnish fighting men were to Alexander II. It was a guard of the Finland regiment which stood between his Majesty and death on the occasion of the Nihilist explosion at the Winter Palace. While St Petersburg and the other big towns were swarming with conspirators, Finland remained perfectly quiet and loyal. Amongst the many thousands who joined the revolutionary movement, there was no Finn save those who had been educated in Russia and thoroughly Russianised. 'When,' says 'Stepniak,' 'the revolutionary propaganda in the army was initiated, it was enough for those conducting it to hear that a certain officer was a born Finn to give up as hopeless the task of converting him to their principles.'[2]

Now, one would have thought that the loyalty of such a people was a thing worth cultivating by Alexander III. But his Majesty himself did not appear to be altogether of this mind. For he had not long been seated on the throne before he began to tamper with and curtail the ancient and chartered privileges of his Finnish people. The flower of their loyalty, he thought, would emit a more charming scent, and exhibit a brighter bloom, if sprinkled daily with the watering-pan of Russian autocracy. It was nothing to him that his predecessors on the throne had sworn to respect the autonomous freedom of the Finns, which had gradually converted them into one of the most prosperous, well-educated, and contented nationalities in all Europe. All these qualities did not bear the national hall-mark of ancient Muscovy, and that was quite enough for the new Tsar.

He loved the Finns and was sorry for them, but they must come into the general fold all the same. The contrast between them and the dark Empire of which they formed so bright a fringe was too great, too dangerous, and they must assume the hue of the general eclipse. For one thing, their free Press must take its orders from the censor at St. Petersburg, and dance to the tune of his dictatorial caprice. Their Post Office must resign itself to violation of the secrecy of private correspondence. Russian must be used as the medium of teaching in the Finnish colleges, and other galling innovations accepted.

'The Finnish Penal Code,' wrote an acute observer,[3] 'drawn up at the Tsar's own desire, and deliberately sanctioned by him, was suddenly revoked, in consequence of a denunciation published in the *Moskovskia Vedomosti*, and a new Code slowly elaborated, in which Finland's absolute dependence on the arbitrary will of the Tsar was affirmed with a frequency and emphasis which bordered on cynicism, and could serve no truly statesmanlike purpose. The Finnish postal system, far superior to the Russian, was completely remodelled; Finnish stamps were abolished; a new Russian archiepiscopal See was founded in Helsingfors; many of the privileges of the Parliament, including that of legislative initiative, were rescinded, although they had been solemnly sanctioned by the Tsar himself in special ukases shortly after his accession; liberty of the Press in the Principality was curtailed; autonomy in matters pertaining to the Customs duties was abolished, and the Finnish nation were treated as rebels on the morrow of an unsuccessful rising.

'The part which Alexander III personally took in this reconquest of Finland is extremely characteristic of the vast difference between the ruler and the man, and illustrative of the impossibility of deducing from the personal character of the latter the motives or, probably, the actions of the former. Alexander III loved the Finns; he passed some of the most pleasant weeks of the summer every year cruising in Finnish waters, listening to the songs of Finnish musical societies. He was really and truly almost as much attached to the people as to his own. And yet he himself gave the first impulse to the movement which, had he been spared a few years longer, would have submerged the last relics of Finnish autonomy. And this he did in obedience to what he honestly believed to be his sacred duty as Tsar, and in spite of the opposite tendency of his own personal leanings.'

In view of all this, was it astonishing that the most loyal of his subjects should have gradually come to harden their hearts against him? At first, the Finns tried to win over Alexander III by their devoted attentions during his annual trips to their beautiful country. 'Now,' says 'Stepniak,' 'we hear of a very different state of things, all the people running away wherever he appeared. No bouquets, no loyal speeches, nothing but cold isolation.' While behaving thus to the Finns, whom he loved, it was scarcely to be expected that Alexander III should have shown much consideration towards the Teutons, whom he positively loathed.

Of these Teutons he had a very large number in his Baltic Provinces - Esthonia, Livonia, and Courland - a race which had supplied his Empire with its very best soldiers and administrators, its Richters, its Adlerbergs, and its Todlebens. The Baltic Provinces, so to speak, had hitherto been the goose which laid most of Russia's golden eggs; and if Alexander III did not altogether aim at killing this goose, he at least cast about to supplant the native feathers of the productive bird with the shaggy hide of a bear. If Germany cast covetous eyes on the Baltic Provinces, the Tsar would at least deprive Germany of one of the motives for her territorial cupidity by stripping them of their Teutonic character. At the same time if these provinces underwent a radical process of Russification, they would surely have all the less craving for assimilation to the old Teutonic Fatherland.

Accordingly the Panslavist mill was set going, and very soon astonishing results had to be recorded in spite of the vehement protests of the German inhabitants of the provinces in question. Their *'nolumus episcopari'* was addressed to deaf ears. The Tsar simply refused to receive from the nobility of Courland a humble petition against all this abolition of their traditional privileges, with the remark that 'the historic rights of the province must yield to the necessities of the Russian State.' In the following year the Russifying process had made such ravages on the ancient rights and customs of the inhabitants that something very like an openly rebellious spirit began to manifest itself amongst them. And then the Tsar commanded all the heads of authorities, the Lutheran clergy, the professors, and the nobility to assemble at Dorpat, where they would hear what he had to say to them.

This message was conveyed by his brother, the Grand Duke Vladimir, who was sent specially into the provinces to proclaim the Imperial will - which was to the effect that there must still be a closer connection between Russia Proper and her Baltic Marches, if for no other reason than the good of these Marches themselves, which formed the object of most affectionate solicitude with the Ruler of All the Russias. It was decreed that German was henceforth to be treated as a 'foreign language,' and Russian was to replace it. 'German was at first restricted, then abolished in all educational establishments; the schools were limited in number, and Russian was made obligatory in all; the University was utterly metamorphosed, and the centre of

Baltic culture and learning changed its historic name from Dorpat to Yosrievo. Here, as in his struggle with Liberalism and Sectarianism, the Tsar was eminently successful, and the Baltic provinces soon differed nowise from the Governments of Kazan or Ufa.'

To complete this policy of Russification it was necessary to prevent the incoming of fresh Teutonic elements to supply the place of those which had been assimilated by the Panslavists; and how could this be better done than by making it next to impossible for foreigners to settle in Russia? Accordingly a ukase was issued prohibiting all foreigners from inheriting, acquiring, or in any other way possessing real property in the Western provinces of the Empire outside the ports and cities. The measure, of course, was chiefly aimed at the Germans, whose success as merchants and and manufacturers in Poland and elsewhere had excited the jealousy and hatred of the Russians. In consequence of this decree many German factories were closed, and the persons employed in them returned to Germany, as the only means of acquiring a right to possess property in Russia was to accept Russian nationality.

These violent anti-German edicts naturally made a very bad impression at Berlin. But Bismarck was all the less able to address remonstrances on the subject to St Petersburg, as the Tsar, in reality, had only been taking a leaf out of his own book in respect to Prussian Poland, which the Iron Chancellor was also Germanising in the most thoroughgoing and masterful manner; and what was sauce for the goose was also sauce for the gander. The Government at Berlin had expelled all Russian Poles from Prussian Poland, and also voted an immense sum of money to buy up Polish estates and parcel them out among German peasant-farmers. But while there was no injustice in one case, there was little but injustice in the other.

Thus the nationalising mill was kept grinding vigorously on both sides of the frontier, though it certainly made the loudest clatter on the Russian side; and Poland, in turn, had to go through the same Panslavising process as Finland and the Baltic Provinces. In 1863, when the Polish insurrection was at its height, General Mouravieff, known as the 'icy-hearted Muscovite' and the 'hangman,' had issued a decree forbidding the transfer of landed property, whether by purchase, mortgage or lease, to any person of Polish extraction. After the suppression of the rebellion this decree practically fell into desuetude, though it was never cancelled, and numerous estates which had changed hands were in the possession of Poles. Alexander III not only revived this decree, but declared all transfers of property made to Poles since it was first issued to be null and void, thereby reducing many families to beggary. The ukase was applied to an area as large almost as that of England. At the same time, also, the Polish language was replaced by Russian for all official purposes, and the Panslavists at last began to chant their paeans of victory. Verily, the European Empire of Alexander III seemed to have been completely Russified. Muscovy had, to all 'appearance, been made one. But the bond of union between the various races which had thus been dragged and dragooned into the national fold was a common feeling of unspeakable hatred towards the unscrupulous Government of the Tsar Panslavist.

The Panslavist policy of which I have thus roughly and rapidly sketched the outstanding features may otherwise be generally characterised in the words of a writer well qualified to speak on such a subject:[4]

'Naturally a man of conservative instincts, and driven partly by circumstances, partly by irresponsibility into illiberal and reactionary extremes, Alexander III has for some time devoted himself to stamping out of Russia all non-Russian elements and setting up an image, before which all must fall down and worship, of a Russia, single, homogeneous, exclusive, self-sufficing, self-contained. Foreign names, foreign tongues, a foreign faith, particularly if the former are Teuton and the other is Lutheran, are vexed, or prohibited, or assailed. Foreign competition in any quarter, commercial or otherwise, is crushed by heavy deadweights hung round its neck. Foreign concessions are as flatly refused as they were once eagerly conceded.

'The Government even declined to allow any but Russian money to be invested in Russian undertakings. Foreign managers and foreign workmen are under a bureaucratic ban. German details are expunged from the national uniform; the German language is forbidden in the schools of the Baltic provinces ; German fashions are proscribed at Court. The stranger that is within thy gates 'is the bugbear and the bête noire of Muscovite statesmanship. There is no cosmopolitanism in the governing system of the Tsar. What Russians call patriotism, what foreigners call rank selfishness is the keynote of the régime. Russia for the Russians' has been adopted as the motto, not of a radical faction, but of an irresponsible autocracy, and is preached, not by wild demagogues, but by an all-powerful despot.'

When Tennyson met the Tsar at Copenhagen, and was urged by his Majesty to recite to him one of his own poems, he should have selected the one which lays it down that -

> 'That man's the best cosmopolite
> Who loves his native country best.'

Otherwise, as to the domestic policy of Alexander III, I can only refer to its salient features and results. The general object of this policy was to strengthen his autocratic power; and as the main pillar of despotism is ever ignorance, so it seemed to be one of the chief objects of the Tsar Panslavist to withhold from his subjects all illumination of their minds. 'Education,' wrote an authority from whom I have already quoted, 'was restricted to a degree that decimated the universities, reduced the number of schools, sent thousands of young Russians abroad, and left tens of thousands in a pitiable state of ignorance and superstition. Higher education in particular was declared to be the exclusive birthright of the higher class; peasants, hucksters, burghers were debarred from entering the universities or the gymnasia; and even the lower orders were gradually compelled to content themselves with the scant instruction promised, but not always given, by the 'parish schools,' which laid greater stress upon psalm-singing than upon reading, writing, and arithmetic.'

But an object of even greater hatred than the 'parish school' with Alexander III was the Press, which he gagged and persecuted with a bitterness which recalled the time of his grandfather Nicholas. One of the most important officials of his Empire was the Press Censor, who had power to extinguish an obnoxious organ of popular enlightenment as completely as if it were a penny candle. When a ship is out at sea, thought Alexander III with his grandfather, does it behove the passengers to advise the captain or criticise the action of the crew? Certainly not; and the Tsar Panslavist deemed to be no less ridiculous than dangerous the tendering of journalistic advice from subject to Sovereign. In the time of Nicholas, as a poet sang, 'there was silence in all languages from the Ural to the Pruth,' and any little sound which might have succeeded to this awful silence in the reign of his grandson was mostly of a hollow and meaningless kind. The nation was virtually dumb, for it had no sort of parliamentary representation, and no Press worth the name.

After the sceptre of Alexander III, the most characteristic symbol of his despotic power was the blacking-brush with which he daubed out in the most vigilant and assiduous manner every article in a foreign journal that might convey a new idea to, or kindle a gleam of intelligence in, the minds of his subjects. This bondage of the Russian Press was one of the main obstacles to the practical carrying out of reforms and the utility of the *zemstvos* (local assemblies) and municipal councils constituting the new self-government, as it was also one of the reasons why government officials, and even the Tsar himself, were often so ill-informed about what was going on in the interior of the Empire. His Majesty had one unfailing means of knowing what was really happening within his dominions, and that was the unmuzzling of the Press; but he chose to keep it gagged, and thus deprived himself of one of the best possible checks on his subordinates. He had apparently not the intelligence to perceive that, in thus muzzling the Press, he was only multiplying the secret societies, and that all that he took from it only went to enrich the underground propaganda which made his life a constant terror and a gilded misery. Surely, if he had been the brave man which some of his eulogists made him out to be, he would at least have repeated the prayer of the Homeric hero who, having to fight the gods, asked but one favour of them - not to remain invisible. When a man has to fight, not with gods, but with devils, as in the case of Alexander III, surely the necessity for such a prayer becomes more urgent than ever.

And what were the consequences of all this obscurantist and enslaving policy? Let us take the testimony of a man, or 'compound man,' who has lived long enough in Russia to command serious attention, at least, if not implicit belief:[5]

'The Government, which is obviously acting with the utmost deliberation, is resolved to reduce the people to a condition of abject unreasoning slavishness, which will permit them to be dealt with like cattle. If the nation were as ready to dispose of its soul, or the remnant of its soul, at the beck of its hundred thousand Tsarlets, the ideal of the Russian Government might be considered realised. But between them and this goal stand a few millions of strong-minded, God-fearing men, known as Raskolniks, on whose victory or defeat depends the future of the Russian Empire. The complete success of this selfish policy is writ large in all departments of public life....The governors of the provinces and other lieutenants of the Tsar are fully abreast of the times, and seem to take a keen pleasure in showing by their life and example what a vast amount of licence is compatible with loyalty....Officials of higher and of the highest political rank are distinguished by the same moral atmosphere which they carry about with them from the schoolroom to their graves. They acknowledge no law but their own caprices and emotions.

'No epoch or country has ever yet offered such a disgraceful spectacle of systematic demoralisation. Shocking instances of the deliberate drowning of intellect and conscience in brutish debauch and intoxication for political purposes have been known to occur on a small scale: the killing of the soul, lest the body should continue inconveniently active. It was in former times part and parcel of the policy of powerful governments and unscrupulous regents. Catherine de Medici was the most celebrated of its patrons, and Louis XVII the most illustrious of its victims. But Russia is the only country in which it has been tried on a vast scale with a *corpus vile* of over one hundred million human beings.'

Here is another touch from the same graphic hand as to the result of the terrible famine which devastated a great part of Russia (a tract of land about 3000 miles long, and from 500 to 1000 miles broad) during the years 1890-91, and proved one of the most galling thorns in the crown of the Emperor, though it must be owned that he and other members of his family made great personal sacrifices to relieve the unspeakable distress of his hunger-stricken subjects:[6]

'Most of these wandering advertisements of squalor are suffering from dysentery, scurvy, and other diseases. Their eyelids are swollen to monstrous dimensions; their faces pinched and withered, and their whole persons shrivelled from the likeness of aught human into horrible ghosts and shadows. Sometimes one meets them stalking silently through deserted villages consisting of the tenantless ruins of burned houses; at other times they drift into hamlets where, instead of almsgivers, they meet their own lean images, still ghastlier shadows of themselves, and then they slink away to a hiding-place which is often their last earthly lodging.'

But as if all this were not enough to knock the hearts out of any poor people and make them submissive enough to their rulers, listen further:

'The Russian authorities are even now carefully considering the advisability of keeping down the pride of the peasants by treating them as an inferior class, and addressing them officially as *thou* and *thee* instead of the more respectful *you*; and another measure is likewise under consideration, compelling all peasants to uncover their heads in the presence of *tshinovniks*, nobles and priests, on the roadside as well as within doors, and condemning those who refuse to comply to be soundly flogged.'

A propos of the famine which drove about twenty millions of the Tsar Panslavist's peasant subjects to the doors of death, let me quote an incident which may be accepted as very characteristic of the way in which things are done under a despotism like that of Russia. M. Doumovo, who succeeded Count Dmitri Tolstoi as Minister of the Interior, summoned to St. Petersburg the Governors of all the famine-stricken provinces to act as a kind of representative assembly in the discussion of the means of relief. The Governors came, each with his memorandum. As a matter of course, they saw the Minister before their reports were shown to the Tsar. The memoranda were examined, and found too gloomy to be presented to his Majesty. They were modified to suit the Minister's taste, and the famine was represented as being almost over at the very time when it was entering upon its severest phase.

To what extent the ways of despotism were responsible for this awful famine may be an open question. But there can, at least, be no doubt that these ways must be held accountable for the prison-system, of which a graphic description inflamed Mr Swinburne to such a pitch of poetical anathema against the Third Alexander. Under his reign his subjects may be said to have suffered from three main sources of comprehensive evil - famine, fetters, and finance. It is true that Alexander III abolished the obnoxious poll-tax on the peasantry, which they had borne so impatiently since the time of Peter the Great. But what he took from one shoulder he shifted on to the other. Figures, I am aware, have been adduced to show that Russian finance has been showing signs of steady progress in recent years. But such figures are taken from Russian budgets, which are subject to no kind of control, and might be the work of a financial *prestidigitateur* for all that the outside world can tell. Of a Russian budget its framers can only say to Europe, as Bismarck once said to M. Thiers about the Evacuation Treaty, '*C'est à prendre, ou à laisser!*'

Whatever the doctored showing of Russian budgets, it will scarcely be denied that from the year of his accession the Imperial revenue went on increasing at an incredible rate, 'utterly disproportioned to the paying powers of the poverty-stricken population....The peasants are still continually flogged to make them pay up their exorbitant taxes; their live stock, furniture, fowls, and huts are sold by auction, and thousands are yearly turned adrift to beg or steal. This is the Achilles' heel of the system of government inaugurated by an honest, veracious, patriotic, and humane ruler, who certainly never realised the sacrifices he was making of all that was nearest and dearest to his heart, in order to train an army and build a navy.'[7]

On this subject I cannot refrain from quoting the following testimony:[8]

'Alexander III is reported to have said to General Vannoffsky, when appointing him to the post of War Minister: 'War is perhaps a necessary evil, and it certainly is a terrible one. But when it ends, as ours has done, in a Treaty of Berlin, it is a national calamity. I trust I shall never have to go to war in my life, but, if I do, I mean to enjoy the fruits of our triumphs. And I want you to assist me.' General Vannoffsky has assisted him, with results of which Western statesmen would seem to have not the faintest notion. The Russian army was always celebrated for its raw material - soldiers who combined the enterprise of adventurers and the enthusiasm of martyrs with the endurance of cast-iron automata. The next war, whenever it breaks out, will obtain for it the reputation of one of the best-trained and best-disciplined armies in Europe, or the world, alter the Germans. Western peoples hear periodically of the annual Russian manoeuvres. They never read anything of the countless exercises, sham fights, marches of 1000 miles, and other movements in which the troops are engaged from year's end to year's end. They know nothing about the severe examinations which a Russian has now to pass before he can receive an officer's epaulettes.

'When Alexander III came to the throne there was in existence a lithographed tariff of the prices of each examination, one of which I possessed. Only one professor at the Academy accepted no bribes, and his subject was of secondary importance. Today, knowledge is the sole passport to the officers' mess; and industry and patience in everyday work the only road to promotion. The Tsar's own brother Vladimir, his cousins, and other relations live exactly the same laborious lives in the Guards as their brother officers. A system of fortresses has been constructed on the west and south-west of Russia which will play an important, possibly a decisive, part in the coming war. Universal conscription, which was introduced by his father in March 1874, has been developed and perfected by Alexander III; old and untrustworthy officers have been gently dropped from the service; merit has been promoted over the head of influence and aristocracy; and the Russian army of 1894, which is by far the largest in numbers of any in Europe, is as superior to the Russian army of 1879 as the latter was to that which was defeated by the allies in the Crimean War. The same thing holds good of the navy, which has ever been the Tsar's own particular hobby.'

It may be added that, a few months before his death, Alexander III formally re-established duelling in his army, which was only in keeping with the rest of his domestic policy. But about the same time he also issued another ukase, according to which all official appointments were thenceforth to be controlled by a special committee in the name of the Tsar himself. By some, this new departure was interpreted to mean that the Emperor had at last resolved to put a stop to the personal wrongs and scandals arising from the corruption of his subordinates; while others could only discern in the new decree a deep distrust of his Majesty's own ministers and provincial governors in the carrying out of his autocratic, Orthodox, and Panslavist policy.

But it is now high time for me to show how this policy was carried out in another field, in which religious persecution was joined to Panslavistic rage.

NOTES

1. The Ministry of War was given to General Vannovsky, Foreign Affairs to M. Giers, and Finance to M Bunge, who gave place to M. Vishnigradsky. Count Woronzoff-Dashkoff was appointed General Aide-de-Camp, while M. Pobedonostseff retained the chair of Procurator of the Holy Synod. In the Palace itself a clean sweep was made of three-fourths of the Aides-de-Camp, Adjutants, and other decorative personages, and strict orders were given to put an end to the reckless expenditure which had marked the closing years of Alexander II's life.
2. Article on Finland in *Free Russia* for September, 1890.
3. St Petersburg Correspondent of the *Daily Telegraph*.
4. The Hon Mr George Curzon in his work on 'Russia in Central Asia.'
5. 'The Demoralisation of Russia, by Mr. E.B. 'Lanin,' in *Fortnightly Review* for October, 1891.
6. *Fortnightly Review* for November, 1891.
7. But the reign of Alexander III was not without its redeeming qualities in the field of national finance. Beginning with the Crown lands and appendages, the Emperor made sweeping changes, and deprived himself of eighteen million roubles of his own Civil List This sum he allotted to the relief of the most distressed villages in the neighbourhood of his lands. In 1888, as the revenues of the Domains continued to increase rapidly under improved management, he made over a third of them to colonists brought in from provinces where the population was growing to excess. In this manner over three million acres were parcelled out. In 1883 his Majesty founded the so-called Peasants' Banks, which advanced money to enable the agricultural poor to pay off the debt incurred towards their former lords at the time of the abolition of serfdom. The peasantry thus became debtors to these State banks instead of to the nobility, and in Russia the State is a very easy-going creditor, wiping off nearly millions of arrears, which it knows it will never encash. The Peasants' Banks were followed by the Nobility Banks, which were founded to save the old landed nobility from the clutches of

the usurers.
8. St Petersburg correspondent of the *Daily Telegraph*, November 2, 1894.

CHAPTER VIII

THE TSAR PERSECUTOR

A new King over Egypt – M. Pobedonostseff - Are the Jews Revolutionists? - Anti-Semitic riots - Ignatieff's circular - The Tsar Jew-baiter - Race or religion? - The Russian Ghetto - The 'May Laws' - Prince Metchersky on microbes - Mr Gladstone and the conscience of England - Guildhall meeting and Memorial - Returned by the Tsar unopened - The Russian Herod - The Tsar Persecutor - Polish Catholics - Baltic Province Lutherans - Barclay de Tolly - The Stundists - History and progress of the sect - Their principles and character - An archiepiscopal anathema - Anti-Stundist alliance between Church and State - 'Gentle pressure' - A modern Torquemada - Mr Swinburne's counter-anathema

'NOW there arose a king over Egypt who knew not Joseph; and he said to his people, Behold, the people of the children of Israel are too many and too mighty for us; come, let us deal wisely with them, lest they multiply, and it come to pass that, when there falleth out any war, they also join themselves unto our enemy.' That was also what Alexander III, who *knew his people*, really said to them on coming to the throne. Of the descendants of Joseph, whom the new King of Egypt knew not, the new Tsar had about five millions within his Empire, and in his Majesty's opinion that was far too many Hebrew subjects by a long way. The politico-theological trinity of the Tsar's worship, as we have already seen, was autocracy, orthodoxy, national homogeneity - one man rule, one religion, one race. His ideal of Empire was to rule over a people one, Russianised, compact - of the same religion, and also, if possible, of the same race - like the man who, having suddenly inherited a large library, and desiring to establish uniformity in the appearance of his bookshelves, sent for the village carpenter to saw off the ends of all such volumes as marred the general symmetry of the rows.

Of these rows in the ethnological collection of Alexander III, the Semitic sections, he thought, were much the most ragged and irregular, and to the sawing-off process the new Tsar and his Ministers now strenuously addressed themselves. Or rather, he sent for his village carpenter in the person of M. Pobedonostseff, Procurator of the Holy Synod, and keeper of the Imperial conscience - a man who had obtained over his quondam pupil, Alexander III, an ascendancy similar to that exercised by Torquemada over Ferdinand and

Isabella, or by Père La Chaise over Louis XIV. And what sort of a man, then, was this Muscovite Torquemada? Let me again cite the testimony of the eloquent and omniscient Mr. 'Lanin,' who had every opportunity of judging:[1]

'In person, M. Pobedonostseff can hardly be called imposing or prepossessing; and one's first feeling is disappointment that the omnipotent statesman, whose name is whispered with mysterious awe, should be as plain, prosaic, and uninteresting as Dominic Sampson. Thin, dry, somewhat pinched features, cast in the Byzantine mould; cold, sharp eyes rendered colder still by the spectacles that shield them, and whose glance is as frigid 'as the cheerless ray of the winter's sun; a jerky, emphatic mode of delivery, and a fidgety demeanour betoken the political algebraist, the lay ascetic whose sharp points and angles have not yet been rounded off by contact with the every-day world.

'His vision is clear, because circumscribed within the limits of one idea where everything is plain, flat, and sterile as the steppe. Hence we seek in vain for breadth of sympathy, to say nothing of that volcanic energy of passion without which there is no genuine greatness - nay, no fulness of human nature. His sole possession in life is a doctrine which, whatever else it may effect, is powerless to neutralise the touch of icy coldness that runs through all he says and does. It is only fair to remember, however, that it is a doctrine which twice, in his hands, has saved the mightiest empire of modern times from the change which some call 'ruin.''

Such was the man who began to act as the village carpenter to the Tsar in the work of sawing his ethnological and theological collections into a semblance of rectilinear form. There were some of the Gentile races in the Empire who required the application of this docking process quite as much as the Jews; but the Jews were the first to be seriously taken in hand, as being of more ancient race and faith than any of their fellow-subjects - *senoires, priores*.

Alexander III had not been many weeks upon the throne before anti-Semitic riots of the most serious kind broke out in various parts of his dominions. What had been the proximate cause of these outbreaks? Was it fury with the Jews, on account of their supposed connection with the crime which had just deprived the people of their Tsar Emancipator? Mr Harold Frederic, who spent a few weeks in Russia, maintains that 'the Jew does not lend himself to the notion of conspiracy - and that in every country he has been the patient, long-suffering, even servile non-resistant, never the rebel.'[2] On the other hand, M. Leroy-Beaulieu, who passed many years of his life in the Empire of the Tsars, and knows it better than almost any foreigner, takes quite the contrary view, and asserts that a very large proportion of those concerned in the Nihilist movement were men and women of Hebrew race.[3]

Be that as it may, it is at least certain that the Jews were believed, both by Alexander III and the bulk of his subjects, to have been largely concerned in the conspiracy which resulted in the murder of his father; and it was to a great extent this conviction (well or ill founded) that acted as a spark to the combustible piles of popular feeling against the Jews which were already lying heaped up, so to speak, all over the Empire. Within six weeks of the crime of March 13, says Mr Frederic, 'the Jewish quarter of Elisabethgrad was sacked and burned, and the reign of terror inaugurated which was to destroy thousands of homes, reduce 100,000 Jews to poverty, and stain the history of the century with incredible records of rapine and savagery....Very soon after came the terrible fires and looting at Kief, where 2000 Jews had the roofs burned over their heads.'

Hereupon General Ignatieff, Minister of the Interior, acting by express orders of his Imperial master, issued a circular to all the provincial governors, in which he pointed out that within the last twenty years the Jews had not only been monopolising trade and commerce, but had also, by lease and purchase, been gradually acquiring a considerable portion of the land, in doing which they did not so much aim at increasing the productive power of the country as of exploiting its Slavonic inhabitants, especially of the poorer class. It was this, he explained, that had caused the late riots; but 'while repressing these acts of violence, the Government at the same time recognised the need of equally rigorous measures for remedying the abnormal relations existing between the Jews and the native population, and for protecting the people from that injurious activity of the Jews which, according to local reports, was the real cause of the agitation.' At the same time the Tsar appointed a Commission, with several Jews in it, to inquire into the question and suggest its solution.

Meanwhile, the rioting and raiding against the Jews continued in other parts of the Empire to an incredible extent, and multitudes of their race began to fly from an Empire which had become something like a fiery furnace of persecution. It was said (but who shall control these figures?) that, between April 1881 and June 1882, 'no fewer than 225,000 Jewish families - comprising over a million souls, and representing a loss to the Empire of £22,000,0000 - fled from Russia.' At Easter, 1882, the town of Balta, in Podolia, was the scene of another anti-Semitic outbreak, resulting in the destruction of 976 houses, the death of eight persons, and the wounding of 211, with robbery and destruction of property amounting to nearly two million roubles. When asked why they thus indulged their hatred of the Jews, the rioters replied: 'They say that our little father, the Tsar, wishes it'; or, 'If the Tsar did not wish us to murder the Jews, he would have long since issued a ukase to that effect.' Throughout all Europe public indignation was roused to fever heat by all those persecutions and barbarities, but nowhere more so than in England, where both Press and platform rang with wrathful protests against all these unheard-of goings-on in Russia.

But the only answer vouchsafed from St Petersburg to these public appeals to the justice and humanity of the Tsar, these Exeter Hall and

Mansion House resolutions and memorials, was, in effect: 'Mind your own business, ye self-conceited, hypocritical, and ignorant islanders, and let us do the same.' Said the *Novoe Vremya*, voicing the sentiments of Panslavist Russia:

'The concern of England, which has beggared the population of India and Egypt, which has poisoned the people of China with opium, which destroyed, like dangerous insects, the natives of Australia, and which, under pretext of abolishing the slave trade, is now exterminating in most wholesale fashion the numerous races of Africa - the concern of a people who do those things is certainly astonishing.'

I said that, in writing thus, the *Novoe Vremya* but voiced the sentiments of Panslavist Russia; for there is a consensus of opinion among all competent authorities that, in proceeding as he did against the Jews, Alexander III, for once in his life at least, constituted himself the exponent and executor of the national will - whatever the value of that was as a reason for and ratification of his acts. 'In the cruel measures adopted against the Jews,' said the *Times* writer of his obituary notice, 'the Tsar unquestionably had the sympathy of the great majority of his subjects.' Again, 'there is little doubt,' wrote Mr Stead, 'that if the anti-Jewish laws were to be submitted to a plebiscite, they would be approved by the enormous majority of the Russian people.'

'Alexander III,' wrote a very able and well-informed observer,[4] 'is an anti-Semite of the most uncompromising type, and the origin of his dislike to the modern Hebrews is to be sought for partly in the prejudice instilled into his mind by his earliest teachers, and partly by the calumnies circulated about the Jews in connection with the vast frauds perpetrated in the commissariat department during the late war by the very men who, although at that time in his confidence, were afterwards transported to Siberia for appropriating the money that should have gone to supply the unfortunate soldiers with boots and biscuits. The latest utterance of the Tsar on the Jewish question was delivered at the beginning of the present year (1894), when reading a report on the results of the famous exodus scheme, which should have transferred his Hebrew subjects to South America: 'It is useless to convert them to Christianity; it is dangerous to turn them loose among my subjects, and it is hopeless to ship them beyond the seas. They are evidently destined to remain the heaviest cross which the Russian people has to bear.'

In the first few years of his reign, at any rate, the Tsar made immense efforts to relieve his people from the burden of what he deemed to be so awful a cross. If we inquire into his motives, we are forced to the conclusion that the question of religion held but a very subordinate place among their number. It was not nearly so much a question of religion as of race. As the Jew-baiters say at Vienna and Berlin:

> *'Was die Juden glauben - das ist einerlei;*
> *In der Rasse steckt Schweinerei.'*

An English publicist only expanded this coarse distich when he wrote:[5]

'The main object pursued by the governing classes in repressing the Jew in Russia is sheer self-defence. Russians hold that the bright Jewish intellect, if allowed free play, would contaminate the whole Empire within a short space of time. It has been calculated that if the repressive laws of Russia were repealed, and the Jews allowed access to any and every post in the service of the Empire, eight years would not pass before every post worth having outside the army and navy would be filled by an official of the Hebrew faith. I believe the statement to be little if at all exaggerated. The average Jew towers above the average Russian. Intellectual jealousy and fear of supersession supply the effective force to anti-Semitic prejudices in Russia. In point of fact, religious antipathy has little part in the measures directed against Russians of the Hebrew faith.'

Rightly or wrongly, Alexander III, with the vast majority of his subjects, 'regarded the Jews as social parasites, demoralising every community into which they penetrated - a species of human vermin whom every Government should seek to extirpate for the general good.' Their usurious habits, it was argued, made them the bane of the Russian peasantry; they refused to amalgamate with the Slavs; they made bad soldiers; they shirked manual and agricultural labour; they exploited vice; they cheated, if they could, in trade; they banded themselves with the Nihilists, and, indeed, formed the brain-power of that revolutionary party; they evaded the laws which had been made from time to time to regulate their existence in Russia; and, above all things, they had overleaped the limits of the vast 'Ghetto,' or 'Pale of Settlement' - fifteen provinces in the south-west, covering an area nearly eight times the size of England and Wales in which they had been assigned a home - and submerged the rest of the Empire like a burst reservoir.

Was a ruler who cared for the welfare of his dear Slavonic subjects to continue tolerating all this? 'No, by Heaven!' cried Alexander III, in effect, and his resolution was embodied in the famous 'May Laws' of 1882, which were issued 'as a temporary measure, and until a general revision has been made in a proper manner of the laws concerning the Jews.' One of these 'provisional' edicts forbade the Jews 'henceforth to settle outside the towns and townlets of the Pale, the only exception admitted being in those Jewish colonies that have existed before, and whose inhabitants are agriculturists.' A second edict suspended all the Jewish mortgages and leases on landed property, and also their powers of attorney for managing estates; while a third forbad them to carry on business on Sundays and Christian holidays.

Such were the Russian 'May Laws.' As some one said of them, 'it was as if all the Jews of Russia were to be violently crowded in and piled on top of each other, like grasshoppers in a ditch. Here they were to be miserably crushed together until the fruitless struggle for life should have done its work.' To M. Pobedonostseff was attributed the saying that of these Jews 'a third would be converted, a third would emigrate, while the rest would die of hunger.' 'When microbes have to be destroyed,' said Prince Metchersky, 'we do not pause to inquire how microbes like the process;' and this, too, was practically the view of the Tsar and his Ministers, especially the Procurator of the Holy Synod, who was animated with a most unbending spirit of Jew-abhorring rigour. A Commission of Inquiry, presided over by Count Pahlen, recommended a policy of leniency, and one of its members, Prince Demidoff San-Donato, even advocated the complete emancipation of God's chosen people. But M. Pobedonostseff, the keeper of the Tsar's conscience, revolted at the very idea, and, with the consent of his Majesty, gave the persecuting screw another succession of truculent twists, which had the effect of filling all the Empire with pitiful havoc and howls of pain.

From 1883 to 1890, the exterminating crusade was conducted in a spasmodic manner, with alternations of mildness and severity; but in this latter year M. Pobedonostseff gave the loose to all his yelling pack, and Europe was horror-struck at the reports of savagery, pillage, expulsion, and pitiless persecution which reached it from Holy Russia. Writing to the *Jewish Chronicle*, Mr Gladstone said that he had 'read with pain and horror the various statements respecting the sufferings of the Jews in Russia, and that the thing to do, if the facts could be established, was to 'rouse the conscience of Russia and Europe in regard to them."

His words caught on, and a meeting of all that was illustrious and humane in the public life of England was convoked at the Guildhall (December 10, 1890). Dukes, bishops, peers, and professors crowded the hall. The Earl of Meath, who 'declined to assume that his Imperial Majesty the Tsar had cognisance of the sufferings to which his Jewish subjects were exposed,' moved (and his motion was adopted by acclamation):

'That a suitable memorial be presented to the Emperor of All the Russias, respectfully praying his Majesty to repeal all the exceptional and restrictive laws and disabilities which afflicted his Jewish subjects, and begging his Majesty to confer upon them equal rights with those enjoyed by the rest of his Majesty's subjects ; and that the said memorial should be signed by the Right Honourable the Lord Mayor in the name of the citizens of London, and be transmitted by his Lordship to his Majesty.'

Accordingly, a memorial to this effect was drawn up, and I will quote its essential passage as showing, better than could any words of mine, the nature of the persecution which had so 'roused the conscience' of England:

'Five millions of your Majesty's subjects groan beneath the yoke of exceptional and restrictive laws....These laws, built up in bygone times, when intolerance was the rule in almost every State, have been intensified by later ordinances, and weigh a grievous burden on the Hebrew subjects of your Majesty, raising a barrier between them and their Christian fellow-subjects, making them a pariah caste degraded and despised as of an accursed race. Pent up in narrow bounds within your Majesty's wide Empire, and even within those bounds forced to reside chiefly in towns that reek and overflow with every form of poverty and wretchedness; forbidden all free movements; hedged in every enterprise by restrictive laws; forbidden tenure of land, or all concern in land, their means of livelihood have become so cramped as to render life for them well-nigh impossible. Nor are they cramped alone in space and action; the higher education is denied them, &c.'

How to transmit this memorial to the Tsar was now the question which occupied the minds of its framers. At first it was thought that the letter had best be taken over by a special deputation, and several courageous gentlemen even volunteered to undertake the risky task. At last, however, it was resolved to convey the missive to the British ambassador in St Petersburg, with a polite request to deliver it to the Tsar. But Sir Robert Morier, deeming himself to be the agent of the English Queen and Government, and not of Guildhall Committees, politely declined to be impressed as a letter-carrier in such a delicate matter, and returned the memorial to its sender. Then the Lord Mayor dropped the memorial into the post-office, and in due time it thus reached its destination. But the Tsar, disdaining even to open such a communication, handed it to M. de Giers, who sent it to the Russian ambassador in London, who passed it on to the Marquis of Salisbury, who gave it to Sir Philip Currie, who returned it to the Lord Mayor (Sir Joseph Savory), who sat down with a most rueful countenance to read the following note:

'My LORD, - The Russian Ambassador has requested the Marquis of Salisbury to cause to be returned to your Lordship the letter which you addressed to his Majesty the Emperor of Russia on the 24th ult, with the memorial which accompanied it, respecting the position of the Jews in Russia, and I am accordingly directed by his Lordship to transmit to you those papers herewith, I am, my Lord, your most obedient servant, - P.W. CURRIE.'

When the Tsar, as Tsarevitch, was in London (1873) he had taken in to supper the Lady Mayoress at the grand ball given at the Guildhall in honour of the Shah. He had shown the Lady Mayoress in then, and now, in effect, he had shown the Lord Mayor out. Nor was the public feeling one of unmitigated surprise that he had done so. For there were many who argued that, as every Englishman claimed to be king in his own castle, so there was also no reason why the Tsar should not equally be allowed the right of managing his own affairs in his own way, and even of pulling down his Empire about his subjects' ears if he chose to do so.

But the truth is that the sense of humanity which moved the Guildhall meeting had completely overmastered its sense of tact. To address a memorial of this land to so mighty a monarch as the Ruler of All the Russias, on the calm assumption that he was ignorant of what was passing within his own dominions, was nothing less than a studied insult which no scrupulously chosen form of respectful address could possibly conceal, and to which a self-respecting Sovereign could return but one reply. On the other hand it was pointed out that as Russia, on a former occasion, had accorded her thanks to the Duke of Westminster when he raised his voice in favour of the oppressed Bulgarians, there was no consistent reason why his present appeal for pity on behalf of the persecuted Jews of Russia should have met with such a pitiless snub.

Far from being deterred by the expression of public opinion all over Europe, especially in England, the Tsar only seemed to harden his heart all the more against his Hebrew subjects, who now became the victims of a harsher persecution than ever. Harsh, indeed, is but a weak word to characterise the new measures that now entangled the poor Jews of Russia in a barbarous and ever-tightening network of extermination, which it would take volumes to detail. Two Commissioners of the United States Government were sent to Europe to inquire into the causes of the ever-increasing immigration of foreigners totally devoid of resources, and their report, in which they embodied the results of their painstaking journey across Poland and Russia, stated that 'in this account will be found a convincing history of the terrible conditions which heretofore have been but partially described and largely disbelieved, because of their incredible character.'

I have not the space to harrow the feelings of my readers with descriptions of the dreadful miseries which resulted from the expulsion from Russia of *all* foreign Jews; of the hunting of all Russian Hebrews, like herds of escaped cattle, back into the pen of the 'Pale,' 'where death or desertion of their country stared them in the face; of incidents like the terrible passover 'purification' of Holy Moscow under the Grand Duke Sergius, brother of the Tsar; and of other heartrending barbarities connected with the anti-Semitic crusade of M. Pobedonostseff and his Imperial master. In a work of this limit I can only deal in generalities,[6] but I think I have now said more than enough to show that if Alexander III ever becomes known to history by any particular title, like his father, who became the 'Tsar Emancipator,' that title is likely to be the 'Tsar Persecutor.'

But his claim to this cognomen is founded on a very much broader and more substantial basis than his persecution of the Jews. To all intents and purposes that was a racial persecution; but it was Alexander III's religious intolerance that formed the most conspicuous and unlovely feature in his character. The Jews he hated, but the Gentiles he positively loathed; and as Gentiles, or 'pagans,' he accounted all those of his subjects who lived and worshipped without the pale of the Orthodox Church. To recover all these lost sheep and force them back into the pale of this Church - which, to the Western mind, seemed to be the embodiment of the most debased and spurious form of Christianity - was his consuming passion; and in the pursuit of this passion he played some of the most fantastic tricks which have ever been performed before the face of high heaven.

I have no space to deal with his manipulation of the Roman Catholics in Poland, though, indeed, he was, perhaps, less of a heretic-hunter in this than in other parts of his Empire; and the diplomatic relations which he finally established with the Vatican showed that he was almost willing to regard the Greek and Romish Churches as estranged sisters not wholly beyond the hope of reconciliation. But wherever the followers of Dr Martin Luther, the heroic monk of Wittenberg, had pitched their Puritanic tents - and this they had done extensively in the Baltic Provinces with their Teutonic population - there it was that the proselytising fury of Alexander III poured itself out like the breath of a fiery furnace.

Let me quote one typical instance of his intolerant zeal, of which the victim was Prince Barclay de Tolly, the son of the man who had driven the French invaders from Russia. True to the faith of his Scottish ancestors - who derived their origin from Tolly in the shire of Aberdeen, and had done great things in their time for the Russian Empire, from the time of Peter the Great downwards - this nobleman had clung to the simple faith of John Knox; and when he married a lady of the Orthodox faith, he had done so on the understanding that any issue of the marriage should belong to the Lutheran faith.

'A private enemy of the young Prince informed the Emperor that he had had his first child christened in the Lutheran Church, notwithstanding the express terms of the law which declares that, if either parent be Orthodox, all the children must likewise be members of the State Church. The Tsar asked Prince Barclay whether that accusation was true. The nobleman replied in the affirmative, and explained his conduct by appealing to the privilege accorded to all the aristocracy of the Baltic Provinces by Alexander II, to bring up their children in their own Church, irrespective of the religion of the mother. The Tsar angrily said that he withdrew this privilege on the spot, and that in future the law that held good in Russia must be enforced in the provinces of the Baltic.

'Soon afterwards Prince Barclay had another child, and he baptised her in like manner in the Lutheran Church, on the ground that he would not have espoused a Russian had he not been convinced that he could bring up his children in the faith of his fathers. Thereupon the Emperor himself, without consulting his adviser, issued an order publicly dismissing Prince Barclay from the Guards and the army. Soon after this the persecution went on apace. Pastors were suspended, fined, imprisoned, banished, for advising the members of their flock to remain steadfast in the Lutheran faith; hints were thrown out that land would be lavishly distributed to all peasants who should spontaneously embrace the religion of the Tsar. But the misguided men who yielded to the temptation discovered the trap that had been cunningly set for them, and, endeavouring to undo their mistake, were punished as apostates or blasphemers.'[7]

In 1888, in reply to the representations of the Evangelical Alliance concerning the persecution of the Protestants in the Baltic Provinces, M. Pobedonostseff, acting with his Imperial master's express approval, had the effrontery to write:

'The Russian Government is convinced that nowhere in Europe do all religions enjoy such liberty as in Russia. This truth is unfortunately not admitted in Europe. Why? Solely because in Europe religious liberty is confounded with an unrestricted right of proselytism. The Western religions in Russia have always been actuated by a mixture of spiritual and secular motives. Catholicism was impregnated with Polonism; Protestantism, as represented by the Livonian Knights, was equally animated by secular motives. The time for a peaceful co-operation of the Christianity of the East with that of the West has unfortunately not yet arrived, for the Western religions are in Russia still not free from worldly objects, and even from attacks on the integrity of the Empire. Russia cannot allow them to tempt her Orthodox sons to depart from their allegiance, and she therefore continues to protect them by her laws.'

How this protection was extended to the Orthodox sons of Russia was well shown in her treatment of the Stundists. But who and what are they? Briefly put, they are what the early Puritans and the Methodists were to England, and the Covenanters to Scotland - the salt and leaven of true religious life in Russia. Their name is derived from a German word, *Stunde*, meaning 'hour' - either because their religious services lasted just so long, or because the German settlers in the South of Russia, from whom they took their form of worship, called the times of their praise and prayer *Stunden*, or hours, irrespective of their length, just as in Germany a school-lesson, which generally lasts an hour, is still called a *Stunde*.

It was in the neighbourhood of Kherson, where our own great philanthropist, John Howard, fell a victim to the plague, that the Stundist movement took its rise about five-and-thirty years ago. In the reign of Catherine great numbers of German peasants had been induced to settle in Southern Russia, and, with the conservatism of their race, they had adhered through many generations to the faith and habits of their simple, pious forefathers.[8] These Swabian peasants were destined to do as much for the social and religious life of Russia as the revoked Edict-of-Nantes victims of

Louis XIV did for the arts and manufactures of the countries where they found a new home.

'In a general way,' says Mr 'Lanin,' 'one may describe the state of the Russian peasantry, when Stundism appeared to regenerate it, as that of brutes rather than men; of chattels sold or pledged to pay a debt, or lost and won over a game of cards. The unfortunate people lay, to use Carlyle's forcible expression, 'in a soak of horrors, sunk like steeping flax under the widespread, foetid hell-waters....addicted to crimes unknown to heathen nations, and unheard of among peoples ignorant of God. Their spiritual guides, gross, grovelling, greedy, were, if possible, in a still less enviable condition than the people. The ranks of the clergy,' declared the Fathers of the Ecumenical Council at Moscow, 'are filled with clodhoppers, unfit to graze cattle, much less to feed flocks of human souls.'....Some of the degraded serfs were driven by stress of hunger to seek work on the farms of certain German colonists settled in the Government of Kherson since the reign of the Empress Catherine – simple, God-fearing Teutons, faithful to the language, traditions, and modes of thought of the Fatherland - and it was while living here as labourers, substituting coffee for vodka, hard work for wasteful idleness, and thrift for improvidence, that these bewitched beasts grew gradually to the fact that they, too, were men like their masters, and, issuing from their subterranean caverns, discovered heaven and earth, God and the devil - above the primal duties shining aloft like stars, and below the charities that soothe, and heal, and bless.'

What may be called the founder of the sect in Russia was a poor peasant, Onishenko by name, a native of Osnova, near the port of Nicolaieff. He had been in the employ of various German farmers, and was one of the most devoted of those who attended the German Stunden, making a special study of the New Testament, pure and simple. In 1858 he declared himself converted, and was admitted to membership with the German brethren. Returning home, he at once began to evangelise his fellow-villagers. His preaching caught on, and the seed which had thus been sown soon began to shoot up abundantly and spread to other districts. In a surprisingly short time the peasants all over the Kherson country had heard the Gospel preached, and the new religious movement began to take something like organised shape. Wherever they went - and they travelled far and near - the propagandists were received with open arms and open hearts. The emancipation of the serfs, in 1861, gave a wonderful impetus to the movement. For previously the peasants had been confined to their communes and villages, and it was only with the utmost difficulty that the preachers could move from place to place as sowers of the new spiritual seed. But now the edict of the Tsar Emancipator removed this local restriction, and enabled the liberated serfs, who wandered forth in search of work, to scatter their knowledge of the true kingdom of God as they went along. Thus it will be seen that Alexander did more than liberate the serfs; for this setting free of their bodies also carried with it the emancipation of their souls.

Masses of people crowded to the meeting-houses. They sang and prayed, and read the Gospels, and multiplied exceedingly. The police were nonplussed, the priests were aghast. It was a tide the force of which they could not stem, the depth of which they could not fathom. 'We must worship God in spirit,' said the new sectaries, 'and the spirit being free, our worship should likewise be free from the fetters of ceremonies and forms. My Saviour is my only priest.' They were the Russian counterpart of the followers of John Wesley and of Fox the Quaker. 'O God, enlighten me! make me a changed man!' Onishenko had prayed. 'I besought Him,' he said, 'with tears and sobs, when all at once it seemed as if some one tore the clothes from off my back, whereupon a marvellous sense of freedom, a feeling of intense joy, came over me, and I knew God thenceforth.'

Old and young, the Stundists set themselves to learn to read and write, and so it soon came to pass that in a land otherwise sunk in brutish ignorance and superstition 'the tiller chanted scraps of Gospel as he walked after his plough, the weaver sang chapters of it to the noisy accompaniment of the shuttle, and the traveller beguiled the tedium of his journey with the thrilling stories of the 'Book.'' The whole monstrous fabric of Russian Orthodoxy, with its debasing image-worship and sacerdotalism, was put away. 'Ceremonies are mummeries' said the Stundist leaders. 'The service of God means our living for others and dying to ourselves. God is love, and what He asks of us is love for each other who are His images, and not temples, and wax-lights, and icons, and myrrh.'

It was computed that by 1870 the Stundist movement had been joined by about 70,000 peasants, spread over the ten provinces between the Austrian frontier and the Volga; and in the next ten years the new creed had made extraordinary progress, numbering as it did about 300,000 members. It had received a decided impetus from the introduction of a rival sect of Baptists - the work also of German missionaries. And what sort of men and women had the new belief produced? Let me quote some impartial evidence on the subject. Said the Police Superintendent of Tarashtshansky:

'The Stundists are distinguished from the rest or the population hy thdr uniforai high standard of morality; and in the villages in which they reside crime has practically disappeared. Owing to their sobriety, their economical condition is incompaiably better than that of the Orthodox population, while no comparison at all need be made between their respective intellectual levels, seeing that almost all Stundists can read and write. Their family life is in all respects exemplary, and their relations with each other are, in the broadest and best sense of the word, Christian.'

This testimony may be supplemented by a writer who bad little sympathy with their religious views:

'Bickerings and wranglings among the Stundists are rare, as are all nianifestations of authority and power. All the members of the family are possessed of equal rights, the husband being in nowise privileged in respect to the wife, nor the parents in respect to their offspring. Parental authority, instead of assuming any of those repulsive forms deemed indispensable for the right bringing up of children, gives way to gentle persuasion, right direction, and, above all, to the powerful example of a truly Christian life.'

Take the following testimony from several Orthodox Russian journals:

'The lofty morality of the Stundists is truly marvellous....Force and violence are foreign to their character; guile and double-dealing banished from their lives ; and such is their natural kind-heartedness that the insults and injustice which they suffer, instead of kindling their anger, evoke their compassion....They set such store by honest labour, that they eschew every kind of pleasure, even the most innocent of all - viz, the squandering of their time away in idleness....The Stundists are a most industrious body of men; they do not steal, neither do they drink nor swear; and in the ups and downs of life they bear themselves like genuine Christians. Crime amongst them is almost unheard of; one of their cherished virtues consists in feeding the hungry, clothing the naked, caring for the sick, sheltering the wanderer; in a word, in helping in every feasible way their necessitous neighbours....An upright, sober, compassionate people.'

On the other hand, the spirit that began to animate the high-placed members of the Russian hierarchy against these simple, fervid folk may be judged from the following verses taken from a leaflet circulated among the faithful, and believed to be the composition of no less a personage than the Archbishop of Kief himself, by whose authority it was issued:

'Boom ye Church thunders,
Flash forth ye curses of the Councils!
Crush with eternal anathemas
The outcast race of Stundists!

'The Stundist strikes at our dogmas,
Scoffs at our traditions,
Loathes our holy icons,
The heretic, the damned Stundist.

'Our lanes and holy temples
That shine throughout the land.
Like stars in the blue finnament,
Are shunned by the damned Stundist

'Cruel and dark as a demon,
He shuns all faithful Christians,
And crawls into darkest comers -
God's foe, the damned Stundist.

'The thoughtless and harmless, who near
The den of this malignant beast,
Are befouled with blasphemies and slanders,
And cajoled by the damned Stundist.'

Such, then, was the spirit which animated the Russian Church against the new sectaries, and which the Church, in turn, managed to infuse into the Government. The clergy soon came to see that, unaided, they were powerless against the growing strength of the Stundists, and, at an episcopal conference held at Kief, it was determined to petition the secular powers to help in suppressing a movement dangerous alike to Church and State. The latter, it must be owned, was at first a little slow to act; but at last, in 1878, the two powers combined their forces, and the persecution began. The infected districts were raided by the police, who closed meeting-houses, confiscated Bibles and hymn-books, 'interned' the leaders in their villages, deprived them of their passports, cast them into prison. For four years this went on, though without any marked effect on the movement, for when the Stundists could no longer meet for worship in their cottages, they took to the solitude of the steppe and there held their secret, sentinel-guarded conventicles, like the Covenanters of old. 'We must sorrowfully confess,' wrote a rural dean in 1888, 'that, notwithstanding the earnest attempts made by the Church to wean these schismatics from their errors, notwithstanding admonition and prayerful entreaty, notwithstanding the gentle and paternal pressure of the wardly powers, they continue in their stiff-necked course, and evince no desire to be reconciled to us.'

'Gentle pressure' was good. But this was written in the year of the accession of Alexander III, and from this time forth the Stundists were to know what persecution really meant. 'My predecessors knouted the Stundists with whips,' said the newly-consecrated Bishop Sergius, 'but I will beat them with scorpions.' With M. Pobedonostseff at his side, the new Tsar determined to do all he could to root out the accursed sect. The local commissaries of police - a rough, ignorant, and tyrannical class -were empowered to levy arbitrary fines on peasants who continued to attend Stundist meetings after a warning not to do so, and to distrain if the fines were not paid. Misery and ruin were thus brought to hundreds of happy homes. All through the winters of 1882 and 1883 it was quite a common thing to see in the villages auctions of the effects of Stundists - their bedding, clothes, and sticks of furniture being sold to liquidate these scandalous fines. We have before us a list of the

Stundists fined and imprisoned in the one village of Nerubalsk. During the space of eighteen months, twelve families here were fined the incredible sum of two thousand six hundred roubles, equivalent in our currency to £260. One man, more than usually obstinate in his views, was fined altogether over seven hundred roubles.'

But the clergy were not yet satisfied, nor the Emperor either. 'It is a national evil, this Stundism,' wrote a minister of religion to the Kief Ecclesiastical Consistory in 1883; 'it is destructive of our best and holiest institution; it aims its shafts at the State as well as at the Church; it seeks to bring about anarchy and Nihilism, and it is therefore the paramount duty of provincial governors to leave no stone unturned in their efforts to purify our beloved fatherland from the stain of these dangerous disturbers of society.' The bishops took precisely this view, and petitioned the Holy Synod to move provincial governors to more drastic measures, and especially to use for this purpose the dreaded power vested in them of 'administrative process,' which empowered the governors of provinces to transport to Siberia or the Caucasus any troublesome or suspected persons, but against whom the evidence was not sufficiently strong to allow of their trial by jury.

Armed with these awful powers, the authorities now began to strike at the leaders of the Stundist movement, thinking thereby to destroy the body by cutting off the head. Soon there was hardly a gaol all over the South of Russia that did not contain martyrs to the new faith, and seldom was there a wretched gang of prisoners on the way to Siberia or Transcaucasia that lacked a Stundist preacher. Awful deserts, like Gerusi, Terter, Yevlach, and other places, were selected as the domicile of the Stundist leaders. They were all sent to their destination per *étape* - walking with ordinary criminals in chains, with shaven heads, and clad in the ordinary prison garb. Pushed and hustled,' they were thrust at with bayonets if they remonstrated, and one hapless wretch had his head caved in. But here we should require to call in the aid of all Mr Kennan's prison horrors in Russia to paint in adequate hues the pains and penalties inflicted on these heroic sufferers for conscience' sake. But hear the anonymous author of *The Stundists*:

'Religious intolerance is just as rampant in Russia to-day as it was in England during the reigns of the Tudors and it is only prevented from going to the extremes of personal torture and the public stake by the dread of Western opinion….The fabric of Russian power is an autocracy based on ignorance and superstition; and, therefore, it is the interest of self-preservation that has always prompted the Tsar's government to crush anything that would bring enlightenment in tu train. Thousands of Stundists and Baptists, of Molokans and Dukhobortsi, are banished to the remotest comers of the vast Empire, and imprisoned and tortured in a variety of ways, only a degree less inhuman than the scouigings and rackings of the Middle Ages. The nations of the West do not seem to be alive to this. They do not seem to realise hat they have at their gates a

Power more intolerant of religious liberty than was Spain in her worst days, and persecutors as unscrupulous and narrow-minded as Alva and Torquemada. How can they know it? Russia works in secret; her methods are underground, and her viaims are voiceless. There is no Press in Russia worthy the name to report and denounce each case of persecution as it occurs. The trials of heretics are conducted with closed doors, the public being carefully excluded. Russians themselves do not know a tenth of what is being done.'

Under the pitiless rule of the 'Tsar Persecutor' and his Torquemada a Stundist became an outlaw; his children were no longer his own; he was excluded from all village life and activity; his passport bore a mark of infamy; he durst not employ an Orthodox servant, nor was he permitted to serve an Orthodox master. Even when dead, the vengeance of the Church followed him; for his body had to be cast into the grave, away from the consecrated earth that held the bones of his fathers.

The 'trials' of some of these poor, persecuted men carry us back to the times of Judge Jeffreys and his Bloody Circuit. 'Ah, you are a Stundist, are you?' shouted Admiral Zelenoi, the Governor of Odessa, to whom a stone-mason applied for leave to go to a neighbouring town, which the loss of his passport debarred him from doing. You are a Stundist, are you? You rascal! How dare you leave the Orthodox Church, you scoundrel? I'll pack you off to Siberia, you son of a ----,' 'As God wills,' the stone-mason answered simply. "As God wills, is it, you ruffian! You presumed to leave the Orthodox Church, did you? Well, by ----, I'll make it hot enough for you outside the Church, you'll find. Leave my presence this moment; begone! son of a ----.'

Boycotted, banished, imprisoned, fined, bankrupted, condemned to loss of civil rights, and torn from the bosoms of their families, these poor martyrs to their religious beliefs could not have been more barbarously treated if they had been conspirators of the most dangerous kind, criminals of the deepest die, instead of being 'the most honest, sober, and moral peasants in the Empire.' Of their brutal treatment on the road to the terrible deserts of their exile some of the Stundist preachers have given accounts quite as horrible as those prison-pictures which moved Mr Swinburne, m his famous ode to Russia, to exclaim:[9]

> 'God or man, be swift; hope sickens with delay!
> Smite and send him howling down his father's way -
>
> Down the way of Tsars, awhile in vain deferred,
> Bid the Second Alexander light the Third.
> How for shame shall men rebuke them? how may we
> Blame, whose fathers died, and slew, to leave us free?
> We, though all the world cry out upon them, know,
> Were our strife as theirs, we could not strike but so.'

'As the rule of Alexander II,' says Mr 'Lanin,' 'was the mildest and most liberal, so that of his son and successor is by far the most despotic experienced by the Russian people since the days of Ivan the Terrible. Especially during the last five or six years, all the legal formalities and other frail barriers that stood between sectarians and ruin have been completely swept away, and flogging, fining, imprisonment, and life-long torture in the Siberian mines can be, and frequently are, meted out, without let or hindrance, or judicial delay, to men and women whom practical Englishmen or Americans would be disposed to regard as good citizens and benefactors to the community.'

Now, was it in the least surprising, in view of all this terrible tyranny and persecution - which must be taken as typical of much more of the same kind directed against other races and religions in the Russian Empire - that the hearts of many of the subjects of Alexander III should have been filled with the deepest hatred of the despotism under which all these dreadful things were possible, and that they should, in consequence, have joined the ranks of those who had sworn to devote their souls and bodies to the work of making Russia a freer and a happier land?

We have seen how Alexander III persecuted millions of his subjects. Let us now see how many of those subjects in turn persecuted him.

NOTES

1. Article on M. Pobedonostseff in *Contemporary Review* for April 1893.
2. 'The New Exodus - A Study of Israel in Russia.' By Harold Frederic. London: William Heinemann. 1892.
3. At p. 196, vol. i, of M Leroy-Beaulieu's work on Russia, I read: 'Among the conspirators many, and not unfrequently the most enterprising, are of Jewish extraction. This gave occasion to certain Russian papers, happy to find an alien scapegoat, to assert that all the trouble came from abroad and from the Jews. This should not be taken seriously. Nihilism is a genuinely Russian thing, although there are numbers of Nihilists outside of Russia. As to the Israelites, it might be said that there exists a kind of Jewish Nihilism which naturally amalgamates with the Slavic Nihilism. The inferior situation created for the numerous Jews of Russia by laws or custom, has, moreover, much to do with their readiness to take part in plots.'
4. The St Petersburg correspondent of the *Daily Telegraph* in an obituary notice of Alexander III.
5. Mr Arnold White in the *Contemporary Review* for May 1892, written as the result of eight months' residence in Russia.
6. If my readers want details, they must refer to such books as Mr Harold Frederic's 'New Exodus' - a work of rare graphic power - or 'The Russian Jews,'

by Professor Erreira, of the University of Brussels.

7. I am here quoting from an obituary notice of Alexander III, contributed to the *Daily Telegraph* by the able and well-informed correspondent of that journal at St Petersburg.

8. For the facts here set forth I have been mainly indebted to a most admirable article on the subject by Mr E.B. 'Lanin,' in the *Contemporary Review* for January 1893; as well as to an equally excellent work, 'The Stundists - the Story of a Great Religious Revolt, with Introduction by John Brown, D.D., Ex-Chairman of the Congregational Union.'

9. 'Russia: an Ode.' By A C. Swinburne, written after reading an account of 'Russian Prisons,' in the *Fortnightly Review* for July 1890.

CHAPTER IX

A REIGN OF TERROR

Assassination and executions - A Terrorist ultimatum - What the Nihilists want - A chat with 'Stepniak' - Party of the 'People's Will' - And of the 'Peoples' Rights' - Spiritual and material means – *De propaganda fide* - Congress of Lipètak - Nihilist organisation - Mass trial of Terrorists - Suchanoff executed - General Strelikoff shot - A basketful of eggs - Coronation of the Tsar - Tactics of the Terrorists at Moscow – 'Nor I either' - Nihilism in the Army - Murder of Colonel Sudeikin - Colonel Aschenbrenner and Baron Stromberg - Vera Filipoff, a tempting Terrorist - Arrests and assassinations - Plots against the Emperor - A life of fear and precaution - Anecdotes - The Grand Morskaia plot, and the Executive Committee - Another mass trial – 'Education to be abolished!' - The Borki catastrophe - 'Oh, papa, they'll come and murder us all!' - A bomb factory at Zurich – 'A paper bullet of the brain' - Madame Tzebrikova's letter - Its consequences to her - Sophie Gunsberg - General Seliverskoff shot at Paris - A French Exhibition at Moscow - Dynamite one of its exhibits - Proof against bribes - The Moujik Tsar - Shaken nerves - A Ministry of personal protection - The greatest Terrorist of all - A revolting manifesto

WE have already seen how Alexander III had not been many days on the throne before there reached him a document in the nature of an ultimatum from the Executive Committee of the Nihilists, and how in all probability it was this document which at last determined him to withhold from the nation the semi-constitutional privileges which had been decreed by his father on the very day of his death. The new Tsar was bent on showing that he would not be terrorised. He might yield to persuasion, but not to threats - the less so as the sight of his poor father's mangled body had filled his heart with such a glowing resentment against the party which had produced the assassins of his sire that his mind, for the time being, was almost bereft of its reasoning powers.

The Nihilists had made six separate attempts to take the life of Alexander II, and at last they had succeeded. But they had to pay dearly for their success. Five of their number, including a woman (Sophie Perofsky), who had been implicated in the regicide of March 13, were summarily tried and executed (April 15) in a very shocking manner. The Government forbore carrying out the capital sentence on another of the conspirators, Jess Helfmann, as she was with child, and commuted her punishment into penal servitude for life. A few days after this execution, the Nihilists contrived to communicate the following to the Tsar:

'On April 15, between 9 and 10 A.M., on the Semeonoff Square, St Petersburg, the following Socialists received the martyr's crown' (names of the five conspirators given). 'Imperial senators sat in judgment over the martyrs, while the Tsar, Alexander III. dictated the sentence and also confirmed it. In this way the new imperialism has characterised itself; the first act of the autocratic win of Alexander III was the command to hang a woman. He sprinkled his throne with the blood of the champions of popular rights before even the time of his coronation had come. As for us, we avouch, in presence of the whole people, by the fresh grave of our dear companions, that we will continue the war of national liberation....While postponing to a near future its estimate of the general policy of Alexander III, the Executive Committee hereby intimates that a policy of reaction, according to the tradition of Alexander II, will inevitably lead to consequences of far graver import for the Government than those of March 13....'

'Knowst thou a murderer?' asked Richard III of his page, as if he had been inquiring for a barber. 'I know a ruined gentleman,' quoth the page, 'whose humble means match not his haughty tastes'; and of such stuff - but stay; let us hear how Prince Peter Dolgoruki once defined the Russian party of revolution. 'Nihilists,' said the Prince, ' are of two kinds - those who have nothing in their heads, and those who have nothing in their pockets.' Touching their purses, I know and care not; but feeling curious, for the purposes of this simple narrative, as to the contents of their heads, I set myself to find out what the Nihilists really want. I applied to 'Stepniak' for information on the point, and got for answer:

'(1) A permanent Representative Assembly, exercising supreme control and direction in all general questions of State.

(2) Provincial autonomy on an ample basis, assured by the election of all public functionaries.

(3) Independence of the village commune (Mir), with economic and administrative unity.

(4) The nationalisation of land.

(5) A series of measures tending to transfer the possession of factories to the workers therein.

(6) Absolute freedom of conscience, speech, Press, public meeting, association, and election.

(7) Extension of the suffrage to all citiiens who have reached their majority, without distinction of class or fortune ; and

(8) The substitution of a territorial militia for a standing army.'

These, added 'Stepniak,' were the demands that had been formulated by the party of the *Narodnaia Volia*, or 'People's Will.'

'Rather a large order,' I remarked, 'Monsieur Stepniak, *n'est ce pas*, to come down with all of a sudden upon the Autocrat of All the Russias? And do the Nihilists expect that such sweeping changes will be granted them all at once?'

'Perhaps not all in a lump,' replied the author of 'Underground Russia'; 'but that is their creed, and if the Liberals in the Empire would only organise a better and more forcible expression of their views, there is no saying but that, under a new *régime*, much might be achieved. I do not mean an outbreak of violence of a revolutionary kind, but a broad and all-permeating movement among the educated classes in the Empire, which ought to be irresistible. Popular discontent is deep and strong, and growing ever more so, and if the present Tsarevitch (Nicholas Alexandrovitch) came to the throne, he might perhaps see the wisdom of doing something to diminish the peck of troubles which always weighed upon his father, and made his life a burden. Things may grow better under a new ruler, I think they will; but they cannot very well be worse. At any rate, it will be wiser of the party of revolution, or call it reform, to utilise the popular discontent at present prevailing as a means of pressure, than to have recourse to acts of violence.'

'You have formulated to me the demands of the 'People's Will' party. But has not another rival, or co-ordinate party, recently sprung up, calling itself that of 'Popular Rights' (*Narodnoe Pravo*) and known in England as the 'Friends of Political Freedom?''

'To be sure there has - a party which, as I gather from its recent manifesto, is based on the belief that autocracy, after receiving its most vivid expression and impersonation in the reign of Alexander III, has with irrefutable clearness proved its impotence to create such an order of things as shall secure the countxy the fullest and most regular development of all her spiritual and material forces.'

'*Très bien*, Monsieur Stepniak. But how, then, does this party propose to confer upon the nation the political blessings which have been denied it by autocracy?'

'Well, to quote again from the manifesto, as there is not, and cannot be, a hope that the Government will willingly enter upon the path indicated, there is but one course remaining to the people: to oppose the force of organised public opinion to the inertness of the Government and the narrow dynastic interests of the autocracy. The party of 'Popular Rights' has in view the creation of this force.'

'And what are its demands as compared with those of the 'People's Will' Party?'

'There is its manifesto, which declares the guarantees of popular right to be -

> "Representative government on the basis of universal suffrage.
> Freedom of religious belief.
> Independence of the courts of justice.
> Freedom of the Press.
> Freedom of meeting and association.
> Inviolability of the individual and his rights as a man."

'Ah, mais c'est bien beau, tout ça!'

'Thus understanding popular rights,' the manifesto goes on to say, 'the party sets itself the task of uniting all the oppositional elements of the country, and of organising an active force which should with all the spiritual and material means at its disposal, attain the overthrow of autocracy and secure to everyone the rights of a citizen and man.'

From all this conversation I had gathered that it was now the intention of the various parties of revolution in Russia to rely more upon 'spiritual' than 'material' force as a means *de propaganda fide*. But if this was the attitude of the Nihilists, Socialists - call them what you will - at the end of the reign of Alexander III, it was at least undeniable that, in order to attain their ends, they had made his reign of thirteen years a Reign of Terror - a despotism tempered with repeated attempts at assassination. The famous 'Executive Committee' of the Nihilists had been formed in 1877, when a number of enthusiastic young men (about fifteen) met at Lipètsk, in the Government of Tambof, and decided to organise an attempt on the Emperor's life, at the same time resolving 'to discard revolver and dagger as obsolete and uncertain weapons, and trust to dynamite and bombs.' This 'Congress of Lipètsk,' as it was ambitiously called, had the effect of splitting the party of revolution into two factions - one, the 'terrorists,' who advocated the 'suppression' of rulers; and the 'moderates,' who were for plain propaganda and opposed to murder.

The former set to work, and by their repeated outrages soon justified their title. 'Bewildered,' says M. Leroy-Beaulieu, 'by the audacity and the gigantic scale of the outrages committed almost simultaneously from end to end of the Empire, public opinion, in the general scare, pictured the terrorists as an immense army, disposing of a costly plant, and operating with perfect ensemble on all points of the Empire. But this was a mistake. The twenty attempts perpetrated from 1878 to 1882 - the mines in the two capitals, in Odessa, in Aleztodrofsk - the explosions at the Moscow railway station and in the Winter Palace - the assassination of the chief of police and the governor - were the deeds of a handful of men.

'As early as 1880, one of the ministers of Alexander II explained how this conviction had been arrived at. As soon as a certain number of conspirators had been arrested, it was noticed that a man implicated in one affair was always implicated in others also. Like supers at a play, the weird actors of the revolutionary drama indefatigably cumulated their parts, passing and repassing from one end to the other of the vast stage comprised between the Black and Baltic seas, continually changing their names, their disguises, their tasks; the same man was - here a miner handling the pick-axe, there a type-setter or a journalist, so that they appeared to be everywhere at once, and, by this seeming ubiquitousness, increased their party's influence tenfold. The hand of Jeliabof and that of Sophie Perofsky, for instance, are shown in all the unsuccessful attempts in the south and in the Moscow explosions, as well as in the final catastrophe in St. Petersburg (March 1881).'

These Nihilists, in fact, would seem to have often played the pluralist *rôle* of the sucking-pig referred to in my character-sketch of Alexander I. But none the less were they a terror to all in authority with the doings and edicts of their Executive Committee, 'the sight of whose seal made people tremble from end to end of the Empire.' Into the secret organisation of the terrorists it is not here necessary to inquire. I must content myself with recording some of the chief manifestations of their activity which made the reign of Alexander III a reign of terror, and so worked upon his nervous system as to generate the illness which ultimately brought him to the grave.

In the spring of the year (1882) succeeding that of his accession, twenty-two persons were tried for complicity in the murder of the late Tsar, for the assassination of General Mezentzeff in 1878, and for the robbery of two and a half million roubles from the Kherson bank in 1879. One of the accused, an ex-officer of the navy, named Suchanoff, declared that the social conditions of life in Russia were such as to drive any sensitive and enlightened man into the ranks of the revolutionists, and drew such a moving picture of the circumstances which had led him to join the Nihilists that even his judges were affected. But in spite of being brilliantly defended by the counsel who had appeared for Vera Sassulitch, the 'Charlotte Corday' of Russia (who had come a long way from the country to shoot General Trepoff, Chief of Police, for beating a prisoner with rods), ten of the accused were found guilty and sentenced to the gallows-tree, the rest being let off with various terms of penal servitude. Suchanoff himself was shot at Cronstadt.

Soon after this the police effected the capture of one Kobozeff, who was believed to be the head of the dreaded Executive Committee; but, nothing daunted by these reverses, the terrorists continued to strike - one of their chief victims about this time being General Strelnikoff, Public Prosecutor at Kief, who was openly assassinated while sitting on the boulevard at Odessa, on the very day (March 30) on which the Tsar had signed Suchanoff's death-warrant. His murderers were at once arrested, tried by court-martial, and hanged three days later, one of them declaring on the scaffold that the General had been killed for opposing the propagation of Nihilist doctrines among the working-men of Odessa.

A few weeks later eighty workmen were arrested in Moscow, a mine, it was said, having been discovered in the Kremlin, where preparations were already being made for the Tsar's coronation in the following year. At the same time the Prefect of Police received a basketful of eggs, several of which were found to be charged with dynamite, while an anonymous note said: 'We have plenty more for the Tsar's coronation.' A mine was also discovered on the Nicolai Railway. In June, forty Nihilists were arrested in St. Petersburg, a large quantity of dynamite, with a plan of the Kremlin, being found in their possession, while a secret printing-press was discovered at the Ministry of Marine with thousands of copies of a seditious proclamation.

But the coronation of the Tsar, in May of the following year (1883), passed off without any sign from the terrorists, who had agreed to hold their hands in the hope that the ceremony might be signalised by some act of Imperial grace - some concession to the popular demands which the Tsar had so sternly refused at his accession, and which even now he would not grant.[1] The surprise expressed in many quarters at the peaceful nature of the coronation was in no wise shared by the Nihilists themselves. To them it was well known that no attempt would be made on that occasion, although, to divert the attention of the police from their real movements, they circulated rumours which greatly alarmed, not merely the Russian Court, but many of its distinguished guests. As a matter of fact, the Nihilist party came to the conclusion that an attempt against the person of the Tsar during the coronation would damage their interests in any case.

They had many good arguments to justify their unexpected neutrality. They urged that the revolutionary movement in Russia embraced many persons of moderate views, whose opinions must be taken into account, for, although rarely producing men of action, they often supplied large sums of money for the purposes of agitation. These moderate partisans looked forward to the coronation as a fitting occasion for the granting of a Constitution, while the extreme faction hoped for some measure of mercy towards the Nihilists in Siberia and in prison. To have hindered such concessions by an untimely blow would have alienated many sympathies; whereas, as matters then stood, whatever reaction of feeling might take place would be in favour of, rather than against, the Nihilists.

It was also calculated that the people who came to the coronation would not be in the right frame of mind, or belong to a class likely to approve of a revolutionary blow. The Nihilists, who were always seeking to win the people over to their cause, would not have increased their popularity by disturbing a popular *fête*. The multitude, intoxicated by the free distribution of beer and spirits, might, on the contrary, have been led to massacre every one of known or suspected Liberal tendencies; and although the power of the autocracy would have lost much of its prestige, the revolutionary party would have been blamed by many of its best friends. On the other hand, the coronation offered an excellent opportunity for the Nihilist party to develop its strength. The whole force of the Government and its most intelligent spies were concentrated at Moscow, and the Nihilists profited by this auspicious occasion to spread their doctrines and to enrol supporters at St. Petersburg and other large centres. When the cat is away, the mouse doth play.

In this work they were amply successful. The strength of the party, at St. Petersburg especially, greatly increased during the preparations for the coronation. The Nihilist agents, free from the presence of the spies who knew them best, propagated their doctrines unchecked, and riots were the result Nor did the Nihilists think that their abstention during the coronation would be taken as a proof of their weakness. Their past was there to speak for them, and the most recent as well as previous arrests showed how they counted partisans in every class of society, among those who were nearest, as well as among those who were farthest removed from, the person of the Tsar.

At the same time, as I myself had reason to know, there were at the coronation officials and others, secretly at the orders of the Nihilist party, near enough to the Emperor to have struck a fatal blow if the dread word of command had been given. Indeed, it was to be feared that some over-zealous partisan would, on his own responsibility, and in defiance of orders to the contrary, throw a small dynamite hand-grenade, or otherwise seek to take the life of the Tsar. Fortunately, however, the discipline of the party was not broken, although to some the temptation to do so must have been great. Apart from these hidden friends of Nihilism, a few well-known conspirators also contrived to be present at the coronation, in spite of all the efforts of the police to discover and capture them. There was no special reason to induce them to be in Moscow at such a time; but the Russian Nihilist is particularly foolhardy, and never seems so happy as when defying fate and the police.

A few years later I made the acquaintance in London of a well-known Russian refugee, who had been connected with the Executive Committee, and the conversation turned on the Tsar's coronation. I remarked that I had never seen a more magnificent pageant. *'Nor I either,'* said my Nihilist friend, who then explained, to my great surprise, that he had also been in the thick of it all.

The coronation period formed but a delusive lull in the fierce warfare between the terrorists and the Tsar. It had been preceded in April by another mass trial at St Petersburg, which showed that the Nihilist organisation could boast of members in the higher ranks of the army, and that its operations were conducted with great ability and daring. Five officers of a Mingrelian regiment had been cashiered on account of their connection with the revolutionary movement; and, at the trial referred to, it was proved that one of the accused was in possession of several treasonable letters, written to him by a Nihilist at the time that the latter was a close prisoner in the island-fortress of Saints Peter and Paul - letters which could not possibly have been penned and sent out without the direct help of the gaol officials. At this trial, too, it came out in evidence that, apart from having organised a Red Cross Committee for helping imprisoned members of the confederacy, the Nihilists had also established a kind of factory for the forging of foreign passports the seals and stamps of the facsimiles produced in court having been imitated so closely that they could barely be distinguished from those issued by the various European Governments.

Towards the end of this year the Tsar was thrown into a state of extreme consternation by the audacious murder of Colonel Soudeikin, chief of the secret police, a man who was hated by the Nihilists as their most active and dangerous foe. As head of the 'Secret Anti-Nihilist Society,' or 'Society for Active Resistance to the Nihilists,' founded in 1882, he had done good service in discovering some of the chief haunts of the terrorists, and tracking down their leaders. He was, therefore, condemned to die, his appointed executioner being one Degaieff, who was employed as a decoy duck to lure Nihilists to his house, where they might be watched by the police. It was in this house that he treacherously shot Colonel Soudeikin and his nephew while drinking tea, which is the beer of Russia. About the same time the Nihilists issued a manifesto contrasting the peaceful life led by the Tsar during his visits to Denmark, with the incessant anxieties of which he was the victim while immured in his palace-prison at Gatchina, and declaring that he would never enjoy peace in his own country until he had granted a Constitution to his long-suffering people.

The following year (1884) was also rendered memorable by another mass trial of Nihilists at St Petersburg (October), which, while letting in more light on their aims and methods, filled the soul of the Tsar with dread and darkness. For it showed him, above all things, that his very army, at once the emanation and the mainstay of his absolute power, was gradually falling a prey to the propagandists of revolution and the practitioners of terror. Among the fourteen Nihilists now put upon their trial for 'high treason' were six officers, one of them a Lieut-Colonel Aschenbrenner, and another a naval man, Baron Stromberg. The former had banded the officers of his regiment into a revolutionary groups and bound them over to the payment of regular money contributions for the promotion of its aims.

But by far the most interesting figure among this group of revolutionaries was a lady, the wife of a physician, Vera Filipoff by name, who had been arrested in the previous year by Colonel Soudeikin, before he was murdered, while on her way from the south of the Empire in order to take part in a plot for assassinating its head in the same way as Sophie Perofsky had participated in the plot to 'remove' Alexander II. The tactics of this Vera Filipoff had been of a singularly bold and original kind Her sphere of action was the army, of which she sought to gain over the officers by offering to surrender her beautiful person to their will in return for a written undertaking on their part to restrain their men from firing on the people in the event of a rising. Such a document made every officer who succumbed to the temptation of her charms - and the number was a large one - the unconditional instrument of her self-sacrificing purpose. Eight of the accused, including Madam Filipoff herself, were condemned to die, and six to imprisonment, though the Tsar only signed the death-warrants of Baron Stromberg and Lieutenant Rogatscheff, commuting the sentences of the others into penal servitude for life.

About this time the police made a great capture in the person of one Lopatin, who had eluded their search for nearly sixteen long years. In his lodging was found a quantity of dynamite and some documents, which enabled the police to make numerous arrests, both in the capital and the provinces. In Odessa (to quote only one of the Nihilist incidents which otherwise marked the course of this terroristic year), Marie Kalyushny, the daughter of a reputable merchant, shot at a *gendarmerie* Colonel Ketansky, but missed her aim, and was drafted off to penal servitude for twenty years.

The year 1885 was a quieter one, on the whole, in the Nihilist camp, though the police again succeeded in unearthing and frustrating several plots against the life of the Tsar. When searching a private house at Kharkoff, where a secret printing-press, weapons, and dynamite were discovered, a police inspector was shot dead by a student named Lissionski, who was thereupon tried and hanged for the crime. But worse than all, Warsaw had been discovered to be the seat of a most serious conspiracy, headed by a justice of the peace called Bardoffski; and about two hundred persons, mostly belonging to the working class, were arrested. Four of the ringleaders were hanged, and others sent to penal servitude or deported. In September another plot against the Emperor was discovered - the third within three months. Again, in October, several officers of various corps and grades were convicted of affiliation to the terrorists - army propaganda being greatly facilitated by the abuses of the military administration, by the spirit prevailing in special schools, by the smallness of the officers' pay, as well as by the inferior social standing enjoyed by the line as compared with the Guards.

In the following year (1886) the Tsar was a good deal on the wing, travelling to Sebastopol, where he issued his stirring appeal to the Black Sea Fleet, as a prelude to his repudiation of the Berlin Treaty clause referring to Batoum; and Europe was now presented with the curious spectacle of a monarch who thus dared to brave the displeasure, and even the active hostility, of the foreign Powers, hurrying from end to end of his Empire through what was virtually a lane of troops to protect him from the bombs, and mines, and other machinations of his own subjects. Every bridge, every culvert, every level-crossing of the railway lines by which he journeyed was guarded by well-tried sentries, and the whole route patrolled by soldiers within sight of each other. The Imperial train itself was always divided into several sections, so as to make it impossible for the public to guess which portion carried the person of the Tsar himself; and his Majesty's destination was never known until he had reached it. Such was the mode of travelling enjoined by fear upon the sovereign who had hoped to build his throne on the hearts and affections of his subjects.

And then, how did he live - at Gatchina, for example? Let the following description show: 'The park surrounding the Castle is admirably planted. Nature, however, has greatly assisted the gardeners in their work. The park, which is surrounded by a strong wall, contains two small lakes and a rivulet. The forest adjoining the park is also enclosed. These enclosures have been constructed within the last five years at enormous cost. The surveillance in the Castle and around the park is extremely strict. The roads leading to Gatchina are constantly patrolled, and no individual is permitted to pass without exhibiting his papers. The railway station, although used exclusively by the Court, is also strictly watched. Persons who are not in the service of the Court cannot enter a train or alight at the Gatchina station.

'Round the wall of the park is stationed a chain of sentries placed at distances of twenty-five metres, who are changed every hour, in order that the surveillance may be vigorously applied. Entry into the park and Caatle is not permitted, even to the servants or to the *employés* of the Imperial Cabinet without the presentation of a special card, the colour of which is changed every week. Besides this, all persons residing in the Castle, whatever their rank and station may be, are forbidden to lock their doors either by day or night General Richter, General Inspector of the Imperial residences, and General Tsherevin, Chief of the Police, are entitled to make investigations in the apartments of the castle whenever they think proper. Gatchina is surrounded by a positive entrenched camp, and one would hardly believe, in passing by it on the railway, that a whole army was there simply to protect the life of one man, the ruler of 240,000,000 of people.'

Of the precautions of every kind which it was thought necessary to take in the Emperor's own home, some idea may be formed from the fact that a scientific man of some eminence was specially employed to search for Mores or other indications of electric batteries in the apartments, corridors, and outlying buildings of the Imperial Palace. Once, so it was said, at Livadia, the Tsar picked up in his palace a beautifully painted Easter egg. On opening it he found a small silver dagger, two ivory-carved death's heads, and a slip of paper, on which, with the customary Easter salutation, 'Christ is risen,' were the words, 'We also shall rise again.'

Here is another story, *ben trovato, si non è vero*: 'The Tsar, while lately turning over an album of family photographs, found in it the signed photograph of a Nihilist who was executed for having been an accomplice in the assassination of his Majesty's father. How the photograph came to be in the album could not be found out, although all the servants were subjected to a strict examination.'

On March 13, 1887, the anniversary of his father's murder, the Emperor and his Court, as usual, attended the commemoration service in the fortress-church of Saints Peter and Paul; and on returning to the station to take train for Gatchina, his Majesty was informed by the Chief of the Police that he had just had another most miraculous escape from assassination. The police had arrested in the Grand Morskaia thoroughfare six young men, who had posted themselves there to take off the Emperor on his way back from church. Three of these student-youths carried bombs made to look like books. The largest of them was found to contain five pounds of dynamite, and 251 small leaden cubes filled with strychnine, the slightest injury from any one of which would have caused immediate death. It can well be imagined how the Tsar felt on receiving this communication, but meanwhile, if we are to believe one of his Majesty's admirers and eulogists, he said nothing to those about him. 'He went down to Gatchina. with his wife and children, laughing and talking in the carriage as if nothing had happened. Not until the children had left for the Palace, and the Emperor and his wife were driving alone through the Park, did he break the news to the Empress. She, poor thing, of less iron nerve than her husband, broke down utterly and wept. Small wonder that a woman, to whom thus suddenly has been revealed the charged mine over which she has so lightly passed, shuddered with horror. Not so her husband. 'I am ready,' he said simply; 'I will do my duty at any cost.'

Shortly after the Tsar received a letter from the Executive Committee informing him that it had decreed his death, and that fifty persons had been entrusted with the execution of this sentence; while he was equally bombarded by manifestoes from the moderate sections of the revolutionary party demanding a Constitution. The trial of those who had been arrested in connection with the plot of March 13 - fifteen in number, including three women and nine University students, mostly Poles and Cossacks - began, with closed doors, on April 27, and lasted till May 10. According to the Crown Prosecutor, these persons had formed a plot to kill the Tsar in the previous autumn, though their purpose was deferred. They were all condemned to death, but only five were strung up, the rest being sent to the mines. A few weeks later another batch of twenty-one terrorists were tried and condemned; while in November of the same year eighteen officers were put upon their trial for having taken part in the Nihilist propaganda and sent to the mines in Siberia, though the Tsar subsequently commuted these sentences into degradation to the ranks.

These Nihilist trials had the usual effect of increasing the stringency of the measures already taken to prevent the spread of Liberal ideas. The 'Women's Higher Educational Institute' at St Petersburg was closed, and several Professors of the Universities of Moscow and Kharkoff respectively were dismissed on a charge of liberal tendencies. But this was not all. On learning that several of those implicated in the plot of March 13 were teachers and students who did not belong to the class of nobles, the Tsar wrote upon the report, with his own hand, the words, 'Education to be abolished!' On the strength of this peremptory demand, it was then decreed (June 18) that the 'children of dependents,' including servants of all kinds, were to be forbidden admission to the middle and higher schools. As the term 'dependents' was a very elastic one, it practically empowered each official to exclude from the schools nearly all the children of his district. The result was to withdraw from the lower classes all opportunity of improving their position, and thus augment the elements of popular discontent from which the Nihilists drew the main elements of their militant power. Mrs Partington's mop was nothing to all this.

In the following year Europe again shuddered on hearing that the special train in which the Imperial family were returning home from the south of Russia had been completely wrecked in a deep cutting near a place called Borki, while rushing along at a speed of about sixty-four versts an hour. Of all who were travelling by the train twenty-one were killed and thirty-seven injured. The Tsar himself had a most miraculous escape, his saloon carriage being terribly wrecked; while the Empress also was only saved by little more than a hair's-breadth. The Tsar's first thought, of course, was that this terrific smash-up had been the work of the Nihilists; but further inquiry seemed to support the theory that the accident was simply due to the rottenness of the sleepers, which had given way and sent the train off the rails. Even the woodwork of this permanent way was no exception to the general condition of rottenness in the State of Russia - 'a nation rotten before it was ripe' - as Cobbett said. On arriving at Moscow their Majesties drove to the cathedral and remained for some time in silent prayer before the image of the Virgin, and now a handsome memorial church stands near the spot where the Ruler of All the Russias was so miraculously preserved. 'May Providence,' he said, in a manifesto on his return home, 'who protected our life, consecrated to the welfare of our beloved fatherland, give us strength to fulfil faithfully to the end all those great duties which, by His will, have been laid upon us!'

By some it was positively asserted that the wrecking of the Imperial train was no accident, but the result of a well-planned plot, and that even its author also fell a victim to his own devilish design. This may or not have been, for in Russia it is next to impossible to get at the truth of such things; but, in any case, the effect which the horrible catastrophe produced upon the mind and nerves of Alexander III was just as great as if he had known it to be work of the Nihilists. For even though the sleepers were proved to be rotten, it could not be disproved that they had not been tampered with, and doubt in such cases is no less terrible than certainty. At any rate, 'from the shock which his nervous system then received the Tsar never thoroughly recovered. It is the taproot of most of the ailments from which he has suffered ever since. An eye-witness of that blood-curdling scene assured me that it was enough to deprive an ordinary man of his reason. His carriage was blown to shreds, his faithful servants lay dead or dying, his loving wife stood trembling like an aspen-leaf amid corpses and blood-stained fragments; and, when he looked around for his children, dreading the terrible possibilities as much as the torturing uncertainty, his little daughter, her bright eyes filled with tears, threw her hands about his neck, and exclaimed, amid sobs: 'Oh, papa dear! now they'll come and murder us all!"

'After this the Emperor grew more moody and reserved than ever before. He lost his confidence in the ability of the most trusted and the devotion of the most intelligent of his Ministers. He avoided even more systematically than before all public ceremonies and amusements. The officers grumbled that he was so seldom to be seen at a review; the aristocracy were dissatisfied that he should avail himself of every slight pretext to stop the annual balls at the Palace, and that, when they were given, supper was always served at half-past twelve A.M., and the apartments deserted before two. From this time forward the Emperor began to show a strong dislike to mount a horse, and his nervousness was painfully manifest to all his attendants. When he appeared at the annual feasts of the Horse Guards and Cavalier Guards, the public was selected with the utmost care, none being admitted except with a card of invitation signed by the Commander of the Regiment; and even among this exclusive set a number of private detectives were judiciously scattered throughout the *manège*.[2]

In his book about Russia, M. Leroy-Beaulieu had written: 'If there is one sure thing, it is that Russian terrorism never had a Mazzini at its head, leisurely conceiving abroad deeds to be executed by blindly obedient agents at home. The political trials have shown that all the great conspiracies were planned on the spot by men who had never breathed the air of the West. Instead of being the starting-point and the cradle of conspiracy, Switzerland and England are its refuge, and often its grave. But presently Switzerland turned out to be more the cradle than the grave of Nihilism. For in March, 1889, the explosion of a bomb at Zürich, which killed one of the Russian students who were experimenting with it, led to the discovery that the terrorists had established here something like a factory of murderous explosives, many of which had undoubtedly found their way into the Russian Empire; and it was even believed that some of the bombs were meant to be used against the Tsar on the occasion of his visit to Berlin that autumn. In any case, numerous arrests were now again made at St Petersburg, Moscow, Odessa, Kharkoff, and Kief, in connection with the discoveries made at Zürich, and traces were found of another clear conspiracy to 'remove' the Emperor. Much valuable information was at this time given to the police by a Nihilist leader named Tikhomiroff, who had come to see the error of his ways, and ratted to the side against which he had hitherto waged incessant and implacable war.

Hitherto the party of reform, of revolution, in Russia had sought to achieve its aims by dynamite bombs and revolver bullets. But now there stepped out of the ranks one who resolved to see what effect could be produced upon the mind, if not the body, of the Tsar by a 'paper bullet of the brain.' This was Madame Tzebrikova, a lady in her fifty-fourth year, who had devoted all her life to writing, and was especially versed in English and American literature. Suddenly the suffering state of her country seized hold upon her heart, and she resolved to do a bold thing and a great. In spite of the law, the custom, which made such an action penal in the highest degree, she would appeal directly to the Tsar, and impeach him of tyranny, injustice, and misrule, before a jury of the whole civilised world.

Accordingly she hastened to repair to Paris, where the printing of her thoughts could be accomplished, and drew up the following letter, of which she sent the manuscript direct to the Emperor, and printed copies to all the Russian newspapers, as well as to the leading journals of England and Europe - a letter of whidi I cannot do better than quote the material parts, as constituting at once the best description and bitterest indictment of the state of Russia under Alexander III which any one has ever penned:

'YOUR MAJESTY,

'The laws of my country forbid free speech. All that is honest in Russia is forced to look on at the arbitrary despotism of the officials, the persecution of thought, the moral and physical ruin of the rising generation, the slavery of the oppressed and plundered people - and to be silent. Liberty is one of the positive needs of society, and, sooner or later, but inevitably, the time will come when the citizens, grown out of tutelage and weary of patience, will speak aloud the daring language of maturity, and authority will be forced to submit. In the life of individuals also comes a moment when the grievous shame of being made, by enforced silence, unwilling accomplices in evil and fialsehood, drives them to risk all that is dear to them, and say to him in whose hands is the power, - one word from whom could destroy so much wrong and shame in our fatherland: 'Take care what you do, and what, knowingly or not knowingly, you let be done.'

'The Russian Emperors see and hear only what they are allowed to see and hear by the officials who stand between them and the masses. The fearful death of Alexander II cast an ominous gloom over your succession to the throne, and your adrisers have persuaded you that his death resulted from the free ideas fostered by the best part of his reign.

'Our terrorists were created, not by the reforms of the last reign, but by the insufficiency of those reforms. Your advisers scare you from a progressive policy, and prompt you with a policy in the spirit of Nicholas I, simply because the former is dangerous to the absolute power of ministers and officials, who find secrecy and despotism to their advantage.

'The publicity of justice has been reduced almost to a cypher. Now, in future, crimes of officials are to be tried in secret The last security which those of your subjects who are not State servants had against the injustice of the authorities is taken from them.

'The result of our censorship is that the young seize eagerly, upon not only what is true in our foreign and 'underground' Press, but upon all the nonsense in it. If free speech is persecuted, that means that the authorities are afraid of truth….The experience, both of former reigns and of your own, should have taught your Majesty that persecution, as internal policy, does not attain its ends. Persecution is the best way to stamp out among the people love for the Tsar. It is already dying out.

'In educated and official society the adoration of the Tsar has died out; its last days were at the beginning of the Crimean war. A large proportion of the official body consists of men who themselves do not believe in the lastingness of the present system. After the 1st (13th) of March 1881 the panic-stricken provincial officials imagined that there was a revolution in St Petersburg, and that the terrorists had founded a constituent assembly. The generality of officers and officials care only to make their career. They themselves see plainly what they are doing, but their motto is: 'It will last our time and our children's, and after us the deluge.'

'But such a motto is unfit to guide the supreme power, which is responsible, not only for the present, but for the future of the land. Intentional evil cannot be its aim, but an autocratic monarch is inevitably responsible for every atom of wrong done in his name.

'The whole system is driving into the ranks of malcontents, into revolutionary propaganda, even those to whom blood and violence are hateful. For one incautious word - for a few pages of 'underground' literature (often taken up out of mere curiosity) a lad - a child - is a political offender. There have been political prisoners, children of fifteen - even of fourteen years old - in solitary confinement. The Government that rules over one hundred millions is afraid even of children. The broken-down, embittered young generation turns to revolution. Blood is horrible to me on which ever side it is shed, but when bloodshed on one side is rewarded with a decoration, and on the other side with a gallows-rope, it is easy to understand which bloodshed will have for the young the charm of heroism.

'Besides the punishments by sentence of a court, we have 'administrative' sentences, by means of which the Government disposes of its enemies when there is not evidence enough to try them. But what is this if not arbitrary lawlessness?

'Political prisoners are the defenceless victims of arbitrary despotism that reaches downright brutality. But no measures of coercion and terror, from administrative' exile to the gallows, attain their end.

'And, after all, what is the use of all this oppression and persecution? Why should free speech be suppressed and public justice abolished? Is it for the sake of the peaceful development of Russia? Or is it for the sake of autocracy - that is, really for the advantage of the officials? Your Majesty's self is proved powerless to struggle against abuses, even if the court for the judging of Ministers should really be instituted. You are inevitably powerless, because all the Imperial measures are founded upon the same slavery and enforced silence of society.

'Freedom of speech, personal security, freedom of meetings, full publicity of justice, education easy of access for all talents, suppression of administrative despotism, the convoking of a National Assembly for which all classes can choose thdr delegates - in these alone is our salvation.

'The measure of patience is overflowing, the future is terrible. If a general revolution, which could overturn the throne, is as yet remote, still district mutinies, such as the Pugachoff riots, are more than possible. The people will grow familiar with blood. Honest citizens await with horror the miseries which this system of all-powerful administration must, sooner or later, inevitably bring, and they are silent; but their children and grandchildren will not be silent.

'You are an autocratic Tsar, limited by laws which you yourself make and alter at your will, more limited by officials whom you yourself appoint and who disobey your laws. One word from you can cause throughout Russia a revolution which will leave a bright trace in history. If, instead, you choose to leave a dark trace, you will not hear the curses of posterity; but your children will hear them, and you are leaving them a terrible heritage.

'You, your Majesty, are one of the most powerful monarchs in the world; I am a working unit in the hundred millions whose fate you hold in your hands; but none the less, I, in my conscience, fully recognise my moral right and duty as a Russian woman to say what I have said.

'Marya Tzebrikova.'

What effect did this letter produce on the mind of Alexander III? After reading it through, the Tsar was said to have exclaimed: 'That is all very well; but what on earth does all this matter to *her?*'! As Madame Tzebrikova was not in his service, he could not understand why she interfered in a matter which did not concern her personally. On returning to Russia, which she at once did after getting her letter written and printed, Madame Tzebrikova was at once arrested, and sentenced to two years' 'internment' at Yarensk, a small town of Vologda, in the North. In the eyes of the authorities her letter was a grave personal affront to the Tsar, *lèse-majesté* and more, and the customary way of dealing with persons guilty of that crime in Russia is to lock them up in a madhouse, where they soon go mad in earnest.

To do this, however, with Madame Tzebrikova would have been impossible; her letter had attracted too much attention, and made too much noise throughout all Europe for that. At the same time, custom demanded that she should be punished somehow, and deportation to a remote comer of the Empire was the form chosen. Her whole conduct had shown that her letter was intended to appeal to public opinion in Russia more than to the Emperor, and in that sense her epistle will doubtless prove an epoch-marking event in the page of Russian history. 'It was an act of high civil courage,' as a writer in *Free Russia* said of it - 'a grand example for those persons who share her views but remain silent, sanctifying by this silence the very things of which they disapprove.'

In this same year (1890) St Petersburg was again the scene of the trial of a batch of terrorists, which ended (November 12) in a sentence of hanging being passed on a woman, Sophie Günsberg, and three of her male accomplices. Another lady implicated in this plot were one Olga Ivanofsky, nearly related to a high-placed official, and several artillery officers. The Emperor commuted the sentence on Sophie Günsberg in consideration of her sex. All these conspirators were proved to have entertained relations with the bomb manufacturers at Zürich, as well as with the Nihilist colony in Paris.

Some members of this latter colony had planned another attempt on the Emperor's life, and were preparing to leave for Russia to carry out their nefarious purpose when they were surprised and seized by the police. Several bombs were in their possession. The Paris tribunal, before which they were at once hailed, sentenced them to three years' imprisonment. A few months later, General Sellverskoff, formerly director of the St Petersburg police, who had come to Paris to watch the movements of the Nihilists, was murdered in the most cunning and audacious manner by a Russian Pole named Padlevski, who, with the help of his French sympathisers, managed to 'plod away o' the hoof, seek shelter, pack.' The Nihilists were determined to show the Tsar that the arm of their organisation was a very long one, and they had done so.

Of course, when the terrible famine afflicted Russia in 1891, the Nihilists were ready with a manifesto, in which they described this calamity as the inevitable consequence of the system of government, against which the only remedy was the convocation of a national assembly. A recrudescence of the revolutionary agitation was the consequence of the famine. In seven towns secret printing presses and numerous copies of proclamations - addressed to the 'persecuted and oppressed nation' - were found by the police ; no fewer than 240 persons belonging to the conspiracy - including fourteen officials, four schoolmasters, and six officers - were arrested at Moscow; while sixty more arrests were made at St Petersburg among the higher classes of society. But perhaps the greatest find of the year was four large boxes of dynamite which had been discovered in the Customs department of the French Exhibition at Moscow, and which were meant for use on the occasion of the Tsar's visit. As a consequence, the very greatest precautions were taken to secure the safety of the Emperor's person when, with his consort, he went to visit the Exhibition in compliment to his ardent political wooers, the French.[3]

The general distress of the country, combined with the harsh, repressive measures taken by the Government against all races and religions, other than the pure ones of ancient and holy Russia, gave a great stimulus to the revolutionary movement throughout the year 1892, though this was meanwhile manifested more by the propagandist agency of the secret word than the open deed. St Petersburg was again flooded with revolutionary leaflets, and the usual arrests were made; but though a reward of a hundred thousand roubles had been offered for such information as would lead to the discovery of the printing office of the *Narodnaia Volia*, or 'People's Will,' the terrorists in the secret remained as proof against the temptation as the followers of Prince Charlie after a price of £30,000 had been put upon his head. 'The people,' said one of the revolutionary leaflets, ' do not understand that all their grievances come from the close bonds between the Tsar and the nobility. Our Tsar is the Tsar of the nobility; he is not the Tsar of the moujiks.'

But it was not only the terrorists who talked and wrote like this. For see what even M. Leroy-Beaulieu says: 'The one and only basis on which social and political order rests in Russia is the people's trust in the Sovereign. But indestructible as this faith of the moujik appears to this day, it were unwise to place entire reliance on it. In the cities, especially the capitals, the audacity of the conspirators, the seeming impotence of the Government, the shrinking attitude of the Tsar, well-nigh invisible in the mazes of his half-desert palace - all these things, prior to the coronation of Alexander III, appeared to have somewhat shaken the prestige that ages have woven round autocracy.' Russia has no Tsar any more,' men of the lower classes said in St Petersburg in the spring of 1882.'

What had been the effect of all this reign of terror on the nerves and character of Alexander III? 'The Tsar,' wrote Mr 'Lanin,' 'has been frequently accused of cowardice - an indictment to which, it must be admitted, many undeniable facts lend a strong colouring of probability. Thus it has been alleged in support of the charge that he seldom drives about the city alone, and when not escorted by a body of Cossacks is usually accompanied by her Majesty the Empress. His profound seclusion at Gatchina, where for a considerable period he hid himself even from the bulk of his own officers, likewise created a most unfavourable impression, which is by no means yet removed. Again, the sight of the armies that guard the railway lines along which he happens to be travelling, the elaborate system of espionage, and the immoral practice of employing agents provocateurs, who sometimes organise the crime which they discover, have contributed to impart consistency to a charge which his creditable career as an oiHcer should have amply sufficed to refute....

'Any man who saw, as he did, his own father mutilated and bleeding to death; who himself, more than once, narrowly escaped a similar fate; whose train and carriage were blown to shreds; whose wife stood trembling in the desolate steppe among fragments and corpses; and whose bright little daughter threw her hands round his neck, and exclaimed with sobs: 'Oh, papa, now theyll come and murder us all' - a man who has had such experiences as these may surely be acquitted of cowardice, even if his nerves be no longer of iron....Whatever his views about fatalism in the abstract, he entertains not the slightest doubt that the hairs of his head are numbered.'

Yet one of his last acts in his terribly wearing and unequal conflict with the secret apostles of terror, was the creation of what might be called a special ministry for his personal protection. In June 1894, General Tcherevin, who, as chief of the political police, had been repeatedly aimed at by the foes of an uncompromising despotism, was appointed General-in-Waiting, a special office revived on this occasion for the purpose of guarding the personal safety of his Majesty. In constant attendance on the Tsar, he was practically invested with dictatorial powers in any town which his Majesty might be visiting or passing through. Not only could he change at will the head police-masters, but, if he chose, he could even interfere in the administration of the Government departments. 'Now,' said a writer in Free Russia, 'what must we think of a monarch who prefers to take such precautions, side by side with reactionary measures, rather than meet the just claims of his subjects for liberty?'

But meanwhile the greatest Terrorist of all struck aside the protecting shield which General Tcherevin had thrown around the person of his apprehensive Sovereign, and laid the sorely-tried Ruler of All the Russias on that bed of physical suffering from which he was destined never to rise again. Yet, even when Alexander III was lying on this bed of death, he continued to be the object of the bitterest opposition and invective on the part of the men who had vainly sought to take his life; and though the following proclamation - plastered with bomb, revolver, and dagger, in some blood-red substance, and signed on behalf of the terrorists - which was dated from Switzerland while the Tsar was already in the Arms of Death - although, I say, this proclamation must revolt the hearts of all right-minded people, nevertheless I feel that I should be doing historical injustice to this impartial record of the Russian Reign of Terror by forbearing to quote it, if for nothing else, as a melancholy proof of the fiendish passions which may inflame the breasts of desperate and disrupted men:

'TO OUR BROTHERS, THE OPPRESSED IN RUSSIA.

'The tyrant Alexander III., the autocrat Tsar and Hangman, the assassin of Michaeleff, Russakoff, Kibaltchik, Jeliaboff, Sophie Perovsky, Jessé Helfmann, and many others, the purveyor of the Siberian galleys, the persecutor of the Jews, is on the point of expiating his crimes.

'He is dying of a mysterious illness. Well-merited punishment! The venal science of his Zacharins, his Hirsches, and his Popoffs can do nothing to prolong a life which has been devoted to violence and oppression.

'At length the monster is going to disappear. Hurrah!

'The day has passed when a man ought to be able, by right of birth, to dispose of the liberty and the lives of a hundred millions of other men.

'Let his son, the Tsarevitch, as well as his ambitious rivals, the Grand Dukes Vladimir and Michael - who are ready to assassinate, in accordance with the traditions of the Romanoff family, to get possession of a bloody heritage - let them all thoroughly understand that every hour, and at every step, they will find themselves face to face with the inflexible will of the Revolutionists.

'Let us leave to the hypocritical Liberals the task of covering with flowers the horrid corpse of the scoundrel who is leaving this world after having too long dishonoured it So long as the Russian slaves do not possess the land, so long as an infernal autocracy, served by a rapacious and shameless feudality, makes Russia a disgrace to the civilised world, we shall always applaud any blow of destiny - or provoke it.

'LONG LIVE LIBERTY AND REVOLUTION!'

NOTES

1. The manifesto issued by the Emperor on this occasion bad no political importance whatever, being only a long list of the remission of taxes, fines, and punishments. These remissions related to the poll-tax and emancipation tax, and to arrears of the peasants' salt, and spirit taxes, and the repayment of sums overdrawn for expenses during the late Turkish war. Criminals condemned, without deprivation of civil rights, had one-third of their terms remitted. Exiles to Siberia for life had their sentences commuted to 20 years' penal servitude, at the discretion of the governor of the province concerned. The application of the manifesto to the cases of State criminals or political refugees was left in the hands of the Minister of the Interior. Those still lying under sentence for the Polish troubles in 1863 were to be free from all further penal consequences; but confiscated property was not to be restored.

Another disappointment and disenchantment now awaited the Nihilists. The secret societies had inscribed their flags with the words 'Land and Liberty' (*Zemlià i Vòlia*); and, in order to keep alive popular illusion and cupidity, the mischief-makers from time to time started rumours as to a new distribution of land among the peasantry, especially about the time of the Tsax's coronation (1883). But at a banquet then given at Moscow to the elders of the niral communes, his Majesty took occasion to say: 'Give no heed to the absurd rumours which are circulate concerning a redistribution of lands and a free extension of the lands belonging to you. These rumours are the work of our enemies. All property - yours as well as other people's - must be inviolable.'

2. I am here quoting from a most admirably written and well-informed article on Alexander III, contributed to the *Daily Telegraph* of October 16, 1894, by its St Petersburg correspondent.

3. A good story was told in connection with the Tsar's visit to the art section of this French Exhibition. By chance somebody placed in the ante-room of the salon where the Exhibition was to take place, the statue of a nude woman. The Marshal of the Court, who preceded the Tsar, frightened by the presence of that

nudity, and fearing that it would shock the modesty of his Majesty or that of the ladies who accompanied him, got hold of a curtain and threw it over the statue. 'Leave it alone,' sadd the Emperor, who had seen everything; 'I know that the costume she wears is one which the French most admire.'

CHAPTER X

ILLNESS AND DEATH

'Weep, Russia!' - A Sore Saint - Monseigneur of Kharkoff *versus* Professor Zacharin - Origin and Course of Illness – Belovishaya - Spala - Story of a Duck - Professor Leyden - Livadia, the Russian Cannes - Father Ivan, the 'Wonder-Worker' - Corfu - Princess Alix of Hesse - Diary of Disease - An Angel on Earth - Death - Last Hours - Nature of Malady - A Funeral-Drama in Five Acts - Yalta—Sebastopol - Moscow - St Petersburg - Processional Pageant - Scene in the Fortress Church - A Prayer *by* the dead – 'The Tsar is dead! Long live the Tsar!'

'WEEP, Russia!' was the title of a fly-sheet threnody issued by a St Petersburg journal, and eagerly bought up by the sorrowing crowds in the streets on the evening of Thursday, Nov. 1, 1894. For at about six o'clock on that evening there had reached the capital from Livadia, on the Crimean shore of the Black Sea, the following telegram: 'The Emperor Alexander III passed to his rest with God at a quarter-past two o'clock this afternoon, peacefully and quietly.' The mighty Colossus of the North, of whom some one had beautifully said, in illustration of the vast breadth of his dominions, that his head was pillowed on snow, while his feet lay swathed in flowers - this Colossus of the North had passed away, leaving his eldest son, Nicholas Alexandrovitch, to reign in his stead.

All this had been comparatively sudden. The Emperor Frederick had lingered for nearly a year after the first diagnosis of his fatal illness. But the Emperor Alexander only remained the object of public solicitude for about a month. It was Oct. 1, 1894, when his state was first known to be really serious, and by November 1 he was a corpse. The best medical science procurable in Europe had been summoned to his bedside, in addition to the most successful 'wonder-worker' in all Russia, in the person of Father Ivan of Cronstadt; but neither science nor religion could arrest the course of his Majesty's malady, which ultimately carried him off on All Saints' Day, of all days in the year. For like David I of Scotland, Alexander III of Russia had been a 'sore saint,' if not for the Crown, at least for many of his subjects.

'Dead the great Tsar, - his hands upon his breast,
   His face unruffled 'mid a world's alarms,

And all his hopes and yearnings laid to rest,
   And all his prowess, all his latent harms;
   For nevermore, when trumpets call to arms,
Shall this man send his legions east or west.

Solemn the scene - and tender and sublime
That last leave-taking, when the requiem bells
Rang out, on All Saints' Day, the dolorous chime
   That spoke of anguish mixed with fond farewells;
   And far and near, in towns and citadels,
The tocsin tolling like the wail of Time.'[1]

For some considerable time prior to the Emperor being struck down, it had been noticed that a curious kind of stagnation had overtaken the course of Russian affairs. The foreign policy of the Empire seemed to have lapsed into a strangely passive state, and it almost looked as if the ship of State were being allowed to drift along with wind and tide. At any rate, the course of that ship no longer appeared to indicate the grasp of a firm and energetic hand on the helm; and then when it became known that the master of the Imperial vessel was really ill, it was seen that these previous impressions had been justified by fact.

When the Emperor himself began to feel the presence of the shadow of the hand of Death we shall probably never know. But it is probable that the course of his fatal malady began towards the end of 1889, when he fell a victim to the influenza; and, on the other hand, the door to this disease was probably opened by the terrible shock to his nervous system which he had experienced at the railway accident of Borki in the previous year. Five years after, this frightful catastrophe (May, 1893), the Imperial family, while again on its way home from the Crimea, stopped at Borki to offer up a thanksgiving prayer in the church which had meanwhile been erected there; to commemorate their miraculous escape; and on this occasion the Emperor was received by the Archbishop of Kharkoff, who thus addressed him: 'The Emperors and Rulers round about thee are growing perplexed, the nations distrustful, and the whole world excited; but thy hand which guides the helm of the Empire trembleth not.'

It is greatly to be feared that, in thus addressing the Emperor, the Archbishop of Kharkoff did not really know what he was talking about, and that his Majesty himself must have felt the bitter mockery of Monseigneur's words; for by this time the Tsar must have been aware that his once powerful constitution had become a prey to the seeds of disease. But it was not till some time later that these seeds began to spring up. For the second time his Majesty fell a victim to influenza, and then Professor Zacharin of Moscow had to be summoned to St Petersburg. And now let this eminent specialist himself take up the tale:[2]

'The attack of influenza in January (1894) undoubtedly weakened the Emperor, but his health was already far from good. He had been severely weakened by an extraordinary bleeding from the nose, in the previous August, after which all the autumn he suffered from fever and bronchitis. The influenza in January was only the third step in the progress of the disease. I say nothing of the constant and excessive labours, accompanied by loss of sleep, which had gradually undermined the health of the Tsar. I was first called in January, and the daily chemical and microscopical examinations I made showed for a few days an insignificant quantity of albumen, a customary symptom of acute fevers; but there were no other signs of nephritis. Before my departure the albumen disappeared, not to reappear for more than a week. The action of the heart was normal.'

Dr Zacharin was then sent to the Caucasus, to attend the Grand Duke George, and on June 2 he returned to report upon the state of the young Prince personally to the Tsar, who permitted himself to be examined, with the following result: - 'I found the appetite good and the digestion quite in order after a supper of sour milk and prostokvasha rusks. There was some oppression of the chest; the lungs were sound, the action of the heart satisfactory. There was a slight cough, proceeding from a catarrh of the glottis, usually present with smokers. The Tsar was thinner, but not more than was desirable. He slept well, his head was clear, and his whole appearance that of a healthy man.'

Dr Zacharin went again to Peterhof in August, when he found certain signs of nephritis, the left ventricle of the heart enlarged, a weak, frequent pulse, sleeplessness, nausea, and urea, owing to the imperfect action of the kidneys. 'From these symptoms a diagnosis was formed, in which subsequently Professor Leyden agreed; and it was fully confirmed by the *post-mortem* examination, which also proved the comparatively short duration of the disease. In a report presented to the Tsar by myself and Dr Hirsch, we stated that the disease of the kidneys and the subsequent weakening of the heart constituted a mortal disease.'

'The contributing causes were overwork, the Tsar's habit of being out in all weathers, and especially the exceeding cold and damp of last summer. Another cause was the damp and cold of the ground floor of the Imperial apartments at Alexandria, near Peterhof; the bedroom there, in particular, was intensely cold, and in the highest degree damp. The Tsar could not bear heat, and always sought a cool place. It was only in August that I first saw these rooms, and I induced the Tsar to change them for a better room on the second floor, but by that time he had occupied the damp room nearly three months - namely, from the end of May to August 18.'

After this, 'the first time that he appeared in public every one who knew him was struck with the change in his appearance, and a whisper went round, 'He is very ill still.' At the launch of the 'Sissoy Veliky' he looked worse; in fact, it was patent to all observers that something much graver than a mere convalescence accounted for the shrunken giant form and the colourless drawn face. The summer trip to Belovishaya Pushta seemed to have a beneficial effect, and, amongst the grand old forests he loved so dearly, the Emperor, for a week or two, regained some of his health and spirit. The amelioration brought about by the change soon wore off, however, and before leaving for Spala, his Majesty was quickly running down again.'[3]

To account for the rapidity of this running-down process several pathetic stories were told about the Emperor having set at naught the advice of his physicians in order to gratify the overmastering impulses of his own parental affection. But from the fact that the incident referred to does not seem to have been alluded to as a *causa contribuens* in any of the medical reports, as well as from the circumstance that a 'duck' - ominous bird! - is made to figure in the more elaborate of the tales in question, I feel that I shall be robbing them neither of personal interest nor of historical dignity by relegating them to the subordinate position of a footnote to this narrative.[4]

In any case, at Spala his Majesty grew rapidly worse, and then it was decided to call in the celebrated specialist, Professor Leyden of Berlin, who fortunately happened to be at Warsaw, not far off, attending on General Gourko, the hero of the Balkans. Professor Leyden at once made his diagnosis, and to Dr Zacharin of Moscow was entrusted the painfully delicate task of communicating the truth to his Imperial patient. 'Your Majesty's malady,' he was reported on credible authority to have said, 'is incurable. With care and attention your valuable life may be prolonged for some months, but it is useless to conceal the fact that no remedies will avail beyond a certain period.' After this, the Emperor went to an adjoining room, where his wife and family were assembled. 'Zacharin,' he said, 'has just told me there is no hope,' and he seemed terribly affected by the intelligence.

For weeks past rumour had been busy with the condition of the Tsar's health, and now the truth became publicly known by the issue of the following official statement: 'Since the severe attack of influenza, from which the Tsar recovered in January last, his Majesty's health has not been fully restored. This summer, disease of the kidneys, nephritis, supervened, and this renders it necessary for his Majesty during the cold season to stay in a warm climate, in order that a cure may be better effected. Acting, therefore, upon the advice of Professors Zacharin and Leyden, the Tsar will make a temporary stay at Livadia.'

'Livadia,' wrote some one who evidently knew it well, 'stands on the eastern undercliff of the Crimea, a romantic strip of coast scenery into which our officers used now and then to make pleasant excursions towards the close of the famous siege. Even at that date there were fine country-houses in the neighbourhood, notably that of the Woronzoffs at Alupka; but Yalta, now a Muscovite rival to Cannes, was as yet a mere squalid collection of Tartar huts, and Alexander II, then heir-apparent to a stalwart, vigorous father, did not dream of the palatial villa in which some curious episodes of his erratic life were enacted. The domain of Livadia lies west of Yalta, within a short drive, the road thither winding between the steepish hill of Aï Petri on the right and the sea on the left, much as does the Corniche as you approach Turbia. Vineyards, olive-groves, plantations of fig-trees and pomegranates, and gardens bright with oleanders, roses, and flowers of all kinds, fringe the way.

'Alexander III does not occupy the palace of his father, which is, however, kept furnished exactly as it was in that Sovereign's lifetime. He has built himself a rather more modest dwelling-place not far distant, in the great park stretching from the thickly wooded mountains to the seashore. Around the two-storied structure gardens are laid out in English fashion, with trim walks and carpet-pattern beds, plenty of Maréchal Niel roses for the Tsarina's special delight, and fragments of classical stonework imported or found on the spot. Further afield may be seen well-stocked orchards, and vines which are said to yield strong and generous wine. The internal arrangements rather suggest comfort than splendour, the rooms being of moderate size and furnished very simply, but with admirable taste.'

This, then, was the sunny southern retreat, the Russian Cannes - lying 'right in the lap of the Black Sea, whose blackness hereabout is blue' to which Alexander III was sent to die. As the Crimea had broken the heart of his grandfather, so it was also destined to be the door of his own descent into the tomb. But the official bulletin which announced the impending removal of the Tsar from Spala to Livadia had not yet revealed the full gravity of his case. This only became apparent on its being announced that the Tsarevitch had now abandoned all idea of proceeding to Darmstadt on a visit to Princess Alix, his bride-elect, for which a special train had been in readiness a week and more, and that he would accompany his father to the South. At Spala the Emperor had been unable to get any sleep for several consecutive nights, in spite of the narcotics administered to him, but he bore the long journey to the Crimea wonderfully well, and even inspected a guard of honour at Sebastopol. After a good night's rest he took a couple of hours' drive with the Empress among the lovely scenery of his southern home, and it began to look as if God had listened to the fervent prayers for the Tsar's recovery which had been offered up by order in all the Russian churches.

But suddenly it was announced that Professor Leyden, who had meanwhile returned to Berlin, had received an urgent summons to repair to Livadia, along with all the members of the Imperial family. A similar message was also addressed to Father Ivan of Cronstadt, an 'upper priest' who was positively known to be a model of his class, and who was popularly believed to have inherited from the Divine Master whom he served some of those superhuman powers whose manifestation formed the basis and justification of the Christian creed.

'The 'miracle-worker,' Father Ivan,' wrote the Russian correspondent of a German journal, 'enjoys the highest authority among all Orthodox Russians. Many successes, and especially cures, are ascribed to the power of his prayers, and Orthodox Russians confidently apply to him in moments of dire distress. I myself have seen a Russian of respectable position, whose wife and child were ill in Odessa, sending a telegram to Ivan begging him to pray for their recovery. They both actually recovered, and the lady emphatically declares that she owes her life and that of her child solely to 'the Holy Man' in Cronstadt. Innumerable stories are told of him: he predicts everything; nothing is hidden from him. He devotes all the presents made to him to the poor, and his wife had, in consequence, to apply for help to the Tsar, who ordered a pension of three thousand roubles a year to be paid to her, and told her to let her husband do as he pleased. Wealthy people in all parts of the Russian Empire summon him when they are ill, and he is reported to be oftener travelling than at home. He is in the forties, and his aspect is that of an ascetic. Russians of the ordinary stamp, and this stamp is found in exceedingly high quarters, revere him as a living saint.'

On October 12 the Emperor and Empress visited Massandra, where they remained an hour and a half, driving through Yalta on their return; but four days later, Professor Leyden having meanwhile arrived, a bulletin declared that 'the disease of the kidneys showed no improvement, and that his Majesty's strength had diminished.' At the same time, the physicians added an expression of their hope 'that the climate of the south coast would have a beneficial effect on the health of the Tsar.' This latter sentence was inferred to imply that the plan of sending him to the island of Corfu had at last been abandoned owing to the already too advanced state of his disease. At Corfu the King of Greece had placed at his Imperial Majesty's disposal his charmingly situated residence of Monrepos, and already his Majesty's Master of the Household, together with a bevy of French upholsterers and other workmen, had gone thither to prepare the chateau for the Emperor's winter sojourn. 'But what is he,' as the first gravedigger says in *Hamlet*, 'that builds stronger than either the mason, the shipwright, or the carpenter?'

In the meantime, while babbling rumour was busy with all kinds of fantastical reports - about the appointment of a Regency among other things, an institution unknown to Russian history - the dying Tsar himself continued struggling manfully with his disease. 'Tell me the whole truth,' he was reported to have said to Professor Leyden. 'How long have I to live?' 'That is in God's hand,' the Professor replied; 'but with this disease I have seen cases of marvellous cures.' 'Can I still live a fortnight?' 'And when the doctor said, 'Yes, certainly,' he begged them to send to Darmstadt for Princess Alix, the bride elect of his son and successor.

Travelling as fast as ever she could. Princess Alix arrived at Livadia on October 22, and was received with great military and other honours. 'The meeting of the Tsar with the Princess Alix, whom he had for a long time been craving to see, strongly excited the patient, in spite of the joy it caused him. The physicians had feared this, but the night passed favourably.' Such was the statement in an official account of the course of the Tsar's illness, from which I may also quote the following:

'The disquieting symptoms which had manifested themselves at Spala became less marked in the early days of the sojourn at Livadia, so that the Emperor was able to attend Divine service, standing up the while, and to drive out.

'Then the symptoms of weakness reappeared, with the falling off of appetite and sleep, the weakening of the heart's action, the increase of albumen, and swelling of the extremities. On the 19th October there was a return of appetite; and on the 20th the necessary sleep was obtained which produced a noticeable increase of strength and reduced the albumen.

'On the same day there arrived with the Queen of Greece the Proto-Presbyter Ivan of Cronstadt, who offered up prayers. The Emperor recdved the Sacrament, which greatly assisted in tranquillising his mind.

'Sunday, October 21. - The Emperor felt strong enough this morning to partake of the highest spiritual consolation which he had long and earnestly desired. He called Father Ivan, and expressed a heartfelt wish to take the Holy Sacrament That day, after dinner, the Sacrament was administered, to the unspeakable comfort and peace of the Tsar. That and the following days were a time of strong though pleasing emotions.

'On Monday (23nd) the Emperor called for Father Ivan of Cronstadt, who prayed with him. The same evening the Princess Alix arrived....

'The Tsar, despite his illness, does not neglect State business. At the urgent instance of his physicians, his Majesty has handed over current affairs and reports requiring examination to the Heir Apparent, but he decides in the most important cases and signs State papers.'

The Empress was almost beside herself with grief, but up to the last minute she nursed her husband with the most devoted care. She took no rest. Day and night she was beside her consort, holding his hand in hers, keeping back her tears with all her strength, and softly whispering words of hope. 'I have even before my death got to know an angel,' the Tsar said, pressing her hand to his lips. For a day or two the bulletins grew a little more favourable, so much so that Corfu again began to be spoken of. But the Tsar himself now knew that his end was near, and expressed a desire to die on Russian soil. During the short improvement in his condition his doctors urgently advised him not to leave his bed in the mornings, even if he had slept well. Nevertheless Professor Zacharin found him up one morning, and, on asking whether another doctor had counselled this, received the very characteristic answer, 'No, no! doctor; but it was done in obedience to the Tsar's own command.'

Autocrat to the very last. The anniversary of Borki (October 29) had been solemnised by another taking of the Sacrament, and the Tsar had replied to a telegram of congratulation from the troops of the Moscow district. But it was the last telegram he ever was to send. For now his state grew rapidly worse, his breathing was hard, he began to spit blood, he could no longer sleep or eat, and finally, about two o'clock on Thursday afternoon, November 1, 1894, Alexander III passed away peacefully, not in his bed, but in his armchair, like Frederick the Great.[5] He was fully conscious to the end. Various versions of this end were given, but I will content myself with quoting the following official account which was published the day after:

'The death of the Emperor was that of an upright man, just as his life, which was inspired by faith, love, and humility, was a life of uprightness.

'For some days before his end, his Majesty felt that death was approaching, and prepared himself for it as a true Christian, without, however, relaxing his solicitude for the affairs of the State. On two occasions, on the 21st and on the 29th, the Emperor received the Holy Sacrament.

'After passing an entirely sleepless night, his Majesty said to the Empress on the morning of the 1st inst, 'I feel the end approaching. Be calm; I am quite calm.'

'All the members of his family having assembled round him, the Tsar sent for his confessor, and received the Holy Communion with great fervour, sitting in his armchair and repeating aloud the customary prayers. During the whole time the Emperor did not lose consciousness for a single moment.

'After morning prayer his Majesty sent for the priest Ivan Szergijeff and prayed with him. Half-an-hour later he again asked for the priest, who engaged in prayer with the Tsar and administered the last sacraments, remaining with him till he passed away.

'At two o'clock the Emperor's pulse became more rapid, and his eyes appeared to brighten. A quarter of an hour later, however, he closed his eyes, leaned back his head, and commended his soul to God, leaving as a legacy to his people the blessings of peace and the bright example of a noble life.'

When all was over the deceased's children and relatives approached the bedside in turn to take a last farewell, the Court officials and members of the suite being afterwards also admitted. The flag over the palace was hoisted at half-mast, and a salute was fired from the vessels lying in the bay. Shortly after four o'clock the ceremony of taking the oath of allegiance to the Emperor Nicholas the Second took place in the square in front of the Palace Chapel. The first to take the oath were the assembled Grand Dukes, and after them followed in order the high Court functionaries, the military officers, and the civil officials.

A post-mortem examination proved that the disease from which the Emperor had suffered was chronic interstitial nephritis, accompanied by progressive cardiac affection and by haemorrhagic infarction in the left lung with inflammation. Death had been more immediately due to paralysis of the heart, consequent upon a degeneration of the muscles, and hypertrophy of the heart and interstitial nephritis (granular atrophy of the kidneys).

As it had taken Alexander III about a month to die, so his obsequies lasted very nearly as long - obsequies which took the form of a grand spectacular funeral-drama in five acts, with a variety of interludes. Of the deceased Emperor it was said that he had aimed, not so much at being a great Sovereign, as at being the Sovereign of a great people; but if the greatness of a monarch might be inferred from the magnificence of his funeral, then certainly the Tsar Peacekeeper may well take rank as one of the greatest rulers who ever swayed a sceptre or sheathed a sword. It was one of the strangest ironies and contradictions of his reign that a Sovereign who had such a hatred of pomp and show in his life, should, at his death, have been made the central, if silent, figure in an altogether unparalleled pageant of the tomb; and as I devoted a whole chapter to the description of how Alexander III was crowned, so the laws of historical consistency compel me to make more than a passing reference to the manner in which he may be said to have been canonised, and which, as I have said, took the form of a grand spectacular funeral-drama in five main acts.

In this drama, the scene of Act First was the modest Byzantine church standing on the cypress-clad slopes of Livadia, to which, on the fifth day after his death, the gorgeously-coffined body of Alexander III was Cossack-borne, by torch and moonlight, to undergo its first lying-in-state – shoulder-borne by stalwart Terek Cossacks, with a procession of white-robed clergy headed by the Bishops of Taurida and Simferopol, a military escort and a foot-following of family mourners - the young Emperor leading his widowed mother, who was deeply veiled, the Grand Dukes Sergius and Vladimir, the Queen of the Hellenes, Princess Alix (the Tsarina-Elect), the Prince and Princess of Wales, the Duchess of Saxe-Coburg-Gotha and her children, the high officials of the Court and military officers. What with the hymn-chanting of the schoolchildren, the tolling of the bells, the solemn strains of the rifle band playing 'How great and glorious is God in Zion,' the flashing of the torches on helmet and bayonet, the bursting out of the moon through a heavy bank of cloud, 'causing the dark mass of the Livadia wood-dad hills to stand out boldly in the background' - nothing could have been more weirdly and solemnly impressive than all this funeral scene by the Black Sea shore. The dead Tsar was attired in the uniform of the Preobrajenski regiment of the Guard - the oldest in the army - over which was partially drawn the Imperial mantle of State. On the lid of the coffin were laid the Imperial crown and the deceased Emperor's sword - that sword which he had wielded in the Russo-Turkish war and retained in its scabbard ever afterwards. Thus arrayed in all the symbolic glory of death, the body of the Emperor lay exposed for two days, the object at once of religious ministration and public reverence.

Act Second in the funeral-drama: the ceremonious transport of the body from the church of Livadia to the deck of the cruiser which was to convey the Imperial remains round to Sebastopol, thence to enter on their solemn procession of about thirteen hundred miles across the entire breadth of the Empire to St Petersburg. It was curiously symbolic of the Russian *'Drang nach Süden'* of the instinct of all dwellers among snow to move away in search of the sun, that both the eldest sons of Alexander II had died in the South. The Tsarevitch Nicholas had expired at Nice, and been taken home by sea, while the first hearse of his brother, who similarly breathed his last at the Russian Cannes, was also a ship of war.

All the way from the jetty at Yalta to the church of Livadia, a distance of about three miles, the soldier-lined roadway had been watered and strewn with cypress branches and laurel leaves. The air was mild as midsummer, the sky cloudless, the sea without a ripple, and all nature smiling with beauty. Stalwart Cossacks had borne the Imperial coffin to the church, and from the church to the cruiser Pamiat Merkuria it was now fitly carried shoulder high by sixteen gigantic man-o'-war's men, the family mourners, as before, following on foot, and the picturesque procession including several battalions of infantry, two squadrons of mounted Tartar riflemen and a field battery, a bare-headed detachment of Yalta merchants, bands of white-robed schoolchildren singing plaintively and crossing themselves as they walked, a bevy of hospital nurses, a group of taper-bearing clergy headed by the Bishop of Simferopol canying a sacred picture of the Madonna, and, most pathetic of all, the deceased Emperor's favourite charger, without trappings of any kind. It took nearly two hours for this slow-moving procession, winding along through dell and cypress-grove to the solemn accompaniment of muffled bells and the booming of minute-guns from the war-vessels, to reach the shore; and then amid farewell salvoes of musketry and the thunder of artillery salutes which had never had any charm for the Emperor in life, the stately vessel, followed by the eager gaze of the onlookers, steamed away, with the dead monarch and his mourning relatives on board - away past the warships now weighing anchor in the bay and on to the famous sea-stronghold of which the calamitous siege had broken the heart of the deceased Sovereign's grandsire.

'The evening shadows,' wrote one correspondent from Sebastopol, 'were adding to the gloom pervading this city when the Russian flotilla escorting the cruiser *Pamiat Merkuria*, conveying the mortal remains of the late Tsar, entered the harbour. The voyage from Yalta had been made at half-speed. The cruiser in which the Tsar's corpse found a temporary resting-place made her own course, no vessels following or preceding her, but on either side of her were six battleships of the Black Sea Fleet, steaming in line and with an unusually long distance between each ship. The cortège was worthy of a Caesar. As the fleet entered the harbour the great guns boomed out the signal of grief. The fleet responded, and during the whole evening the cannons' testimony to the dead ruler continued at stated intervals.'

After a series of interludes at Simferopol, Paulograd, Borki (the scene of the terrible railway disaster of 1888), Kharkoff, and other places along the soldier-lined railway route, where the Imperial train stopped that requiem masses might be said for the soul of the departed, the curtain again rose on the Third Act of the funeral drama at Moscow, into which, but eleven short years before, Alexander III had made his triumphal entry in order to be crowned - with the symbol of earthly power and glory then, and now with the still more gorgeous diadem of death. But I have no space to describe the appearance presented by Moscow on this the occasion of the Tsar's second grand triumphal entry into the andent Mother City of his Empire, or to dwell on the sombre magnificence of the ceremonious procession which conducted the remains of the Emperor from the railway station to the Archangel Cathedral in the Kremlin, there to lie in splendidly sepulchral state for a day, and be gazed at by a deep, continuous stream of his subjects.

'It is difficult,' wrote a correspondent,[6] 'to do justice to the impressiveness of the scene from the moment of the arrival of the train imtil the deposit of the coffin on its bier in the Cathedral. The absolute silence of the thousands who lined the roads and windows, and crowded the roofs was broken only by the sound of the bells and the minute guns. The grey, still cold of the Russian winter gave a spectral aspect to the snow-covered houses, which were draped with black, and displayed fluttering black and white flags, through which passed the stately mourners, representing every class and every age of this colossal Empire, from the Emperor to the village Mayor, from tottering old age to the freshest youth. All combined to form a picture which will be ineffaceable from the memories of those who witnessed it.'

But still more impressive was the scene inside the Archangel Cathedral, where, to quote the words of another graphic eye-witness,[7] 'the beautiful coffin was deposited reverently in front of a gorgeous catafalque all glittering in gold, the pall being so disposed as to show the head. Then the elaborate Service for the Dead was chanted antiphonally by Metropolitan and clergy. The scene was resplendent. The silver-gilt ikons vied with the silver and gold panelling of the walls in reflecting the light of countless tapers burning within the sacrarium, by the picture-screen, and around the catafalque. Anything more solemn than the office it was impossible to imagine. Many of those present were unable to restrain their emotion. Tears were seen rolling down the cheeks of noble ladies. Sobs broke on the ear almost riiythmically with the cadences of the sacred music. Evidently the late Tsar was deeply esteemed and beloved by those within his circle.' Nor were some of the heart-rejoicing incidents of an Irish wake entirely absent from this touching scene of Imperial sorrow, seeing that, by order of the new Tsar, five-and-twenty thousand poor people were twice treated to a free dinner at some score of the monasteries of Moscow, thus giving them substantial reason to reflect that it is an ill wind which blows good to no one.

The same reflection must have also occurred repeatedly to fifty thousand similarly treated poor people at St Petersburg to which the scene now changes (Act Fourth of the funeral drama), showing us a long processional line of route of several miles from the Nicholas Railway Station down the Nevski Prospect and across the ice-encumbered Neva to the island-fortress church of Saints Peter and Paul,[8] which forms the mausoleum of the Romanoffs - a line of route lugubrious with the hangings of undertakers' woe and dismal with slush and mud, and a drizzle falling from a sullen, leaden-hued sky. On a scale hitherto unequalled, the procession - which took about two hours to pass any particular point - consisted of thirteen sections, subdivided into one hundred and fifty-six distinct groups.

Of all these groups, perhaps, the one which created most interest was 'the gay and imposing figure of a mounted man-at-arms in golden armour and showy plumes with drawn sword, his horse being richly harnessed and led by two gaudily clad grooms, and then a second knight on foot in jet-black armour, carrying his crape-pointed sword reversed, figures which were supposed to symbolise the sentiment expressed in the saying, *'Le Roi est mort; vive le Roi!'* The sight of the Imperial hearse itself was declared by another observer to be no less theatrical. 'The small dimensions of the vehicle and the over-abundance of cheap gilding and of gold hangings, under which it almost disappeared, with the four aides-de-camp sitting at the corners, involuntarily recalled one of the chariots in which the fairies are drawn in a Drury Lane pantomime.' But in spite of these and other scenic imperfections, the procession, with its rich representative variety, was one of the most impressive things of the kind which had ever been witnessed in the pile-built capital of the Great Peter. "The demeanour of the people was eminently respectful - nay, even reverent,' wrote the discriminating correspondent from whom I have already quoted,[9] 'but there were not such external marks of devotion as impressed me at Moscow.'

Most of the devotion was reserved for the fortress-church, to which the Imperial corpse had thus been borne with such unparalleled processional pomp, and of which the interior, according to the same authority, had simply been transfigured:

'The porch was hung with black and silver and gold. From the middle roof of the nave suspended by a golden cord was a superb tent formed of cloth of silver, internally resembling ennine, the traditional royal fur being bordered with gold bullion fringe. The circular top was emblazoned with shields bearing for device the double-headed Russian eagle. Thin curtains fell in lovely curves, caught up by four great pillars of the nave, whence they descended to the ground in a sheen of silver.

'Gold curtains covered the huge daïs occupying the whole floor-space of the middle of the nave. It was approached on each side by cherry velvet steps. The estrade of the dais was laid with crimson cloth, which reflected a pale pink glow on the ermined curtains. Approached by three steps from the dais was the bier, covered with cherry velvet emblazoned with the arms of the Romanoffs and of the Empire. At the corners of the estrade were exquisitely modelled white and gold candelabra, draped with crape, nine feet high. The interior was a-blaze with wax tapers, what with the golden candelabra at the four corners of the dais and the silver candelabra, four feet high, which were dispersed over the church, chiefly near the Sanctuary, and Peter the Great's pendant candelabra illumining the upper part of the interior. Weird was the effect of the pale daylight straggling through the aisle windows and the windows of the west front, which were draped darkly with crimson velvet. The emblazoned curtains and the Ikonostas - all the glory of gold and colour not specially prepared, not even touched for the occasion, revealed latent glories and became doubly resplendent under the light of a thousand tapers.

'The ensemble at the moment of the commencement of the service of prayer was indescribably superb. The ladies in deep mourning kneeling near the bier; the deep intoning of the Metropolitan, and the wailing responses of the priests and the choir; the glitter of the silver and the glow of gold; the occasional sobs; the innumerable waxlights; the hand of the dead just resting on the edge of the coffin; the rapt attention of the illustrious congregation - all combined to furnish a composition never surpassed in electric vitality with sorrowful charm.'

'As the strains of the glorious anthem, 'Rest with the Blessed,' rang out as only a Russian choir could render them,' said another writer, 'all fell upon their knees, and many sobbed aloud. Then came the closing scene. The living representatives of earth's power and glory gathered together to honour the mighty dead, slowly, one by one, mounted the catafalque and kissed the strong, still hand which no longer held the olive-branch. With this token of respect to the dead, the members of the Imperial family left the building' - but only to return to it several times a day during the interval before the final entombment and go through the same painfully pathetic scenes of religious service and leave-taking.

Historians may afterwards differ as to the character and acts of Alexander III. But I feel quite sure that, to some at least of the foreign Princes who attended his obsequies, the most memorable feature of his reign will be the long and elaborate Masses for the soul of the deceased Sovereign at which etiquette compelled them so frequently to assist.

'His Majesty had died on the 1st of November, but it was the 19th of this month before the fortress-church became the scene of the Fifth and final Act in the funeral drama - a scene which utterly beggared all that had gone before in its indescribable magnificence and moving power. Certainly, Death had never sat upon a more gorgeous throne, or been more gloriously arrayed, than it now was in that transfigured mausoleum of the Autocrats of All the Russias. The scene has already been but it now seemed to have assumed quite a different aspect from the piles of wreaths,[10] of Nature's richest flowers and richest metals, lying around, as well as from the brilliant assemblage of mourners representing all the rank and station of Russia and Europe which stood around the Imperial bier.[11]

'The Requiem was commenced with a magnificent chant, at whose opening notes all the congregation fell on their knees and noiselessly lighted their tapers by passing one swiftly from hand to hand. When all rose from their knees, the Cathedral was, for the first time, lighted through its whole extent, with an effect which baffles description. A thousand glimmering candles were reflected in the silver wreaths, the majestic brocade of the canopy, and the star-spangled breasts of the uniforms, producing a scene of such splendour as is seldom witnessed.'

While lighted tapers were being distributed to all present, the Metropolitan laid upon the forehead of the deceased Emperor a rich band of silk bearing the traditional sacred emblems of the Russian Church, and then placed in his hands a document setting forth the customary indulgences. This done, the chief mourners advanced one by one to the coffin and paid their last reverences to the remains of Alexander III, the young Tsar passing first, then the Empress, the other members of the Imperial family, and the Kings and Princes in the order of precedence in which they had entered the Church, each kissing the face and hands of the dead Monarch. This moving scene took place amid the most solemn silence. Many of those who witnessed it were overcome with emotion.

The Tsar having deposited on the coffin his father's Imperial mantle, it was carried to the altar by eight Generals, and the lid having been fastened down, the remains were solemnly borne to the tomb by the Tsar and his immediate relatives. When the coffin had been deposited by the side of the open grave, the chief mourners fell upon their knees in front of the tomb, and while the fortress artillery thundered forth a Royal salute, the Burial Service was begun by the Metropolitan, its chief feature being the following address as from the lips of the departed Tsar:

'Me lying voiceless and deprived of breath beholding, bewail ye, O brethren and friends, O kinsfolk and acquaintances, for yesterday I spake with you, and suddenly on me came the dread hour of death. But come ye all that love me and kiss me with the final kiss, for never shall I go with you again, or further converse hold with you. For I depart unto the Judge where no respect of persons is, where slave and lord together stand, the King and warrior, rich and poor in equal worthiness, for each according to his deeds is glorified or shamed. But I beg all and entreat all unceasingly to pray Christ-God for me, that for my sins I be not bidden unto the place of torments, but that He may appoint my lot where is the light of life.'

As the reciting of this went on, the living Tsar and his mother, with the other chief mourners, were completely overwhelmed by their emotions; and as soon as the Metropolitan had uttered the last words of the Burial Service, with its thrice-repeated: 'May thy memory endure for ever, O our brother, who art worthy to be blest, and to be had in remembrance!' the Palace Grenadiers and the Sergeant-Majors representing the various regiments of which Alexander II was the chief, finally lowered the coffin into its vault, while the thunder of cannon, the crash of musketry, the acclaiming shouts of the soldiery as they greeted their new Emperor, the rolling away of the carriages through the vast multitudes outside, and the bursting out of the bands into lively tunes as the troops marched away back to their barracks - all proclaimed, *urbi et* orbi, with a sense of relief like that produced by the knocking at the door in Macbeth, that Alexander III had at last been laid to his everlasting rest. To parody the closing couplet of the *Iliad;*

Such honours Russia to her ruler paid,
And peaceful slept the 'Tsar Peace-keeper's' shade.

NOTES

1. Ode to 'The Dead Tsar,' by Mr Eric Mackay, in the *Daily Chronicle*, Nov. 2, 1894.
2. I am here quoting from a letter which was addressed by Professor Zacharin to the Moscow Gazette after the Tsar's death, and which gave the fullest account of the progress of his Majesty's illness. The letter was intended as a reply to numerous articles and more rumours implying blame upon the Moscow Professor for his treatment of the case.
3. St Petersburg Correspondent of the *Daily Telegraph.*
4. According to a Vienna paper which claimed to have derived its information from a trustworthy source, the Tsar, on reaching Spala, pressingly desired that his son George should be sent for, and, though the Empress begged him with tears not to risk his son's life by the long journey, the Tsar insisted, and the Grand Duke George arrived in Spala. The first interview between the father and son there was touching in the extreme. It was during the first night of their sleeping under one roof that the following incident occurred: 'The Empress, as usual, remained near her husband's bedside till after midnight, and when she retired for a few hours' rest the Tsar rose, dressed very slightly, and ordered his valet to conduct him to the bedroom of Prince George, which was situated some distance from his own chamber through a cold passage. The Prince was fast asleep, and the Tsar remained several minutes to watch him in his sleep. Thereupon he returned to his room, having caught a chill, which made his own condition

worse.'

This was improved upon by Mr T. W. Stead, who, in his *Review of Reviews* for November 1894, offered the following version of the story:

'It is not generally known that the fatal chill which carried him off was due to his paternal tenderness. When at Spala the Tsar and his son, the Grand Duke George, whose delicate constitution has always been a source of anxiety to his parents, went out shooting in the woods. The boy shot and dropped a duck. The bird fell in what seemed, to the lad's inexperienced eye, a grassy glade, but on approaching the bird he found to his horror that he had walked into a treacherous marsh. He began to sink with great rapidity, and before his cries of alarm brought his father to the spot he had sunk up to his neck in the bog. The Tsar rushed to his rescue, and succeeded in extricating his son from the bog by putting forth his immense strength, but not until he had been thoroughly saturated by the moisture. They hastened home. The young Grand Duke showed signs of fever, while his father was conscious of a chill. The palace of Spala is an extensive building, and it so happened that the Grand Duke's rooms were at the end of one wing, while the Tsar's bedchamber was in the centre. At night the Tsar wished to get up and visit his boy. The Tsarina strongly opposed this desire, declaring that his health was of quite as much importance as that of his son's, and, considering the chill which he had received, it would be dangerous for him to get out of bed. The Tsar, who always shrank from opposing the will of the Empress, pretended to go to sleep. His wife, satisfied that he was slumbering peacefully, went to her own room. No sooner was the coast clear than the Tsar got up and traversed the long draughty corridors of the palace in dressing-gown and slippers until he reached his son's apartments. After remaining there for a short time he returned, with the result that the chill which he had received in extricating his boy from the bog settled upon his vital organs, and from that day is dated the acute stage of the malady which ultimately carried him off.'

5. On hearing that the Emperor was nearing his end, the Prince and Princess of Wales started off from London, travelling day and night to reach Livadia, but the news of his Majesty's death met them before their arrival at Vienna.

6. Of the *Standard*.

7. The Special Correspondent of the *Daily Chronicle*.

8. All the Sovereigns of Russia since the building of St Petersburg lie buried in this Cathedral with the exception of Peter II, who died and was buried at Moscow. The bodies are deposited in vaults under the floor, the marble tombs above only marking the sites of the graves. The Cathedral on ordinary occasions lacks all special grandeur or richness of decoration.

9. Of the *Daily Chronicle*.

10. Five thousand wreaths had been sent from France alone; while the special mission had taken with it to St Petersburg, for distribution among the populace, ten thousand bunches of artificial flowers tied with crape and tricolour, and ticketed with portraits of the late President Carnot and the deceased Tsar bearing the legend 'United in sentiments and death.' During the last two days of the lying in State four French officers had formed part of the Guard of Honour in the

church. The Queen's wreath was of natural lilies and violets, and bore the dedication: 'To my well-beloved and never-to-be-forgotten brother.' 'The French wreaths,' said the correspondent of the *Daily Chronicle*, 'were the most numerous, and the English the most simple.' Just so.

11. The following Sovereigns and Princes were present at the funeral: - The King of Denmark, the King and Queen of Greece, the King of Servia, the Grand Duke of Hesse, the Duchess of Saxe-Coburg Gotha, the Grand Duchess of Mecklenburg, Prince Nicholas of Montenegro, Prince and Princess Henry of Prussia, the Archduke Charles Louis, the Prince and Princess of Baden, Prince Ludwig of Bavaria, Prince Valdemar of Denmark, the Prince and Princess of Wales, the Duke of York, Prince George of Greece, the Prince of Naples, the Hereditary Grand Duke of Luxemburg, the Hereditary Prince of Oldenburg, Prince Ferdinand of Roumama, Prince Frederick Augustus of Saxony, Prince Eugene of Sweden, the brother of the King of Siam, Duke Albert and the Duchess Vera of Würtemberg. Great Britain was represented by Lord Carrington (Lord Chamberlain) and Major-General Ellis, Equeny to the Prince of Wales, while France sent a special military mission, under General Boisdeffre, including Admiral Gervais of Cronstadt fame.

CHAPTER XI

CHARACTERISTICS

A 'psychological enigma' - A compound monarch - Not a military one - The 'Peace-keeper' of Europe - Examination of his Claim to the Title - A treaty-breaker if a peace-keeper - European Peace and Russian War - A Second Ivan the Terrible - A 'Moujik Tsar' - The 'Tsar Prisoner' - Truth-lover and Truth-teller - His real Feelings towards France -The Great Mistake of his Reign - The Dumb Ruler of a Voiceless People - Model Husband and Father - Family Life - Denmark an Asylum - 'Uncle Sasha' - Contemporary, not of Queen Victoria, but of Queen Isabel - The 'Two Alexanders' - Opinions of Lords Rosebery and Salisbury - M. Leroy-Beaulieu - Mr Harold Frederic - Processor Geffcken - The *Times* - A Personal as well as a Political Autocrat - Lady Randolph Churchill - His daily Habits described by Mr 'Lanin' - General Richter, the 'Sandalphon of the Empire' - Great Physical Strength - Fondness for Animals – 'Sullen, Taciturn, Curt' - Intellectual Tastes - Domestic Habits – *De mortuis nil nisi bonum* - Canon Wilberforce - 'Resistance to Tyranny is Obedience to God'

IT will be impossible to form a true estimate of the character of Alexander III until facts and documents and motives, which are still a sealed book, are given to the world, and in Russia they wait long before revealing the contents of their State archives. The personality of the late Tsar, in spite of his simplicity in some things, was a most perplexing one. Some one aptly described him as a 'psychological enigma.' He was a large but by no means a luminous figure on the canvas of his time, and it was hard to say which of his ancestors he most resembled. Perhaps it would be near the truth to say that he was a kind of 'Frankenstein monster,' compounded of fragments of the characters of some of his predecessors on the throne of the Romanoffs. In his prime he enjoyed the physical strength of the Great Peter without Peter's tremendous energy; and his physical courage was never of the highest. There were some traits in his mental composition which reminded one of his great-grandfather Paul, who was deposed and strangled as a kind of dangerous lunatic; nor was he altogether without a taint of that dreamy idealism which distinguished his grand-uncle, Alexander I, of whom Madame de Staël said that his 'character was a constitution to his subjects.' Again, he had much in common with his grandfather, the despotic and reactionary Nicholas; while, on the other hand, his tendencies at one time betrayed the benevolent and reforming spirit of his father, the 'Tsar Emancipator.'

It may be said with perfect truth that Nature never intended the late Emperor to be the absolute and irresponsible ruler of one hundred millions of his fellow-beings. But by the death of his elder brother, Nicholas, he had greatness suddenly thrust upon him. He was trained for the career, not of a Sovereign, but of a soldier, and yet it never appeared that Nature even intended him to be a soldier. He had the bulk and look of a dour, heavy dragoon, and that was all. In this respect he resembled the late Emperor Frederick of Germany, who looked the most martial figure of his age, but in reality had neither taste nor capacity for the career of arms, and was content to let his Chief of the Staff all the battles for which he got the credit. Like Frederick III, whom he also resembled in his tragic fate, Alexander III had a positive distaste for soldiering, and was not in the least infected by that mania for marching-past, that *defilirium tremens*, as it has wittily been called, which possesses the heart of his fellow-sovereign at Berlin.

But doubtless this disinclination of the Tsar to make a show at the head of his troops was as much due to the dread of appearing in public as to lack of passion for military pomp. The master of the largest army in Europe, Alexander III was nevertheless not a military monarch like his grandfather Nicholas. From the campaign against Turkey, in which he had been the nominal commander of the Army of the Lom, and achieved successes that were more due to the blunders of his opponents than to his own brilliancy as a strategist, he returned home with a holy hatred of war and all its ways. Besides, his own experience in the field may have honestly convinced him that he had no great talent for war, and that another campaign, with himself as necessary Commander-in-Chief, might only result in proving his unfitness for the post. His reign of thirteen years was passed without a war, and he was justly called the 'Peace-keeper' of Europe. But this title he gained less, perhaps, from his innate love of peace than from his acquired horror of war.

Nor must it ever be forgotten that this magnificent title had been still more justly applied to the old Emperor William and his Bismarck before Alexander's accession to the throne; and that the real 'Peace-keeper' of Europe was the Triple Alliance, which must have convinced the Russian Emperor of the utter hopelessness of carrying to success any schemes of adventure or aggression, which he might have cherished.

'This master of many legions never waged a war,' as was finely said of him by Lord Rosebery. It is true he never waged a war with any European nation, though the course of Russian conquest in Central Asia showed that the Russian sword, even in his day, was never continuously in its scabbard. But, at the same time, it must be said that Alexander III's policy in Bulgaria was at one time perilously near provoking a European war; and. If his masterful and illegal repudiation of the Batoum clause of the Treaty of Berlin did not end in hostilities, that was due - as none knew better than Lord Rosebery himself - more to the forbearance of the other Powers than to the Russian love of peace. If Alexander III never broke the public peace, he at least broke a public treaty, and that was the next thing to it.

His Majesty was a mass of apparent contradictions. He was much belauded for keeping the peace so long, for the issues or peace and war lay in the hollow of his hand, though not more so than in that of the German Emperor or the Government of the French Republic. But surely that was a very peculiar love of peace which, while sparing Europe the calamity of an awful war, nevertheless plunged his own Empire into domestic struggles of the most internecine kind. This was a form of war which involved no risk to his own military reputation, but yet it was war of the most savage and relentless, if one-sided kind all the same, a war of positive extermination against obnoxious races and religions. It was also a war prompted by ignorance and stupidity, seeing that the Stundists, or Methodists, formed the salt and social leaven of the great mass of Alexander's brutalised and degraded subjects, the true apostles of the Kingdom of God in an Empire groaning under all the odious devilries of a mediaeval despotism. Alexander III was frequently credited with great kindliness of heart, and yet he lent his countenance to cruelties which placed him on the level of a Philip and a Torquemada.

From beginning to end his reign was one painful tragedy of racial and religious persecutions, which can scarcely be paralleled out of the cruellest page of all history. It is of no use telling us that Alexander III was a sincere and honest man, and that all his actions sprang from the most exalted patriotism, the purest piety. The same apology might be tendered on behalf of Nero, or Nana Sahib, or the Bloody Mary. Piety is no doubt a fine thing in itself, and so is patriotism; yet, if these abstract virtues are not prompted to express themselves in concrete form by the spirit of tolerance and enlightenment; it is possible for them to become vices of the most odious kind. But the intellectual and moral atmosphere always breathed by Alexander III was more that of the time of Ivan the Terrible than of the latter half of the nineteenth century; nor do the annals of this century contain any more shameful and distressing pages than the record of the late Tsar's persecution of the Jews and the Nonconformists in his Empire (Stundists and Lutherans), as well as of all the non-Slavonic elements amongst his subjects - Finns, Poles, and Teutons. His Panslavism was the Procrustes-bed on which he forced all his people, without exception, to lie, heedless of their prayers, their protests, and their howls of pain.

And then, as for civic freedom under Alexander III, where was it? What, I ask, did he do to inspire his subjects with a sense of their human dignity? What, indeed, in the field of domestic policy, did he do which was not. calculated, to demoralise, degrade, and debase the millions of human beings subject to his stupid, his obscurantist, and his reactionary sway? Alexander III would have needed to be a hundred times at least the man he was to sway with anything like success the sceptre which, had been placed in his hands by a cruel and capricious fate. With all his virtues as a man, he was no more capable of ruling, as it should have been ruled, his colossal Empire than one of his own average moujiks, or peasants. He claimed, and had his claim allowed, to be the 'Moujik Tsar.' On his head sat one of the most magnificent of crowns; but his brows were not encircled with the still more dazzling aureole of bright intelligence, enlightenment, and lofty aims.

If he becomes known to history by any special title at all, it will not be so much the 'Tsar Peacekeeper' as the 'Tsar Persecutor,' or perhaps even the 'Tsar Prisoner.' For he ever lived in a state of real or imaginary siege, and his palaces were prisons. His journeys were hurried, furtive; and when he had occasion to travel from St Petersburg to Moscow, or from Moscow to the Crimea, he simply passed through a lane of guardian troops. When he went to his coronation it was like passing to his execution. The Nihilists murdered his father with bombs, and they also made his own life so great a misery to him as to precipitate his end. There can be no doubt about it. The secret apostles of revolution, the underground advocates of reform, were as directly responsible for the death of Alexander III as of Alexander II. His was a reign of terror, and terror of the kind that kills. Never at the best endowed with physical courage of the highest kind, his nerves proved quite unequal to the double strain of coping with his secret foes and at the same time of carrying on the colossal business of his one-man rule. He attempted an impossible task, and he broke his back with the effort.

Fear had a deep hold of his nature, side by side with a capacity for courage; just as strange irresolution marked many of the acts of the monarch who looked the incarnation of human will. Doubtless he was a truth-loving and truth-telling man, and yet he frequently allowed himself to be made the tool of the lying and the dishonest. The circumstances connected with the *Prinzenraub* form a case in point. And what can be thought of the intelligence and perspicacity of the man who was imposed upon by the famous forged dispatches relating to Bulgaria? Count Herbert Bismarck made no secret of his opinion that Alexander III was endowed with no more than the mind of one of his own moujiks, a 'Mujik-verstand' and M. Stambuloff endorsed the judgment in a manner more emphatic than discreet.

With an intellectual outfit scarcely equal to the task of ruling a hundred of his fellow-men, Alexander had been saddled with the responsibility of ruling a hundred millions of them. No one ever doubted his perfect honesty and his determination to govern well according to his lights, but the worst of him was that he let himself be guided by the counsel of men who, his superiors in mind, were inferior to him in the qualities of the heart. The exigencies of political expediency sometimes gave his words and actions the semblance of personal insincerity. This was the case, for instance, with the relations of France and Russia. The French persuaded themselves that they had a true friend and warm admirer in Alexander III, while, as a matter of fact,, there was no one who entertained a deeper horror of Republican France, as being the hotbed of anarchy, irreligion, and all other modem abominations. The idea of entering into a formal alliance, a political *mariage de convenance*, with such a godless, reckless, and revolutionary people was never seriously entertained for a moment by the autocratic and Orthodox Tsar of All the Russias.

The great mistake of his reign, the missing of the tide which, taken at the flood, would have helped him on to happiness, was the withholding of the quasi-parliamentary privileges which his father had actually decreed on the very day of his death. At first also he was for confirming this bequest, but reactionary counsels gained the upper hand over him, and he refused to grant concessions which might seem to have been wrung from him by the threats of the terrorists. It was his one great chance, and he missed it. Certainly he did much to cleanse the Augean stable of his Empire from its foul administrative abuses; but, on the whole, the tendency of his reign was more in the direction of reaction than of reform. He gave his people no voice to express their grievances, their hopes, their aspirations. The nation continued dumb, and its mouthpiece was seldom anything but mute himself. Yet, even though he kept the mouth of his people muzzled, he would have stirred their enthusiasm had he but spoken out with the freedom and fervour which characterise the frequent utterances of his fellow-monarch in Germany; for those who are led, and even those who are driven, love to hear from time to time the voice of their leader or their driver.

Whatever his failings as an autocrat, his domestic life was at once an exception and an example to all the other members of his family. A devoted husband and a doting father, he would have made a model subject. But, in making him a Sovereign, capricious Face imposed on him a burden which he found it quite impossible to bear, and he succumbed to the effort, just as his deceased brother Nicholas, who would in all probability have proved a better Emperor, ultimately fell a victim to the physical strain or wrench which had been imparted to his constitution in a playful wrestling match with his cousin.

I have said that the late Tsar was a devoted husband, and scandal never once breathed on his conjugal relations, as it had done on those of his father. His domestic life was as simple as it was pure; and he caused his children to be trained and educated with a severe absence of all softening luxury. About eleven years ago I chanced to be in St Petersburg, and had the privilege of being conducted all over the Anitchkoff Palace, which was then the town residence of their Majesties. I was much struck by the quiet simplicity of everything. The schoolroom was severity itself, a parish schoolroom, indeed, more than an Imperial one. The walls, I remember, where not hung with maps, were pasted over with pictures of the chief battles in the Russo-Turkish War, taken from *The Illustrated London News* and other illustrated English papers. The aide-de-camp who acted as my guide spoke in the most touching terms about the tender relations existing between their Majesties, and above all things of the Tsar's fond devotion, to his children. No matter how late he might return, home, he always made a point of coming to the cots of his little ones to kiss them in their sleep and cross himself over them.

Perhaps the reign of Alexander III cannot be better characterised than by saying that the happiest hours of his life were those which he spent out of his own dominions. As Denmark had given him a wife, so it also afforded him an asylum; and the lawns of Fredensborg were much dearer to him than the terraces of Peterhof, the woods of Zarskoe Selo, or the embowered walks of Gatchina - Fredensborg, with its château fronted by a statue to the Goddess of Peace, and the Tsar's study there emblazoned with the motto, '*Fortissima consilia tutissima.*' It would have been his boldest, and perhaps also his safest, policy to show himself to his subjects; but he dreaded those over whom he domineered, and loved to exchange the perils of rule for the pleasure of romping on the sequestered lawns of Denmark with the numerous children of his royal relatives, who only knew and adored him as 'Uncle Sasha.' At the close of one of these annual visits to Denmark he was saying good-bye to his favourite nieces, the daughters of the Prince and Princess of Wales. 'Good-bye, my dears,' he said as he kissed them, 'you are going back to your happy English home, and I to my Russian prison.' Alexander III loved Denmark for the same reason and to the same extent as France was loved by Mary Queen of Scots, whose portrait hung over his writing-table at Fredensborg, opposite to that of Catherine II.

But I must seek to illustrate my subject from as many points of view as possible, and focus upon it the light of other judgments. Says M. Leroy-Beaulieu, in the preface to the American edition of his great work on 'The Empire of the Tsars and the Russians' - a work which is forbidden in Russia: - 'The Tsar Alexander Alexandrovitch, crowned in the Kremlin of Moscow, is not so much the contemporary of Queen Victoria as of Queen Isabel of Castile. The uprightness of his intentions, the loftiness of his character, are beyond all doubt, but neither he nor his people live in the same intellectual atmosphere with ourselves. He can, with a good conscience, sign *ukàses* that our conscience condemns. If, at the distance of four centuries, the Russian Tsar takes against his Jewish subjects measures which recall the edicts issued in 1492 by *los Reyes Catolicos*, it is because Orthodox Russia is not unlike Catholic Spain of the fifteenth century. For the last two centuries his country's history has been that of a pendulum drawn alternately towards two opposite poles. It oscillates between European imitation and Muscovite tradition.

'Just now the attraction of Moscow and the Russian pole prevails, as it did at one time under Nicholas. The current is no longer, as under Catherine, Alexander I, and Alexander II, set towards Europe. Alexander III prides himself in being, first and foremost, a national ruler. He is the Orthodox Tsar of popular tradition - Russian, and nothing if not Russian. He seeks for no glory save that of embodying in himself his people. To him the Russian Tsar is Russia incarnate. With whatever feelings we may regard certain of his acts, it is impossible to deny the dignity of his personal character. Never, perhaps, has Russia had a ruler more profoundly imbued with his duties, more earnestly thoughtful for the welfare of his people. His qualities as a Sovereign, his virtues as a man, are his own; his government methods are not. They are the outcome of the soil, of the autocratic system of which he is the representative, and which he deems it his mission to maintain in its integrity. This man, invested with the omnipotence which breeds the Neros and the Caligulas of the world, is an upright, honourable man. He is brave, simple, modest; he is calm and patient. He has shown a quality most rare with those possessed of absolute power - 'self-control.'

Once in particular he lost this self-control, and that was when he made up his mind, at all costs and hazards, to get his cousin, Prince Alexander of Battenberg, removed from the Bulgarian throne. In an age rich in sensations, none was ever more engrossing than the drama, the tragedy of 'The Two Alexanders.' Mediaeval still in most things, the Russia of Alexander III never showed itself more startlingly so than in the methods it employed to compass its will with respect to the ruler who, while ready to show his patrons every mark of gratitude and consideration, most emphatically refused to become their tool. The Emperor's implacable rage and spite were due to the fact that he had been grossly deceived. And so he had. But the deceit was much more on the side of his own servants than on that of the Prince, whom they wished to dragoon into being a mere unquestioning instrument of their imperious master, and rage almost bereft him of his reason. Alexander III kept the peace for thirteen years; but he was as near as possible causing it to be broken then. He kept the peace, no matter what his motives - whether physical fear of war, humanity, irresolution, helplessness, dread of having himself to take the field - it is quite impossible to say. Motives are generally mixed. But he did keep the peace of Europe during all his melancholy reign, and that must always be placed to his credit as a set-off against the cruel and stupid persecutions of which he allowed so many of his own subjects to be made the victims.[1]

Some one wittily remarked of Alexander III that his merits might be summed up by saying that he kept two things - the Seventh Commandment and the peace of Europe. On the latter subject let us take the testimony of the British Premier, Lord Rosebery:[2]

'There is not a thoughtful mind in Europe at this moment which is not turned to the sick-bed at Livadia. We have had in times past subjects of difference, but I am certain of this that there is no one who knows what has passed in Europe for the last twelve years who does not feel the immeasurable debt of obligation under which we lie to the Emperor of Russia. Gentlemen, it is not my concern to-night to say one word as to the relations of the Emperor and his own Empire. But we have a right to concern ourselves with the Emperor as he appears to foreign countries, and we have in him a monarch the watchword of whose reign and character have been the worship of peace. I do not say that he will rank, or does rank, among the Caesars and Napoleons of history - the great conquerors of whom history, perhaps, makes too much account.

'But if 'peace hath her victories no less renowned than war,' the Emperor of Russia will reign in history with a title not less undisputed than the titles of Caesar and of Napoleon. It is something for a Sovereign of unbounded power to have introduced - not to have introduced altogether, perhaps, but to have made more respected in the realms of diplomacy - an absolutely conscientious devotion to truth. I have not the honour of the Sovereign's acquaintance, but all who have united to say that the one sin he never forgives is that of personal deceit and untruthfulness; and, on the other hand, he has by his influence done that which few men in his position have been able to do to guarantee in his own person and by his own character that inestimable blessing, the peace of Europe. It is now some twenty-four years ago since we had a great European war, and it is not too much to say that if peace has not been broken in more than one instance during late years it is due as much to the character and influence of the Emperor of Russia as to any other cause you may mention.'

The Marquis of Salisbury's tribute was no less flattering:

'His reign has not been a long one, and during, I think I may say, the greater part of it, I was in a position to appreciate the working of his character and the motives of his acts; and beginning, as I confess I did, with some doubt of the attitude that he would assume, the force of facts and of constant experience strongly convinced me, long before my official connection with foreign affairs had terminated, that Europe owed to him a debt which it was difficult to express for the peace which is self-restraint and his high Christian character had secured to us. On more than one occasion a man of lower motives might have yielded to a temporary irritation - and irritation in an autocrat is a terrible thing - and but for his self-restraint Europe might have been plunged into war. He has left behind him a diameter for which all nations are bound to be grateful, and which future rulers in all lands, whether monarchical or popular, will do well to study and to follow.'

So much, then, for the character of the Emperor in the field of foreign policy. And now - for my witness-box must be open to all kinds of honest and independent testimony - let me supplement this by again quoting M. Leroy-Beaulieu with regard to his Majesty's merits as an administrator:

'The Emperor Alexander III, on ascending the throne, set before himself, as his first task, the eradication of the abuses of which neither his father nor his grandfather had been able to cleanse the soil of the Empire. Could the success of such an undertaking be prejudged from the loyalty of one man's intentions and the uprightness of his character no Sovereign ever was better equipped for his work. At all times the sworn enemy of abuses and of corrupt men - profoundly honest himself, and unable to tolerate dishonesty around him, impervious to the feminine blandishments to which his father so easily succumbed, combining, unlike the latter, the virtues of the private man with the Sovereign's noble aspirations, incapable of any weakness or low compromise with conscience for the benefit of favourites of either sex, scrupulously thrifty in the use of the public wealth, and filled with the sense of the sacredness of his mission, Alexander III appears to be, personally, better qualified than any of his predecessors to deliver the State from the hideous canker that gnaws at its vitals; but what can one man do, however resolute and austere, in a State of over 12,000,000 square miles?

'Such an Empire does not come under the class of those domains where the master's eye can see everything and reach everywhere. Whatever his energy, the Sovereign is doomed to impotency; after a few efforts, usually made with a novice's ardour and ingenuity, the most hopeful almost fatally ends by getting discouraged, tired, and by giving in to the evil which it is not in his power to prevent. For a Sovereign, indeed, can govern - especially as regards administration - only through the eyes and by the hands of others, and it is precisely the central administration, the Court, and the higher circles of bureaucracy which are most interested in maintaining the old practices and abuses. If we are to believe public rumour, peculation and prevarication, stock gambling and unclean dabblings, have already quietly resumed their course around the pure and honest Alexander, unbeknown to him.'

On the other hand, take the following remarks on the same aspect of the Emperor's character by another acute critic. 'Alexander III,' says Mr Harold Frederic (in his 'New Exodus'), 'is a man of rather limited mental endowments and acquirements, who does not easily see more than one thing at a time, and who gets to see that slowly....He has no idea of system and no executive talent. He would not be selected to manage the affairs of a village if he were an ordinary citizen. It is the very irony of fate that he has been made responsible for the management of a half a million villages. He has an abiding sense of the sacredness of this responsibility, and he toils assiduously over the task as it is given him to comprehend it. Save for brief periods of holiday-making with his family, he works till two or three in the morning, examining papers, reading suggestions, and signing papers. No man in the Empire is busier than he.

'The misery of it is that all this irksome labour is of no use whatever. So far as the real government of Russia is concerned, he might as well be employed in wheeling bricks from one end of the yard to the other, and then back again. Even when one tries to realise what 'Russian government' is like - with its vast bureaucracy essaying the stupendous task of maintaining an absolute personal supervision over every individual human unit in a mass of a hundred millions, and that through the least capable and most uniformly corrupt agents to be found in the world - the mind cannot grasp the utter hopelessness of it all. The ablest man ever born of woman could do next to nothing with it; at least until he had cleared the ground by slaying some scores of thousands of officials. Alexander III simply struggles on at one little corner of the towering pyramid of routine business which his Ministers pile up before him. Compared with him, Sisyphus was a gentleman of leisure.'

Professor Geffcken, who knew the Emperor Frederick so well, thus also hit off certain phases in the character of the equally unfortunate Alexander:

'Personally, the Emperor is said to be kind-hearted, though at the same time hot-tempered, while a strange vein of timidity pervades his character. He does not like new faces, and prefers to communicate with his Ministers and Generals by writing rather than by word of mouth, because he does not like discussions for which he is not prepared. He is, of course, obliged to receive hundreds of persons, but avoids long conversations if he feels unable to cope in argument with his interlocutors.

'His personal commerce with those in whom he has confidence is therefore very limited, and he dislikes intercourse with eminent men because he fears the influence they may exercise upon him, being very desirous of appearing independent. For instance, he has discarded Count Adlerberg, a real man of business, who always accompanied Alexander II on his travels, and when he goes abroad he is surrounded only by those who have no opinions of their own. Yet the Emperor is very accessible to the advice of lunatics like Pobedonostseff, because their resolute convictions impose upon him, and because, above all, he fears foreign influence.'

'Some acute physiognomists,' said a writer in the *Times*, 'imagined they could perceive in his features traces of his descent from Paul I, and some of the people who knew him best believed they could detect in him, especially in his later years, symptoms of the impatient waywardness and dislike of even the most respectful suggestions which characterised that eccentric and unfortunate monarch. Certainly he had not much in common with his liberal-minded, kind-hearted, well-intentioned father, Alexander II, and still less with his refined, philosophic, sentimental, chivalrous, yet cunning grand-uncle, Alexander I, who coveted the title of 'the first gentleman of Europe.' With high culture, exquisite refinement, polished manners, and studied elegance, he had no sympathy, and never affected to have any. Indeed, he rather gloried in the idea of being of the same rough texture as the great majority of his subjects; and, if he knew that he was sometimes disrespectfully called behind his back 'the Peasant Tsar' (*Muzhitski Tsar*), he probably regarded the epithet as a compliment.

'His straightforward, abrupt manner, savouring sometimes of gruffness, and his direct, unadorned method of expressing himself, harmonised well with his rough-hewn, immobile features and somewhat sluggish movements. The impression which he generally made in conversation was that of a good, honest, moderately intelligent, strong-willed man, who might perhaps listen to explanations or objections, but who would certainly stand no nonsense, whether from subordinates or from any one else. It was as a man rather than as an Emperor that his amiable qualities became apparent. All the world knows in a general way that he was the incarnation of all the domestic virtues; but only those who had the privilege of observing him in the unrestrained intimacy of the family circle, especially when he had an opportunity of romping with children, or amusing himself with his four-footed pets, could fully realise what a simple, kindly, affectionate nature was concealed behind the by no means sympathetic exterior which was presented to the world at large.'

As in politics, so in personal respects, Alexander III was an autocrat, especially towards his family. His father always kept open house for his relations. Every Grand Duke and Duchess could always come to him uninvited. Soon after his accession to the throne his successor restricted this liberty to his own children. Even his brothers did not go uninvited to dine with him. New family statutes were drawn up, according to which the degree of relationship to the Tsar became of the greatest importance. Only the children and grandchildren of a Tsar were allowed to bear the title of Grand Duke and Imperial Highness. Those who came after these were only princes of the blood-royal and 'Highness.' The appanage was also dependent on the degree of relationship to the Tsar.

The Grand Duke Vladimir was formerly wont, during his military tours of inspection, to be accompanied by the Grand Duchess Marie, his wife, whose beauty and kind-heartedness made her very popular. Alexander III soon heard of this. Fearing that a member of the family might thus gain too much influence in the country, he ordered the Grand Duke Vladimir to make his tours of inspection for the future without his wife. He also feared that his relations, and especially the above-named Grand Duchess, might have an influence over the troops. He therefore gave orders that members of the Imperial family were to greet by word of mouth only troops to which they were specially attached. If they did so to others, the men were not to answer.

All authorities agree in describing the late Tsar as a man of extremely simple habits and tastes. Lady Randolph Churchill, writing in 1889, shortly after her visit to Russia, mentioned, in her description of the Palace of Gatchina, 'a hall worthy of an old English country-house, full of comfortable writing-tables, games, and toys; I even spied a swing. In this hall their Majesties often dine, even when they have guests, and after dinner the table is removed and they pass the remainder of the evening there. The Emperor and the Empress elect to live with the greatest simplicity in the smallest of rooms, which are rather at variance with the Emperor's towering frame and majestic bearing. His Majesty's manner is as simple as his tastes, and, if rather shy, impresses one with a conviction of his honesty and earnestness.' 'There are,' she goes on, 'some curious customs at the Russian Court which do not harmonise with the idea of a despotic and autocratic Sovereign. To see the Tsar standing, while supper is going on, talking perhaps to a young officer who remains seated all the time, is startling. But tradition is everything in this country, and as it was the habit of Peter the Great to dislike ceremony of any kind, it is religiously kept. The etiquette of the Russian Court is much less rigid in some respects than in England or Germany.'

The truth of this will appear from the following account of how the Tsar spent his day, from the pen of Mr 'Lanin':[3]

'The Tsar's daily habits of life are those of a Pope rather than of a secular monarch, his relaxations those of a prisoner rather than of a potentate. When residing at Gatchina he generally rises at 7 A.M., whereas few noblemen in the capital leave their beds much before midday; and I am personally acquainted with two who rise with the regularity of clockwork at three o'clock every day. He then takes a quiet stroll in the uninteresting, well-watched palace park, returns to early breakfast, and engages in severe manual labour as a preparation for the official work of the day. The latter consists mainly in the reading and signing of enormous piles of edicts, ukases, laws, and reports, all of which he conscientiously endeavours to understand. Upon the margins of these documents he writes his decision or his impressions with a frankness and abandon which laughs prudence and propriety to scorn. He writes down the thoughts suggested by what he reads just as they occur, employing the picturesque phraseology in which they embody themselves. And the former are not always very correct nor the latter very refined. 'They are a set of hogs,' is a phrase that recurs more frequently than most. 'What a beast he is!' is another (*ekaya skotina*). The account of a fire, of a failure of the crops, of a famine, or of some other calamity, is almost invariably commented upon in the one stereotyped word, 'discouraging' (ncyooteshitelno).[4]

'Lunch is always served at one o'clock, and consists of three courses, including soup, in the preparation of which Russian cookery is far ahead of that of the rest of Europe. After lunch the Emperor takes his recreation in the park, walking or working, conversing with the members of his family or with General Richter, General Tcherevin, or one of his adjutants. He generally reads the newspapers at this time of the day - viz, the *Grashdanin* and the Moscow Gazette (the *Novoe Vremya*, which is presented to him each day on special paper, he rarely honours with a glance), and listens to the reading of the summary of the previous day's news, which consists of extracts from the Russian and foreign papers selected by officials and copied out in a caligraphic hand on the finest paper in the Empire. Beside these *précis*, one of foreign the other of home news, he takes a keen delight in hearing the gossip and scandal of the fashionable world of the capital.

'Recreation over, the Emperor gives audience to those Ministers whose reports are due on that day, discusses the matters laid before him, and reads over the edicts drawn up for his signature, signing them or putting them aside for future consideration. At 8 P.M., dinner, consisting of four courses, is served *en famille*. After dinner the Tsar takes tea in the private apartments of the Empress, where he invariably appears in a check blouse and leather belt, which would impart a rude shock to the notions of Court etiquette prevalent in most European countries.'

Mention is made in the above extract of General Richter, and I cannot refrain from supplementing it by quoting the following description of this functionary from the graphic pen of Mr Stead:

'The Emperor's letter-bag is almost the only means by which the mass of his subjects can make known to the man who is their natural and appointed Tribune their grievances or their complaints. The department of the Imperial Chancery which attends to this Tribunitial side of the Emperor's daily work is presided over by General de Richter, one of the best men in Russia. General Richter is from the Baltic provinces, a Lutheran, and a sincerely pious and devoted Christian. He commanded in Sebastopol during the Russo-Turkish war as a general in the artillery. Few men whom I met in Russia impressed me more favourably. An honester and more straightforward man never breathed, or one more full of all the better and nobler aspirations of humanity. He has an office under him which is concerned with answering petitions and attending to applicants for the Imperial intervention. To him the Emperor refers the 106 petitions per day which arrive on an average every twenty-four hours, and to him come, in long *queue*, the petitioners who seek to bring their troubles before the Emperor. He is, as it were, the Tsar's secretary, and no better man could be found for the place. A high-minded man of stem integrity, his selection for the responsible post which) he occupies in the Imperial *entourage*, and the confidence which the Emperor places in him are an indication that Alexander III is a better judge of men than some of his critics are disposed to admit.

'That portfolio of General Richter,' said a dashing young officer whom I met on my way to Gatchina, 'should be made of waterproof, for it is watered with tears of the suppliants of a whole nation.' General Richter is the Sandalphon of the Empire. He listens to the sounds that ascend from below:

> 'From the spirits on earth that adore,
> From the souls that entreat and implore
> In the fervour and passion of prayer,
> From the hearts that are broken with losses,
> And weary with dragging of crosses
> Too heavy for mortals to bear.'

He is the doorkeeper of the Earthly Providence whom men call the Tsar. He has to read the petitions, to receive the petitioners, to be the ear and the voice of the Emperor. It is heart-breaking work; for, after all, the extent to which a Sovereign, even when he is an autocrat, can intervene between mortals and adverse fortune is very limited; and yet, as Titus said, no man should approach the person of Caesar and go away unsatisfied.'

Alexander III was the first Emperor after the two Romanoffs - Feodor and John Alexeiwitch - to wear a beard. He took a great delight in manual labour, which, in his case, was a physical necessity no less than a favourite pastime. He unhesitatingly put his hand to any kind of work that had to be done, but his usual occupation was to fell huge trees, saw them into planks, plane them, and generally prepare them for the cabinet-maker. He was also fond of shovelling away show. Like some members of the Orloff family, including the one who, in 1856, signed the Treaty of Paris, he had wrists of iron, or, rather, of steel, and he could roll up a silver plate like a scroll of paper. He could tear asunder a pack of cards, or a horseshoe, or even, it was said, a rouble piece (not the paper, but the silver kind). Like Mr Gladstone, he cut down trees, he practised gymnastics, mowed the grass in his garden, shovelled snow, and chopped wood. He would also sometimes help the workmen who were occupied in the palace, especially the joiners and upholsterers. He laid the greatest store on having his rooms comfortably and suitably furnished, and he was very fond of arranging the pictures on his walls and hanging them differently.

'The Tsar's physique,' wrote a correspondent, 'is exceptionally powerful. The feats of physical strength with which he was wont to amuse himself in his youth would make the fortune of any of his subjects. He has twisted and broken thick iron pokers and bars with his hands, has bent pewter tankards into bouquet-holders, has burst open doors, raised heavy burdens, and accomplished enough to justify his claim to the title of the 'Russian Samson.'" 'In person,' says Mr 'Lanin,' 'the Tsar is tall and powerful, strong and muscular; in his younger days he was able to bend a bar of iron across his knees, or to burst in a strong door with his shoulder. He possesses one of those heavy, unwieldy figures whose awkward movements, resulting largely from morbid self-consciousness and consequent shyness, no calisthenics could subdue to the easy bearing which characterises the ordinary man of the world. His manner is cold, constrained, abrupt, and so suggestive of churlishness as often to deprive spontaneous favours of the honey of friendship for the sake of which they are accorded.'

Like most large-hearted men, he was devotedly fond of animals. He would tramp for miles through forest and marsh, with his favourite setters, Spot and Juno, for sole companions, and the Imperial kennels and stables were models of order and propriety. The stables at Gatchina were, indeed, inferior in magnificence and comfort only to the Palace itself; and, though not himself given much to riding, the Emperor did all in his power to encourage horse-breeding and horsemanship, especially among his officers. He invariably presided at the annual race-meeting at Krasnoe Selo, and all the prizes offered at it were given by the Imperial family. He was even a regular visitor to the circus, and, though he did not restrain a smile when a performer came to grief, never failed to acknowledge with a kindly bow the salute of the crestfallen rider on leaving the ring. He will also be greatly missed at the French Theatre, where the Imperial box was seldom empty on Saturday nights. Oh these occasions the whole company played to the Emperor, and the actor or actress who won his applause was happy and envied for weeks. One performer, who appeared in a secondary *rôle*, tells with honest pride how he once succeeded, small as his part was, in provoking the Imperial mirth. 'I may not be a great artist,' he is wont to say, 'but when I came on the Tsar laughed till he cried. That is quite enough for me.'[5]

Outside the narrow circle of his family the Tsar was never very communicative or cordial. 'His distrustful look, which has often been confounded with a scowl; the knitting of his brows, which signifies active thought quite as much as dissatisfaction or anger; his sullen taciturnity, curt, blunt replies, and brusque movement when finishing a conversation, have contributed more than aught else to raise an impassable barrier between himself and his subjects. 'I entered into his Majesty's presence with feelings very different from those connoted by the words fear and trembling,' said a friend of mine - a journalist who once went to thank the Tsar for a decoration bestowed upon him, as he fancied, for his literary and historical researches, but in reality for a very different reason. 'I felt grateful to him with a gratitude which I cannot express in words. Affection, loyalty, sympathy, devotion vied with each other for the mastery in my soul. I would have thrown myself down a precipice at his nod. But the moment I beheld him a cold blast of icy wind froze my very soul. I thanked him for his kind recognition of my journal, which had done its best to turn a searchlight upon the sombre past; but before I could finish the sentence he said: 'Aye, and on the present, too; and I would have you understand that I will stand no more of this!' He then turned upon his heel, and I was left alone with my thoughts, which were somewhat different from those I had on entering the apartment.'[6]

'The Tsar's intellectual occupations,' says Mr 'Lanin, 'are not nearly so fatiguing as his physical labours, and his reading is less varied and extensive than that of many of the ladies who frequent his Court. Besides the two newspapers already named and two historical reviews, he confines his reading to Russian, French, and English novels. Among the novelists of his own country he prefers Count Tolstoi, little though he relishes him as a preacher. Music has a soothing effect upon him, as it had upon Saul, but, like Kant, he displays a particular fondness for loud music. He himself plays the trombone with as much success as any specialist in his military band, and occasionally organises quartettes at the palace, in which he takes an active part with his favourite instrument. His love for the fine arts is moderately developed, and is excelled by the correct taste which he has uniformly displayed in all the purchases of pictures he has ever effected at home or abroad. For science the Tsar has no appreciative organ. Russian history, where it merges into romance - the Russian history painted by Repin and dramatised by Count A. Tolstoi - possesses powerful attractions for a monarch the dream of whose life it is to resuscitate the spirit, if not the outward form, of the forgotten past.' According to another authority the Emperor's favourite authors were Pierre Loti, George Meredith, Stevenson, Oscar Wilde, and Wilhehn Hauff. Wilde and Meredith may both be doubted.

Partly in consequence of his isolated position, and partly on account of his natural inclination, which made family life attractive to him, the Tsar did not mix much with his people, and few came to him.[7] Many a Grand Duke and Grand Duchess did not see him for months, as he neither gave nor accepted invitations. But in spite of this he knew quite well what was going on in the world. His Ambassadors abroad sent extremely exact and detailed reports, not only about political events, but also about life at the respective Courts and in society. General Tcherevin brought the Tsar all the town gossip, and he listened with the greatest interest to his piquant anecdotes. His Majesty did not read the newspapers himself; he generally had the *Imperial Review* read to him in the afternoon by the *aide-de-camp du jour*, and also a collection of cuttings from Russian and foreign journals, copies of which were laid before him in place of the originals, this being according to old-established custom. The clerks of a special office had to make these copies.

When not with his family he was taciturn, and as he always felt uncomfortable, was rather awkward. He never understood how to hold a reception, and it was just as difficult for him to say a few simple friendly words to any one whom he wanted to praise. He understood much better how to show his displeasure, and many a Minister and General knew from experience that the Tsar was thoroughly master of the Russian language, especially of its coarse and strong expressions. He was always kind and considerate to his domestics. He did not like changing; and sometimes, improbable as it may seem, quietly allowed a servant to answer him improperly, and even rudely, rather than send him away and be forced to have another.

As years advanced, the Tsar's increasing love of ease, nutritious food, with very little bodily exercise, the suspicion and fears of attempts on his life, anxiety about the Tsarina's health, who of late years had been a victim of nervous attacks, and the condition of his second son - who was suffering from consumption - all this in time undermined the otherwise strong and robust health of this Herculean monarch. He became more silent and unapproachable than ever. His nervous excitement showed itself on every trivial occasion. This was especially seen in the dislike he took to riding, and the manner in which he avoided taking part in military ceremonies. The officers grumbled in private that the Tsar had withdrawn himself from them and their sphere of activity; the aristocracy became dissatisfied that the number of Court festivities was continually decreasing. Everywhere it was believed that the reason for all this was the increasing ill-humour of the monarch, and nobody had any idea that a malignant disease was gnawing at the apparently robust man in the prime of life.

De mortuis nil nisi bonum is a maxim that was never better observed than on the occasion of Alexander III's death; and to such an extent was indiscriminate eulogy of his character carried in some quarters, where good sense might have been expected to guide the expression of sentiment, that the first magistrate of the city of London, for example, lauded as 'illustrious and *enlightened*' the very monarch whose lack of enlightenment had formed the subject of the famous Guildhall memorial of only four years before. It was the pulpit, more perhaps than the Press this time, which held evenly the scales of critical truth. Preaching in Westminster Abbey, Canon Wilberforce said: 'It is impossible to think of that lonely, incarcerated life which has just ended, without the deepest compassion. Never could death, the last earthly gift of God, 'tired nature's sweet restorer,' have been more welcome to weary mortal than to him - *the man in the iron mask*, bound hand and foot by the exigencies of an autocracy which it was death in life to maintain, and to him, disobedience to the divine will to modify or abandon. Imagination can conjure up no sadder picture than that of the mighty ruler of millions pressing his face against the window-panes of the Anitchkoff Palace, wistfully gazing upon the careless throng below, in speechless, guarded solitude. And now death has set him free, and our earnest prayers are offered for the consolation of those who loved him well, in the bitterness of their bereavement.

'It would, however, be irrational and unjust to withhold at the same time the expression of our compassion for the thousands who have groaned and suffered under the system of which he was the unwilling embodiment, which he solemnly believed it was his sacred duty to maintain. Naturally of a kindly, affectionate disposition, transparently truthful, a lover of peace, rectitude, and order, it was his doom, as the inheritor of a throne based on irresponsible dominion, to crush by banishment and persecution that quenchless instinct of dvil and religious liberty which, when guided, changes for the better the face of the world, and when trodden under foot rallies under the motto, 'Resistance to tyranny is obedience to God.'"

NOTES

1. So far, most of this character-sketch was contributed by the writer to the *Illustrated London News*, the proprietors of which he thanks for permission to reproduce it.
2. Speaking at the Cutlers' Feast in Sheffield while the Tsar was dying.
3. *Contemporary Review* for January 1893.
4. Once the introduction of lifts was recommended by the Council of the Empire. A small minority was against it because it was alleged that foreigners were at the back of the undertaking. The Tsar did not confirm the Bill, and remarked on the margin: 'I am astonished that a majority could be found to sell Russia.'
5. From a character-sketch in *Standard*.
6. St Petersburg Correspondent of the *Daily Telegraph*.
7. For the evidence as to the character and habits of Alexander III given in this and the following two paragraphs, I am indebted to a personal sketch of his Majesty furnished by a 'Russian writer' to a German journal (the *Strassburger Post*) quoted in the *Daily News*.

CHAPTER XII

NICHOLAS II

'What is Nicholas II?' - His Teachers - A Panslavist Tutor - General Danilovitch and his Method - Not much of a Soldier - Youthful Characteristics - His Tastes and Reading - Nothing but good to say of Him' - 'Good all Round' - A 'Globe-trotter' - Visit to India - In Japan - Narrow Escape at Ossu - His Saviour describes the Incident - 'I admired Nicky's Pluck' - At Vladivostock - The Trans-Siberian Railway - The Great Famine Anecdote by 'An Englishman' - The Princesses of Hesse-Darmstadt - 'Every one to Heaven in his own way!' - Betrothal - The Royal Wedding at Coburg - Second Visit to England - Sketch of in the House of Commons - Accession Manifesto - What will he do? - The Finns - The Jews - Dr Geffcken the New Tsar - His Foreign Policy - The Kaiser and the Tsar - Nicholas II less anti-German than his Father - Two Thousand Telegrams from France - The Emperor and the President - 'Grovelling before the Tsar' - England and Russia - Marriage - 'Nonsense about me' - See-saw System of Russian Government - A Tsar-Emancipator of his subjects' souls?

WHEN Alexander III breathed his last, by far the most interesting personality in all Europe in all the world, was his eldest son, on whom the mantle of his father's mighty Empire, with the 'terrible responsibilities of that awful crown,' had suddenly fallen.[1] 'What is Nicholas II?' asked a French statesman, M. Clemenceau. 'Nobody knows, possibly not even himself.'

The world meanwhile only knew who he was - the eldest son of his father, born 6/18 May 1868, and consequently now only in his twenty-sixth year - a very green age surely at which to be entrusted with the weal or woe of so many millions of his fellow-creatures. Of his childhood little or nothing is known except that, like his brother George, he betrayed a certain delicacy of constitution, which sometimes caused no slight anxiety to his parents. Alexander III was a giant; while his successor - well, the physical contrast between father and son was so great that they positively did not seem to be of the same race. Though Nicholas II gradually outgrew the more marked symptoms of his earlier weakness, he remained pallid, frail, and of nervous disposition. He never showed the exuberant vitality of youth, and an explanation of his extreme shyness and reserve was possibly to be found in constitutional peculiarities. M. Flameng, a French artist, who had been employed by the late Tsar in painting the portraits of the family, informed a correspondent in Paris that he often had long conversations with the Tsarevitch, and was 'much impressed with his cleverness and good sense.' The young Prince, he said, is naturally shy, 'but when he becomes animated he is quite another man.' M. Flameng believed that the Tsarevitch 'would yet surprise many persons who had no great idea of his mental qualities.'

It is worth noting and remembering that the preceptors of the future Emperor included such a fiery and uncompromising Panslavist as M. Katkoff, the famous Moscow editor. My authority for this statement is a trustworthy German writer, who, in referring to the violent attacks that were made upon Ignatieff by the Moscow journalist[2] in connection with the former's anti-Jewish policy, said: 'Katkoff, who had hitherto borne the title of Councillor of State, was elevated to the rank of Privy Councillor, and undertook the education and mental development of the fourteen-year-old Crown Prince, Nicholas Alexandrovitch, a position, of course, which brought him into very close connection with the Court.' Possibly M. Katkoff had been sent for to ground the Tsarevitch in one or more special subjects. But his education as a whole was conducted by General Danilovitch, and of the nature of this general education the following interesting (and I have no doubt accurate) account was given by the St Petersburg Correspondent of the *Kölnische Zeitung* (Cologne Gazette):

'The scientific training of the young Prince was superintended by his governor and tutor, General Danilovitch, a man keenly alive to a sense of duty, highly educated, and with a habit of looking at all things in a very gentlemanly manner, although of a somewhat dry temperament. He brought up his pupil free from prejudices of any kind, which was greatly to his credit, since this early education had to be carried out at a time when the hatred of Germany and Germans was at its height in Russia. The scientific education was excellent, but not after the fashion of a German gymnasium.

'At the wish of the Tsar more attention was given to modem sciences than to classical work. Dead languages were not taught at all, and ancient history only up to a certain point; whilst, on the other hand, the records of recent centuries, especially so far as they bore upon Russia, were carefully read. At the same time, a good deal of Muscovite history and much that pertained to the rise of his own family was kept back from the Prince. The necessary amount of mathematics and a very thorough knowledge of geography was instilled into him, and particular attention was given to the language and literature of his own country as well as of Germany, France, and England. All these languages the Tsarevitch speaks and writes fluently. He was also thoroughly instructed in constitutional history, law, the administration of the country, finance, and political and social economy. The best masters were selected, and care was taken that their instruction should not be warped by political views.

'He entered the army at eighteen, and was little more than a child as regards his way of looking upon life at that time. He abhorred the homage of Court and official life, and was only happy when he could frolic in an innocent fashion with his younger fellow-officers, the elder ones, especially his tutor - for whom he has always entertained the greatest esteem - being out of the way. In this manner his character became more independent. He became a good officer, and, although anything but a passionate soldier, he is able to recognise mistakes and to appreciate efficiency. He is devoted to duty, and does everything that he undertakes thoroughly.

'In many ways he resembles his father, but is, in scientific knowledge, in advance of him, and has this advantage over Alexander III, that from his earliest years he has been brought up as Heir Apparent, whereas the latter was twenty years of age before he came into that position. He has also, like his father, a certain shyness, which, in his case also, has been mistaken for haughtiness. At home he was brought up in the most loving manner, like all the other children of the Imperial family; but a sense of the dignity of the Tsar's position was more deeply impressed upon him than upon his brothers. To him the Tsar was higher than the father.

'One day, for example, the Tsarevitch, when a lieutenant, returned to Peterhof very tired after a long day's exercise with the troops, withdrew to his room, took off his uniform and boots, and lay down on his bed to rest. As he was on the point of sleeping, the Tsar entered his room. Afterwards, when telling the story to his friends, he remarked: 'You can imagine my terror when I saw the Tsar before me and I had no boots on.'

'The Tsarevitch still sees everything through his father's eyes, and from him he has learnt to look down upon all other countries and nations without exception. In this respect the Tsarevitch is noted for the harmless jokes he makes, especially about Germans. Germans, he thinks, are so utterly incapable, in society, of accommodating themselves to the manners and customs of the country they are residing in; they are stiff, have a high opinion of themselves, and ostentatiously display their astonishment abroad, especially in Russia, at all that seems grand to them. The young Tsarevitch did not fail to notice this German weakness, and just because he sometimes made fun of it, it was rumoured that he hated Germany. But this is not at all the case. Germans are just as indifferent to him as Frenchmen, Englishmen, or any other foreigners.

'He has never yet displayed an opinion contrary to that of his father, audit may be pretty positively affirmed Chat he will tread in his footsteps when he comes to the throne. But one must reckon with one factor - namely, the Tsarevitch is very easily influenced, and there is a fear lest his younger counsellors, whom he will have to select later on, should not be inspired with such pacific intentions as the majority of the well-proved counsellors of Alexander III, in whom, though unconsciously, the traditional feeling for Germany still slumbers.'

'Russians here,' wrote the Paris correspondent of the *Daily News*, 'who know the Tsarevitch, say that he is affable and amiable, and in all respects the Tsarina's son. She is likely to retain, when he comes to the throne, the influence that she has been in the habit of exercising. Like her, the coming Emperor is extremely fond of music and dancing, and has a lively disposition. Anything amuses him. One of his jokes as a youth was that if he had ever to join the Kings in exile he would be courted for his musical talents and tenor voice. He does not care for sculpture or painting, but neither did Nicholas I or Alexander II. The Tsarevitch has a nervous twitch in the eyes, which otherwise are fine. So had Paul I, whom in this one respect, and his small stature, he resembles.'

And again: 'I have been given some personal impressions of Nicholas II by a French author who was presented to him during a tour in Russia. The Tsarevitch regretted that he had not been able to go to Paris in the summer of 1889. He spoke of many French composers, and of their esprit. He thought Gounod the Racine of the musical world. The conversation then turned on literature. His Imperial Highness owned himself a great reader of French novels. He thought M. Zola overdid description, and spoke of M. Daudet as exquisite. Travels were touched upon. Some objects picked up in Cochin-China and Tonkin were shown. There was a very beautiful box in gold, of Indian workmanship. This brought the Tsarevitch to talk of India, and the influence of England in the world. His visitor was surprised to hear him speak with marked sympathy of that influence. The genius of Russia, of England, of France, of Germany, ran in such different directions that he did not see why they should clash. Each, it seemed to him, had a different work to do. 'You believe, then,' said the visitor, 'that there is a power above the world which sets each nation its appointed task? 'Certainly,' said the Tsarevitch; 'and, for the great sake of peace, it would be a blessing were statesmen well imbued with this idea.'

The above may be supplemented by what was said to a journalist at Livadia by an Englishman, who 'was for years in constant communication with the new Tsar and knows him thoroughly':[3]

'He was taught an immense variety of subjects, and showed great aptitude in them all. English and French he speaks and writes with ease, and he is also a good German scholar, while he is thoroughly conversant with the literature of all three countries. In mathematics, history, geography, law, political economy, and chemistry he is especially proficient.

In addition to all the other branches of bis education he has bad a capital military training in all branches of the service.

'He completed his general studies under English and French tutors, while each special science was taught by the best available St Petersburg professor.

'As a child he was thoroughly conscientious, and went to his lessons unbidden. He has a wonderfully receptive mind, an excellent memory, sound judgment, and great common sense. From his earliest childhood he has been remarkable for his truthfulness in the smallest matters. He has never made a resolution in haste, but, when he has made a resolution, he has never swerved from it. The Prince had unbounded confidence in and respect for his father....

His mother has great influence with the present Tsar, in whose education she took the keenest interest. Nicholas, though he knows how to command respect, is gentle with those around him. Physically he may be described as 'good all round,' delighting in shooting, riding, and rowing....

'I have nothing but good to say of him, and I am convinced he will cut a great figure in history. Europe can look upon him with the greatest confidence, trusting every word he utters.'

Mr Heath, of St Petersburg, his English tutor, told Mr Stead the following anecdote: The boys had been reading with him 'The Lady of the Lake,' and Nicholas was much delighted with the description of the popularity of Scotland's James V. The stanza is the twenty-first of the fifth canto, which begins:

> 'The castle gates were open flung,
> The quivering drawbridge rock'd and rung,
> As slowly down the steep descent
> Fair Scotland's king and nobles went,
> While all along the crowded way
> Was jubilee and loud huzza,
> And ever James was bending low
> To his white jenet's saddle-bow.
> Gravely he greets each city sire,
> Notes each pageant's quaint attire.
> Gives to the dancers thanks aloud,
> And smiles and nods upon the crowd,
> Who rend the heaven with their acclaims,
> Long live the Commons; King, King James.'

'That,' said the boy, flushing with pride, 'that is what I should like to be.'

A St Petersburg friend of my own said to me: 'As a boy he (the Tsarevitch) was rather sickly, but of late years he has enjoyed the best of health, is an eager rider and shot, and devoted to all kinds of athletic sports. By no means without natural abilities, he is a diligent student, and has amassed a very considerable stock of knowledge. His views were greatly enlarged by his grand tour of the world, which had a most favourable effect on his general development, inspiring him with self-confidence and imbuing him with notions about men and things that seem much too liberal to many Old Russians. At the same time he has a very amiable disposition; in social intercourse he does not show the least trace of 'side,' and among his comrades he is immensely popular.'

The 'grand tour' above referred to was undertaken by the Tsarevitch Nicholas in 1890-91, and extended round the world - a form of education which his father before him had never enjoyed. Alexander III had limited his travels to the Courts of Europe, whereas his Heir Apparent, up to date in all things pertaining to the illumination of his mind, joined the ever-increasing ranks of the 'globe-trotters.' In the course of his tour he visited India. He landed at Bombay in December, 1890, and spent several weeks in the country. At Calcutta he was entertained with befitting honour, and was reported to have made a distinctly favourable impression upon those whom he met. Leaving India, he travelled through Japan, his companion being Prince George of Greece.

In Japan the Tsarevitch was very near falling a victim to the rage of a fanatic. The Princes reached Kioto on May 9, 1891, and a few days later they made an excursion to the classic Lake Biwa. After seeing the lake they paid a short visit to the Prefect of Shiga at Ossu, and then prepared to see the outskirts of the town in a 'jinrikisha.' The streets of Ossu were well lined with police, and as the Princes were being drawn along, one of the officers drew his sabre and aimed a violent blow at the Tsarevitch's neck. Fortunately, however, the danger was averted by the presence of mind of Prince George of Greece, who partly warded off the blow with his cane, and at once threw himself on the would-be murderer. With the aid of the 'jinrikisha' runners and the police, the assailant of the Tsarevitch was finally secured. The incident was described by Prince George in a letter to his father, the King of the Hellenes, as follows:

'We passed through a narrow street, decorated with flags and filled with crowds of people on both sides of the thoroughfare. I was looking towards the left when I suddenly heard something like a shriek in front of me, and saw a policeman hitting Nicky (the Tsarevitch) a blow on the head with his sword, which he held with both hands. Nicky jumped out of the cart, and the man ran after him, Nicky with the blood streaming down his face. When I saw this, I too jumped out, with my stick in my hand, and ran after the man, who was about fifteen paces in front of me. Nicky ran into a shop, but came out again immediately, which enabled the man to overtake him; but I thank God that I was there the same moment, and while the policeman still had the sword high in the air I gave him a blow straight on the head, a blow so hard that he has probably never experienced a similar one before. He now turned against me, but fainted and fell to the ground; then two of our jinrikisha-pullers appeared on the scene; one got hold of his legs, while the other took the sword and gave him a wound in the back of the head. It was God who placed me there at that moment, and who gave me the strength to deal that blow, for had I been a little later the policeman had perhaps cut off Nicky's head, and had the blow missed the assailant's head he would have cut off mine.'

Though he had two large wounds above the ear, which happily failed to penetrate the skull, and had lost much blood, he did not faint or lose his self-command. 'I must say that I admired Nicky's pluck,' wrote his companion. 'Nicky stood it splendidly.' His head was hastily bandaged, and the party was escorted by soldiers to the railway station and returned to Kioto. He soon recovered from the superficial scalp-wounds, and was well enough the next day to receive a visit from the Mikado, who travelled over two hundred miles to visit the wounded Prince, and convey to him personally the expression of his regret at the outrage. When the news first reached Europe it was feared that the Tsarevitch might have been made the object of a Nihilist attack, and much relief was felt when it was found that this had not been the case, but that the outrage had simply been prompted by sectarian fanaticism at some supposed breach of religious etiquette on the part of an alien.

Nevertheless, the incident had the effect of making the Tsarevitch shorten his stay in Japan and hurry on to Vladivostock, where what should he find awaiting him but a letter from his father appointing him Chief of the East Siberian Jäger, in honour of his return to Russian soil, and further marking the happy occasion by commuting the punishment of some Siberian exiles. At Urussi he performed a memorable act by turning the first sod of that end of the great Trans-Siberian Railway, a scheme in which he had always been most warmly interested, and indeed had acted as President of the Committee appointed to report upon the project.[4]

On another occasion the Tsarevitch was prominently engaged in a work of great public importance. This was during the terrible famine of 1890-91, when several millions of the Russian people were suffering from the horrors of hunger in their acutest form. The Grand Duke Nicholas was then at the head of the Help Committee, and in that position he displayed the utmost activity. It was generally believed, moreover, that a sum of 50,000 roubles, sent anonymously to Count Tolstoi for the purpose of establishing free kitchens in some of the most famished districts, came from the Tsarevitch's private purse. His active connection with the Trans-Siberian Railway and Famine Committees had given him much insight into public business - insight which was supplemented by his regular attendance for some time at Councils of State. Travelling overland by way of Tobolsk and Moscow, the Tsarevitch rejoined his parents about the middle of August 1891, bringing home with him a knowledge of the Empire over which he was destined to rule such as was not even possessed by his father.

In connection with this tour of the world, the following testimony deserves to be quoted. Writing to the *Times* from Pau, 'An Englishman' said:

'When, some years ago, the Tsarevitch, now the Tsar Nicholas II, was on a visit of some days' duration to a certain port in the East, a friend of mine had the honour of several conversations with him. In the course of these, mention having been made of the great popularity in England of his aunt, her Royal Highness the Princess of Wales, the young Prince at once claimed for his mother, the Tsarina, a similar popularity in Russia, while altogether his expressions respecting her, especially as being used to a stranger, were indicative of a very strong affection. After the stiffness of first introduction had worn off, his manner to my friend and his family was all that is charming, and when he had taken what he had intended as his final leave, he left behind him an impression of amiability of chamcter decidedly above the average. This impression was much confirmed by what followed. The Prince went away on an expedition, it being arranged that on his return the following day the Russian warships would take their departure fpr the next port. But during his absence my fnend was taken seriously ill, and on hearing of this the Tsarevitch at once put off the departure of the squadron for some hours and came ashore *incognito* to pay him a visit. Sitting for a considerable time beside the sick man's sofa he displayed a tenderness of manner and a genuineness of concern which my friend is not likely to forget. My friend thought he perceived in the young Prince indications of other qualities which, to the ruler of a great Empire, are of more value than amiability; but as there occurred no opportunity for the confirmation of this judgment, I confine myself to what was sufficiently proved.'

Having thus seen the world, it now behoved the Grand Duke Nicholas to find a wife, and this he ultimately did at the Court of Darmstadt, which had already furnished consorts to his grandfather, Alexander II, as well as to his uncle, the Grand Duke Sergius. The latter, in 1884, had married Princess Elizabeth, second daughter of Queen Victoria's Hessian son-in-law; while the third daughter, Irene, had become the wife of her cousin, the sailor-Prince Henry of Prussia. Only one daughter was left, Princess Alix, and for several years her name had been connected in a matrimonial sense with the heir to the Russian throne. Long before the Tsarevitch had set out upon his travels, Princess Alix had accompanied her father to St Petersburg on a visit to her sister, the Grand Duchess Sergius, and rumour had anticipated her engagement for years before it became an accomplished fact.

Of course the opera-singer, or even *danseuse*, who generally intervenes to provoke a desperate and long-enduring conflict in the hearts of princes between real affection for the lowly objects of their love and respectful attachment to a high-born but uncongenial beauty, with whom union would at best be a marriage of convenience - such a theatrical siren, I say, failed not (in the imagination of the cackling quid-nuncs) to appear upon the scene at St Petersburg. On one side there was the bewitching siren who acted as a bar to the hoped-for union of hands, while on the other religious scruples were supposed to have for a long time stood in the way of the expected engagement - as if, forsooth, they did not believe at Dannstadt, as at Berlin, in the words of the Great Frederick, that *'Jedermann kann nach seiner Façon selig werden,'* and that Dr Pobedonostseff could open the door of heaven just as well as Dr Martin Luther.

But all this tittle-tattle was put an end to by the final engagement of the Tsarevitch to Princess Alix - a fact in itself which proved that the Princess had previously consented to adopt the Orthodox faith, though certain relaxations of form were afterwards made in her favour. A law had long existed in Russia by which the Emperor and the Heir Apparent could only marry a Princess professing the Orthodox religion; and its application was extended under Alexander III (1886) to the Heir Presumptive and the Heir Presumptive's eldest son - a fact which accounted for the importance attached to the conversion of the Princess Alix before her marriage.

The engagement was officially made known at Coburg on the occasion of the marriage of the Grand Duke of Hesse to his cousin, the Princess Victoria Melita of Edinburgh, which the Tsarevitch came to attend, and to prove the truth of the maxim that one wedding generally produces another. It was the German Emperor who, with a beaming face, first let out the secret to an English officer in Coburg, and his Majesty looked as happy at the event as if he had suddenly succeeded in adding another party to the Triple Alliance. In the previous year the Tsarevitch had been his guest for about a week at Potsdam, where he was made the object of all imaginable honour, and there were indeed pretty sure signs of more natural affinity between the Kaiser and the son than between the Kaiser and the father. At any rate, the engagement of the Tsarevitch was everywhere (except, of course, in France) hailed with the utmost satisfaction as an additional bond of union between Germany and Russia on one hand, and between Russia and England on the other.

After spending some time at Darmstadt with his bride-elect, the Tsarevitch paid a visit to his English relatives, and was the guest of the Prince and Princess of Wales. In the previous year he had also come over to attend the wedding of his cousin, the Duke of York, as well as to thank the Queen personally for the reception which had everywhere been accorded him in India. On the occasion of his engagement-visit to our Court he spent his time in seeing as much as possible of our national life in all its phases, and was treated, among other things, to a review at Aldershot. He even spent an evening in the gallery of the House of Commons (a thing, I think, which his father had ominously omitted to do when in London at the same time as the Shah in 1873); and it is to be hoped that nothing was said or done on this occasion by our 'fierce democracy' of a kind calculated to inspire the heir to the greatest despotism in the world with a justifiable hatred and distrust of parliamentary institutions.

I cannot do better than here present my readers - by way of some bright additional rays to the scattered light which I am tiying to focus on the personality of Nicholas II - with the following little character-sketch from one of the deftest and most incisive of our descriptive pens, that of Mr T. P. O'Connor, MP:

'I saw the Tsarevitch during his trip to this country. One day he paid a visit to the Peers' Gallery of the House of Commons. I was immediately struck - as everybody was - with his extraordinary resemblance to the Duke of York. It is curious how persistent some family strains are. The little royalty of Denmark has created more replicas of the original type than any other living Royal House. And thus when you see the children of one Danish princess, you see the very picture of the children of the other princess - though the fathers be of two such different types in every respect as the Prince of Wales and Alexander III. The type appears to me more persistent, however, than vigorous. The Tsarevitch certainly did not give the impression of either mental or physical vigour. It was hard to realise that this slim, not very tall, and decidedly delicate-looking stripling was the son of the giant who could twist tin plates in the hollow of one of his brawny hands.

'There was something singular, and even a little sinister and foreboding, in the manner in which the Tsarevitch entered the gallery. He was accompanied, of course, by a small group of gentlemen-in-waiting; they remained a little behind, giving him the opportunity to advance forward to the seat over the clock in front which is reserved for Royalties. He seemed shy, uncertain, indecisive, looked back as if to get a hint; and altogether went to his place with much awkwardness and shame-fincedness. There was something suggestive of the lonely and perilous elevation to which he will so soon attain in this little scene - of all its solitude, desertion, and uncertainty in the midst of the millions of adoring subjects and thousands of servile courtiers.'

Such was the young Prince who, nevertheless, by his personal qualities, succeeded in inspiring the Queen with a feeling of 'sincere affection and regard,' as the Court Circular informed us on his accession to the throne. But Nicholas II must not be solely judged by the words of others, which have, so far, been the only sources of enlightenment as to his character at our command. Let us now examine him in the light of his own utterances and his own acts - first of all, of the proclamation by which he announced his accession to the throne - a document, in all probability, which was penned for his Majesty by the Procurator of the Holy Synod, whom we all know:

'We hereby proclaim to all our faithful subjects that God, in His inscrutable providence, has seen fit to assign a limit to the precious life of our dearly beloved Imperial father. His grievous suffering yielding neither to medical skill nor to the beneficent climate of the Crimea, he died at Livadia on the 20th of October (O.S.) surrounded by his family, and in the arms of the Tsarina and of ourselves.

'Our grief is not to be expressed in words, but that grief every Russian heart will understand. And we believe that there is no spot throughout the vast Russian Empire in which hot tears will not flow for the Emperor, thus prematurely called away, who has parted from that country which he loved with all the power of his Russian soul, and in the welfare of which, sparing neither health nor life, he centred all his thoughts.

'But, also, far beyond the borders of Russia the memory of the Tsar, who was the incarnation of unswerving loyalty and of peace, which during his reign was not once broken, will not cease to be respected.

'The will of the Most High be done! May our unshaken faith in the wisdom of Providence give us strength! May we be consoled by the consciousness that our sorrow is the sorrow of the whole of our beloved people, and may our people not forget that the strength and stability of Holy Russia lie in her unity with us, and in her unbounded devotion to us.

'We, however, in this sad but solenm hour, when ascending the ancestral throne of the Russian Empire and of the Tsardom of Poland, and the Grand Duchy of Finland, indissolubly connected with it, remember the legacy left to us by our departed father, and, inspired by it, we, in the presence of the Most High, record the solemn vow always to make our sole aim the peaceful development of the power and glory of our beloved Russia and the happiness of all our faithful subjects. May the Almighty, who has chosen us for this high calling, vouchsafe us His aid, while we offer before the throne of the Almighty Ruler our heartfelt prayers for the unstained soul of the departed.

'We command our subjects to take the oath of allegiance to ourselves and to our successor, the Grand Duke George Alexandrovitch, who will bear the title of Crown Prince and Tsarevitch, until it please God to bless our approaching union with the Princess Alix of Hesse-Darmstadt with the birth of a son.

'Given at Livadia this 20th day of October 1894.

'NICHOLAS.'

At St Petersburg, we were told, this document was received 'with an open delight probably unparalleled in the history of Russian official declarations.' Its tone,' said another authority there, 'is softer and less autocratic than that of the proclamations issued by the late Alexander III. There is a strong inclination to believe that it may perhaps indicate a milder and somewhat less autocratic reign.' Deep satisfaction was felt at the remark that his first aim would be the 'peaceful progress of the nation,' which was placed before 'the strength and glory of the Empire.'

Still the proclamation abounded in carefully-worded generalities, and afforded no precise due to the policy that would be followed by the new Emperor in the various fields of his sovereign activity. Very unlike his father in person, would Nicholas II resemble him in his policy? We all know what that policy was - peace abroad, with autocratic reaction, Panslavism, and persecution at home. Now, what said the new Tsar in reply to the message of homage sent him by the Senate?

'Assured of the feelings of devotion which the Senate has expressed to me, I do not doubt that I shall have its co-operation in the service of my dear country, *in the path marked out by my ever-lamented father.*'

Again, how did his Majesty's answer to the Holy Synod run?

'I heartily thank you for the sentiments and sympathy expressed to me at a moment of my deep sorrow. Inspired by ardent love for my departed father, I shall, following his example, devote all my strength to the service of my dear country and of the Orthodox Church.'

Do these two assurances increase or diminish the hopes of the Jews, the Stundists, the Poles, the Finlanders, the exiles in Siberia, and the dumb masses of the suffering Russian people?

As for the Finlanders, their hopes of the future were decidedly raised by the new Emperor's special proclamation to them in which he solemnly promised to 'maintain all their privileges and Constitutions strictly unimpaired both in effect and value.'[5] His father, on succeeding to the throne, made the same vow, but broke it repeatedly in pursuance of his Panslavist-Procrustean policy. In this respect, at least, Nicholas II. will surely not follow in his father's footsteps. If, indeed, this Finnish manifesto carries with it the sense of its words, it may be taken perhaps, as a sign that the domestic policy of the new reign will in general be a little more liberal, to begin with, than that of the late Tsar.

And then the Jews, poor, persecuted race! What said the Vienna correspondent of a London journal? 'In one respect, however, I am able to confirm the estimate generally formed of the young Emperor. I spoke not long ago with a Russian, who was a member of a deputation to the Tsarevitch which petitioned him to intervene on behalf of the Russian Jews. The reply the present Emperor then made was, textually, as follows: 'I despise and condemn the expulsion of your countrymen, but my hands are tied.'

Now that his hands are free, we shall see what use his Majesty will make of them.

'Of the Tsarevitch I formed a very high opinion,' said the Rev Dr Talmage of Brooklyn,[6] for every little bit of such evidence is valuable. 'Many people now are wondering what will happen should he come to the throne - whether he will act in a belligerent or in a peaceful spirit. *I can testify that his sentiments are the sentiments of his father.* He is a most loveable young man, thoroughly cultured, and with a mind broadened by travel. Neither Russian nor European need fear anything from him in the way of antagonisms or asperities.'

And what says Dr Geffcken, the friend, the indiscreet friend and diary-divulger, of the Emperor Frederick? 'The Tsarewitch is a noble, generous character, opposed to every kind of persecution, and especially to religious fanaticism. He has already prevented a great deal of mischief, and has softened down many a strong measure. He is a decided opponent of Pobedonostseff, and the latter would probably be among the first to disappear under a new *régime*....Whether the next Tsar will be sufficiently energetic to carry out his strong opposition to the present bureaucratic regme, and to introduce such reforms as are possible in Russia, remains to be seen.

But in his efforts towards that end he will have a valuable assistant in his uncle, Grand Duke Vladimir. The rest of the Imperial family do not count. Outwardly there will be few changes. If the Tsar was a lover of peace, who only pushed onward where he knew that England would not dare to act (in Asia, for instance), the Tsarevitch is still more opposed to war.'

Turning now to other nations, what will be the attitude of Nicholas II to Germany, to France, to England, to Bulgaria, and other countries?[7] His father was known to be at heart rather anti-German. What will the new Emperor be? Will he be as devoted to Kaiser William as the latter declared himself to be to him? For on hearing of the death of Alexander III, what must the German Emperor do but deliver at a military banquet in Stettin the following harangue:[8]

'The news of a far-reaching and grave event has just come to our ears. His Majesty the Tsar is dead. Nicholas II. has ascended the throne of his fathers - one of the most arduous heritages, I suppose, on which a Sovereign can enter. We who are here assembled, and who have just glanced back on our traditions, remember also the relations that united us of old with the Russian Imperial House. We combine our sympathy with the new Emperor who has just mounted the throne, with the wish that Heaven may grant him strength to bear the heavy burden he has just assumed. Long live the Emperor Nicholas II. Hurrah!'

Does Nicholas II reciprocate the ardent friendship thus expressed for him by William II? Let us hear Dr Geffcken again:

'Alexander III was not always a friend of Germany. At the time when the then German Crown Prince (Frederick III) went to St Petersburg to the funeral of Alexander II, and said something about the friendly relations of the two countries, the Tsar remarked, *'Mais il y a pourtant le plan de Bismarck,'* who, he considered, was anxious to annex the Baltic Provinces. And even after the Crown Prince had convinced him of the utter futility of the idea, he remained suspicious while the anti-German elements in Russia fostered the feeling.

'The Tsarevitch goes further. He is distinctly friendly to Germany, and is warmly attached to the Emperor William. The French have nothing to hope from him, and the Triple Alliance has nothing to fear. Hence, it is only the home-politics in Rusua which will undergo a great change under a new ruler, and if the future Tsar has the strength to carry these changes through, they will be for the welfare of the great Empire, and will lead to the pacification of the discontented elements in Russia.'

'The French have nothing to hope from him.' This may be the conviction of Dr Geffcken, but it certainly is not the belief of the French themselves. For the breath had not been long out of the body of 'the noble and magnanimous monarch,' who had 'saved them from mutilation,' from isolation, and from a thousand other ills, than with one accord they again rose and hurled themselves at the head of his successor.

Within a few days of the death of Alexander III more than two thousand telegrams of sympathy, of devotion, of hope, of homage, of the Lord knows all what, had been flashed from France to Livadia. To some extent Nicholas II was to blame for this, for on the day after his father's death he telegraphed to M. Casimir-Perrier:

'I am grieved to inform you of the cruel loss which I and Russia have just sustained in the person of my father Alexander III, who died yesterday.

'I am certain of the active share which will be taken by the entire French nation in our mourning.'

To which the French President replied:

'By announcing to me the cruel loss which you have just experienced, your Majesty enlists the participation of France in the national mourning in Russia.

'The two great peoples remember Alexander III, who, a year ago to-day, sent a telegram to President Carnot, which drew still closer the bonds between the two countries. I am confident that I am speaking in the name of France when I assure you of the feelings of respect and grief which inspire all hearts. I am anxious also to repeat to your Majesty and to the Imperial family the assurance that I share in the grief which afflicts you.'

But that was only the prologue to the omen coming on. For now the tale was taken up by the French Premier, M. Dupuy and M. de Giers, the French Minister of Foreign Affairs and the French Ambassador at St Petersburg. But the finest flower in the whole French bouquet thrown at the new Tsar came from General Mercier, Minister of War:

'SIRE, - The entire French army lays at the feet of your Majesty and of your august mother the assurance of its profound grief, and expresses the unanimous and lasting sorrow occasioned by the recollection of your glorious father. We weep with our comrades of the Russian Army. The memory of their revered chief, who has been so cruelly called away, will ever live in our hearts.'

In view of all this, was it surprising that the Press of Vienna should have bitterly commented on what it termed 'the prostration of France at the feet of the new Emperor,' and that the expression once used by Prince Bismarck about 'grovelling before the Tsar' (*Das Wettkriechen*) was to be found in nearly every Vienna leader, in one case being employed as the title of the article? 'The French people,' remarked a London newspaper,[9] 'can hardly be wrong in interpreting the (new Tsar's) telegram in consonance with their own dearest wishes. The alliance of Russia and France will be precisely what it was during the late reign. Indeed, the Emperor Nicholas would be conspicuously wanting in the most ordinary statecraft if he dreamed of changing anything in an arrangement of such enormous value to Russia. For what have time and experience shown to be the nature of the Franco-Russian friendship? They have shown that Russia can count on all the benefits of French sympathy, French credit, and, in case of necessity, French military and naval assistance, without pledging itself to give anything in return but pleasant words and Imperial smiles.'

As for Russia's relations to England under the new Tsar, it is not to be doubted that they will go on improving, and when he came to the throne these relations had never been better. Said Lord Rosebery at the Guildhall banquet (Nov. 9, 1894):

'Ever since this Government has been in power our relations with Russia have been more cordial than I can ever remember them to have been. We have as nearly as possible, I hope and believe, terminated that long-standing difficulty with regard to the limitation of our spheres in Central Asia, which removes in Asia, I hope, almost the last dangerous question that arose between us.'

On the occasion of the marriage of the Duke of Edinburgh to the Grand Duchess Marie, Lord Granville said that, though such dynastic alliances might be powerless to prevent war, they nevertheless helped to preserve peace, and it is pretty certain that English court influence will now be much stronger at St Petersburg than ever it was before. Nicholas II seems to be sincerely devoted to his English relatives especially to his cousin, our heir-presumptive; while his mother is said to have an unbounded influence over him and that influence can only be for good. Of his father it was said that, if questioned by any of the Princesses in Denmark as to his excursion plans for the morrow, he would reply, not altogether in jest, 'I never let women know what I am going to do.' Alexander III never discussed affairs of State with his wife. But it may safely be assumed, from all that is known of him, that his son will not prove quite so unimpressionable to feminine influence, especially to that of his consort, the graces of whose person would seem to be set off by a considerable share of those mental endowments which made her English mother an ornament to her sex.

On the day after his father's death Nicholas II was formally betrothed to Princess Alix after she had embraced the Greek faith;[10] and a week after Alexander III. had been finally laid to his rest, 'the funeral baked meats did coldly furnish forth the marriage tables' of his son and successor. For it was held that, in such cases, reasons of State must override etiquette and appearances, and that the period of mourning woe should be interrupted by a brief term of wedding mirth.

It said much for the strength of will and lofty principle of the Princess Alix that she had objected to comply with the rule exacted of all converts to the Orthodox creed which compels them to abjure and curse the faith of their fathers. On the other hand, that the new Emperor should have waived the observance of this rigorous rule betrayed a spirit of compromise and toleration which augurs well for the religious policy of his reign. 'I cannot understand,' he was said to have remarked to his ex-tutor, 'how the people of the capital allow themselves to talk such nonsense and form such opinions about me. They will soon find out how wrong they have been.' The people of the capital made the same discovery when Alexander III came to the throne. As Tsarevitch he had been Liberal; as Emperor he was reactionary. Let us trust, for the sake of Russia, that it will just be the other way about with his successor; and the chances, on the whole, are that it will be so.

For there is a fairly well-founded hope that Nicholas II will continue what might be called the rule of Government in Russia by the same kind of alternation, or see-saw, as we witness in our own House of Commons, Tories succeeding Liberals, and Liberals Tories. In Russia this custom has already acquired something like the force of a natural law since the time of the madly despotic Emperor Paul. His son Alexander I proved a mild and sentimental Sovereign, enamoured of reform; while the next Emperor, Nicholas I, again caused the pendulum of one-man power to swing, or rather bump, back to its extreme angle of oscillation. It was now the turn of Alexander II, the 'Tsar Emancipator,' to resume the cycle of liberal reforms, thus preparing the way for his reactionary son, and we all know in which direction he made the political pendulum to fly. It only now remains for his successor, Nicholas II, to observe this apparent law of Russian government, and there is a fair hope, I repeat, that he will see the wisdom of doing so.

On the other hand, if Nicholas II continues to tread in the domestic tracks of his father, he will be laying up for himself a still more insufferable crown of thorns than that which galled his father to the grave. For some time, no doubt, he will be distracted between the promptings of filial piety and the dictates of a policy of statesmanlike expediency; but, in the long run, the wisdom of more enlightened counsellors than ever were listened to by his father must surely prevail with the new Autocrat of All the Russias. He brings with him to the throne the progressive ideas of the younger generation, and he has seen more of the world than ever his father did. Much will depend on the counsellors who manage to catch his ear.

The character of Nicholas II does not seem to be cast in a strong mould; but this very weakness of his may become a source of happiness to his subjects in the hands of those who can influence him most; and among the number of those, his mother and his wife will doubtless hold a foremost place. A ruler who allows himself to be swayed by good women cannot prove a bad one. Nicholas I used to say of 'Sasha,' his son and successor, that 'he was an old woman,' and that, nothing great would ever be done in his time. But this little old woman turned out to be the liberator of the serfs. Let us hope that, as Alexander II set free the bodies of the serfs, so Nicholas II will ultimately see the wisdom of emancipating the souls of all his subjects, who are still in a most abject state of civil and religious slavery, no less degrading to its victims than dangerous in the highest degree to the throne of which this servitude is made the pedestal.

NOTES

1. Speaking at the Lord Mayor's banquet in the Guildhall, Lord Rosebery said: 'I think we may only now express the pious hope that that young head on whom has fallen the terrible responsibilities of that awful crown - a crown that involves so much of the destinies and the happiness of the human race - may not prove unequal to that burden. I think he must find some consolation in the universal tribute of regret, and even sorrow, with which his father's death has been received. And in that fact I think that we also, who try to look forward to the future of the hunum race, may find something to rejoice in too, because, after all, while it is a tribute to the Emperor, it was quite as much a tribute to peace.'
2. Professor Wilhelm Müller of Tubingen, in his *Politische Geschichte der Gegenwart*, for '82.
3. Special Correspondent of the *Pall Mall Gazette*.
4. One remarkable characteristic of the active life of Alexander III was his love of great engineering enterprises. In his vast undeveloped empire Alexander III found ample scope for the newest developments of scientific daring and practical mechanics. The great Siberian Railway was one of his favourite schemes. Since the Tsarevitch opened the eastern end of the route the work on the various sections of the 6000 miles or so of line has progressed with regularity and economy. A journey can now be made direct from St Petersburg to Omsk, and it is stated that on this section of 300 miles no less than 3,000,000 roubles have been saved on the estimate by economies in alignment and construction. Many other great works of the kind might be mentioned as typical of the reign of Alexander III., notably the drainage of the Pinsk Marshes, a huge swamp, bigger than Scotland, in South-Westem Russia; and the re-irrigation of the sometime fertile plains north of the Murghab River, which were declared an appanage of the Crown for this purpose.
5. The following was the text of this proclamation:
'Having by the dispensation of God come into the hereditary possession of the Grand Duchy of Finland, we desire to confirm the religion and fundamental laws of the country, as well as the rights and privileges which every class and inhabitant, both high and low, have hitherto enjoyed in the aforesaid Grand Duchy, according to the Constitution of the country, promising to maintain all these privileges and Constitutions strictly unimpaired, both in effect and value.'
6. Dr Talmage saw a good deal of the Imperial family while at St Petersburg in connection with the distribution of some American charity to the famine-stricken in Russia.

7. The following was the foreign policy circular issued by M de Giers at the beginning of the new reign to the Russian representatives abroad: -

'Our illustrious Sovereign, on assuming the supreme power conferred upon him by the inscrutable decrees of Providence, has firmly resolved to take upon himself in all its details the exalted task which his beloved father of imperishable memory had undertaken. His Majesty will devote all his strength to the development of the internal welfare of Russia, and will in no way deviate from the completely pacific, loyal, and firm policy which, to so great a degree, has contributed to the general pacification. Russia will remain faithful to her traditions, and endeavour to maintain friendly relations with all Powers, recognising as hitherto, in respect for right and lawful order, the best guarantee for the safety of States.

At the opening of that glorious rule, which now belongs to history, the objects of the Ruler consisted simply in the ideal of a strong and happy Russia, having proper regard for her own good, without at the same time injuring any one. To-day, at the beginning of a new reign, we avow the same principles with equal sincerity, and implore the Lord's blessing, so that these principles may be carried out without modification for many years, and may be invariably productive of good.'

8. 'At the same time the Emperor hastened to appoint Nicholas II Chief of the Alexander Regiment of the Guard, and to decree fourteen days' mourning throughout the army, 'which will thus testify that it shares the deep sorrow felt,' for my true friend, the most sincere protector of European peace, and ever remember with gratitude the goodwill always manifestrd towards my army by the departed Emperor.'

9. *The Standard.* Said M. Clemenceau in the *Justice*; 'With Alexander III a guarantee for peace has disappeared. This genial giant, by interposing his massive bulk, checked all adventurous undertakings, all reckless designs calculated to bring about dangerous complications. The German Emperor now passes from the second rank to the first, as it cannot be expected that the youthful Nicholas II can address the Emperor William in tones of authority.'

An inspired writer in the *Temps* said: 'There is every indication that he will steadily pursue the path laid down by Alexander III. By persevering in that path, he will be sure to reap, together with the legitimate pride of having done his duty, the gratitude of his subjects, the respect of Europe, and that proud position of arbiter of peace which his father so ably occupied. We may add that, by following that course, be may rely on the affectionate gratitude of the French people, who are earnestly desirous to continue to pay the son the homage they readily paid to the father, and to contribute, with Nicholas II, firmly to establish the balance of power initiated with Alexander III.'

10. Said his Majesty in a manifesto:

'The bride of our choice has to-day been anointed with the holy chrism and has accepted our Orthodox faith under the name of Alexandra, to the great comfort of ourselves and all Russia.

'After the painful trial imposed upon us by the inscrutable will of God, we believe, together with our people, that the soul of our well-beloved father from its celestiad abode has sent down a blessing upon the choice of his heart and of our own for consenting to share in a faithful and loving spirit our incessant solicitude for the welfare and prosperity of our Fatherland.

'All our loyal subjects join with us in imploring God's blessing upon our destiny and that of the people confided to our care.

'In announcing this **much-wished for event** to all our faithful subjects we command that henceforth our august betrothed Princess Alix be called by the name and title of her Imperial Highness the Orthodox Grand Duchess Alexandra Feodorovna. - Given at Livadia, November 2.

'NICHOLAS.'

Also available

FREDERICK, CROWN PRINCE AND EMPEROR, Rennell Rodd

Frederick III, second German Emperor, reigned for only three months, from March to June 1888. Having been Crown Prince for twenty-seven years, he was stricken with cancer of the larynx, and by the time he succeeded his elderly father on the throne he was unable to speak above a whisper. Married to Victoria, Princess Royal of Great Britain, he was the hope of liberals throughout Germany and Europe. Had he ruled for longer in good health, the war of 1914-18 would almost certainly have been avoided. Rodd's brief biographical essay, first published in November 1888, was the first life of him to appear. This new edition contains the original text, with a foreword which includes the background to the writing of the book and a note on the life of the author, and additional illustrations.

153pp, paperback

ISBN 10: 151765923X
ISBN 13: 978-1517659233

Made in United States
Orlando, FL
20 April 2024